AN INTRODUCTION TO
POLITICAL
PHILOSOPHY

THIRD EDITION

JONATHAN WOLFF

OXFORD
UNIVERSITY PRESS

OXFORD
UNIVERSITY PRESS

Great Clarendon Street, Oxford OX2 6DP,
United Kingdom

Oxford University Press is a department of the University of Oxford.
It furthers the University's objective of excellence in research, scholarship,
and education by publishing worldwide. Oxford is a registered trade mark of
Oxford University Press in the UK and in certain other countries

Published in the United States of America by Oxford University Press
198 Madison Avenue, New York, NY 10016, United States of America

British Library Cataloguing in Publication Data

Data available

Library of Congress Control Number: 2015953856

ISBN 978–0–19–965801–5

Printed in Great Britain by
Clays Ltd, St Ives plc

AN LOSOPHY,
3RD EDN

This book is due for return on or before the last date shown below.

For Elaine and Max

CONTENTS

PREFACE TO THE THIRD EDITION

In the Preface to the revised edition of this book I wrote 'Ten years after first publication most books that have not outlived their usefulness will at least be ready for a spring clean.' Well, another ten years have passed and something more than a spring clean and an update to the further reading seemed required this time. The first five chapters have been given a light edit: changing some wording that seemed to me ambiguous or a bit clunky, updating some examples, changing references from 'this century' to 'last century', and making a few minor additions or clarifications in the light of comments received over the years. I have also replaced references to out-of-print editions of primary texts with more recent editions, which in the case of Rousseau has also meant using newer, if, regrettably, somewhat less poetic, translations. The most significant revisions, however, have been made to the final chapter. Previously called 'Individualism, Justice, Feminism', it is now called 'Justice for Everyone, Everywhere?' (with a deliberate question mark, at the welcome suggestion of one of the reviewers of the new chapter). In the twenty years since the first edition was published, a number of issues have moved from the periphery of political philosophy to its centre: racial justice, sexual orientation, disability, multiculturalism, global justice, immigration, and climate change. Issues about gender justice have not disappeared and so a good part of the earlier discussion on that topic remains, but it is now set in a context where it is one of a number of issues discussed. The cost is that there is much less on the critique of liberal individualism than there was in the earlier editions, although a very small amount of material on that topic has been moved to the discussion of communitarianism in Chapter 4, and a short section remains in Chapter 6. The idea, then, of Chapter 6 is to give a brief introduction to the issues that are increasingly occupying the time and attention of contemporary political philosophers. And it is no coincidence that these are some of the most urgent problems that face the world today.

In preparing this third edition for the press I have greatly benefited from reports from five referees, both on how they would like to see the book changed, and their responses to a draft of the final chapter. I would like to thank Mark Garnett, James Hampshire, David McNaughton, Raino Sverre Malnes, and Christian Schemmel for their enormous help.

Elaine Collins has also, once again, saved me from myself in her astute commentary on the draft, and I would also like to record my thanks to Sarah Iles and Fiona Barry at Oxford University Press for seeing the book safely through the press. But most of all, I'd like to thank the teachers, students, and other readers who, remarkably, seem just as interested in this book as their predecessors were twenty years ago.

PREFACE TO THE REVISED EDITION

Ten years after first publication most books that have not outlived their usefulness will at least be ready for a spring clean. Re-reading this one I see that there is much that could be changed. After much agonizing, though, I have decided against major revisions, so that it remains substantially the same book, and recognizably so for readers familiar with the original edition. On first publication the book seemed to fill a need for an introductory text that shows the way in which the works of the great political philosophers can illuminate many of the problems that still dominate contemporary political philosophy today. It has proved popular with teachers and students, all round the world, at a variety of levels, and even with 'the general reader'. Although if I were starting again now I am sure I would do things differently, I do not want to run the risk of destroying whatever it is that makes it of use, and hence have resisted the temptation to make changes. The Guide for Further Reading, however, had become seriously out of date. Since 1996 there have been various useful publications that deserve to be included, and accordingly it has been updated.

To the main text there are a number of minor alterations and corrections, but only one of significance. Shortly after publication my colleague Bob Heinaman pointed out that I had somewhat misread Plato's 'navigation' analogy, although, he kindly reassured me, not in a way that affects the argument. This is now corrected, and I offer my thanks to Bob and my apologies to anyone who wrote, or assessed, an essay based on the mistaken reading.

PREFACE TO THE
FIRST EDITION

My purpose in this book is to give the reader a sense of the central problems of political philosophy, and the most interesting attempts, throughout its history, to solve them. In doing so I have explored the subject through a series of linked questions, raiding the treasure houses of political philosophy in search of answers and approaches. Rather than trying to provide a systematic account of contemporary debates, or a thorough and scholarly history, I have often jumped centuries (sometimes millennia) to explore the most thought-provoking writings on the most important topics—or so I think.

Some will disagree with my choice of the central problems, with my view of the relations between these problems, and with my choice of thinkers to take seriously. This is no bad thing. The last thing I want to do is to present the illusion of a finished or completed subject, or even one that is straightforward to chart. Too many introductory books give the impression that the area of study was created by decree, and that understanding is a matter of mastering the manual or rule book. I have tried to avoid this type of over-simplification.

The book is written so that each chapter develops a theme arising from the previous one, but I also hope that any of the chapters can be read as a self-standing unit, as an introduction to a particular issue. Readers often feel that they have virtually a moral obligation to start at the beginning of any book and read it page by page (my grandmother used to say that Hitler would always read the last page of a book first). In the case of this book the reader is hereby invited to follow his or her own interests.

Much of the material has been presented as lectures to students at University College London and Birkbeck College, and to students on the London Inter-Collegiate Lecture Programme. In return I have received many helpful criticisms. Indeed, I have managed to amass an almost indecent amount of help and advice for such a short book. Those who xiv | PREFACE TO THE FIRST EDITION

have discussed parts of the book with me, or have commented on all or part of drafts (in some cases, on many versions) include Paul Ashwin, Richard Bellamy, Alan Carter, Elaine Collins, Issi Cotton, Virginia Cox, Tim Crane, Brad Hooker, Alya Khan, Dudley Knowles, Annabelle Lever, Veronique Muñoz Dardé, Mike Martin, Lucy O'Brien, Sarah Richmond, Mike Rosen, Mike Saward, Mario Scannella, Raj Sehgal, John Skorupski, Philip Smelt, Bob Stern, and Nigel Warburton. I am very grateful to them all.

INTRODUCTION

We do not say that a man who shows no interest in politics is a man who minds his own business; we say that he has no business here at all.

Pericles' funeral oration, in Thucydides, *The Peloponnesian War* ([431 BCE], London: Penguin, 1973), 147

It has been said that there are only two questions in political philosophy: 'Who gets what?', and 'Says who?' Not quite true, but close enough to be a useful starting-point. The first of these questions is about the distribution of material goods, and of rights and liberties. On what basis should people possess property? What rights and liberties should they enjoy? The second question concerns the distribution of another good: political power. Locke defined political power as '*a Right* of Making Laws with Penalties of Death, and consequently all less Penalties' (John Locke, *Second Treatise of Civil Government*, ed. Peter Laslett ([1689], student edn, Cambridge: Cambridge University Press, 1988, s. 3, 268). This probably goes further than we need, but we can see the point. Political power includes the right to command others, and to subject them to punishment if they disobey. Who should hold this power?

As soon as we reflect on these questions puzzles emerge. Is there any good reason why one person should have more property than another? Are there any justified limits to my liberty? What should the relation be between political power and economic success? In some countries few obtain political power unless they are already wealthy. In others, those who gain political power soon find themselves rich. But should there be any connection at all between possession of wealth and enjoyment of political power?

Political power is puzzling enough on its own. Someone with legitimate political power over me has the right to force me to do various things. But how could another person justify the claim to have such rights over me? It can seem outrageous that someone else should tell me what to do, and worse still that they think they are entitled to punish me if I disobey. Yet there is, of course, another side to this. Perhaps I should also consider how others might behave—how unpleasant they could make my life—if they were left unrestrained by the law and the threat of punishment. Perhaps there is something to be said, after all, for the existence of political power. It seems we can identify with both the anarchist's plea for the autonomy of the individual, and the authoritarian's claims for the power of the state.

One task for the political philosopher, then, is to determine the correct balance between autonomy and authority, or, in other words, to determine the proper extent and distribution of political power. This example also illustrates what is distinctive about political philosophy. Political philosophy is a *normative* discipline, meaning that it tries to establish norms (rules or ideal standards). We can contrast the normative with the *descriptive*. Descriptive studies attempt to find out how things are. Normative studies try to discover how things should be: what is right, just, or morally correct. Politics can be studied from both a descriptive and a normative standpoint.

Characteristically, descriptive political studies are undertaken by the political scientist, the sociologist, and the historian. So, for example, some political scientists ask questions about the *actual* distribution of goods within a given society. Who in the United States of America holds wealth? Who in the European Union holds power? The political philosopher, like all of us, has good reason to be interested in the answers to these questions, but his or her primary concern is elsewhere: *what rules or principles should govern how we live together, including the distribution of property, power, rights, and liberty.* The political philosopher will ask, not 'How is property distributed?', but 'What would be a just or fair distribution of property?' Not 'What rights and liberties do people have?', but 'What rights and liberties *should* people have?' What ideal standards, or norms, should govern the distribution of goods within society?

The partition between normative and descriptive studies, though, is not quite as clear-cut as it might seem. Consider again the question 'Who holds wealth?' Why are we interested in this descriptive question? We are interested primarily because the distribution of wealth is relevant to normative questions about *justice*. (Compare the question 'Who holds string?'— inequalities in the possession of string are rarely of political interest.)

Furthermore, questions about human behaviour often seem to straddle the descriptive/normative divide. A sociologist seeking to explain why people generally obey the law, for example, is likely to appeal at some point to the fact that many people believe that they *ought* to obey. Equally, factual questions about human behaviour are just as relevant to normative issues. For example, there is no point in putting forward a theory of the just society without having some knowledge of human behaviour and motivation. Some theories of justice, for example, might make unrealistic assumptions about people's capacity (or lack of capacity) for altruism. In short, studying how things are helps to explain how things can be, and studying how they can be is indispensable for assessing how they ought to be.

But how can we answer the question of how things ought to be? We know, broadly, how to go about answering purely descriptive questions: we go and look. This is not to say that political science or history is easy, for very subtle and detailed work is often involved. But in principle we do think we know how to do it, even if often we cannot find the information we seek. But what can we do to find out how things ought to be? Where can we look?

The uncomfortable fact is that there is no easy answer. But, despite this, very many philosophers have attempted to solve these normative political problems, and they have not been short of things to say. We will examine some of the most important contributions throughout this book, and we will see that, by and large, philosophers reason about politics in just the way they do about other philosophical issues. They draw distinctions, they examine whether propositions are self-contradictory, or whether two or more propositions are logically consistent. They try to show that surprising theses can be deduced from more obvious ones. In short, they present arguments.

And philosophers argue about politics for good reason. In political philosophy, unlike many other areas of philosophy, there is no hiding-place. In philosophy, agnosticism ('The English translate their ignorance into Greek and call it agnosticism', said Engels) is often a respectable position.

Perhaps I cannot find a satisfactory position on the question of whether or not we have free will, so I profess no view. In a wider context this hardly matters. But in political philosophy agnosticism is self-defeating. It may not matter if a society has no official policy on the solution to the problem of free will, but in every society someone (or no one) holds political power, and property is distributed in some way or other. Of course, any one individual's influence on society's decisions is likely to be minute. But potentially we all have some say, if not by voting then by making our views known through debate and discussion, whether on the public stage, or by 'underground' means. Those who prefer not to participate will find their political decisions made for them, whether they like it or not. To say or do nothing is, in practice, to endorse the present situation, however repellent.

In the course of this book we raise and discuss the main questions of political philosophy, examining some of the most influential answers, from the ancient Greeks to the present day. Each chapter takes on a particular question or controversy. The natural starting-point is political power, the right to command. Why should some have the right to pass laws to regulate the behaviour of others? Well, suppose no one had such a right. What would life be like? This is the question pursued in the first chapter: what would happen in a 'state of nature' without government? Would life be unbearable? Or would it be an improvement on how things are now?

Suppose we come to accept that life under government is preferable to life in the state of nature. Does it follow from this that we have the moral duty to do as the state decrees? Or is there some other way of justifying the state? This is the problem of political obligation, which we shall discuss in Chapter 2.

If we have a state, how should it be organized? Should it be democratic? What does it even mean to say that the state is democratic? Is there any rationale for preferring rule by the people to rule by an expert: perhaps a benevolent dictator? These are the questions pursued in Chapter 3.

How much power should the state have? Or, viewed from the other side, how much liberty should the citizen enjoy? Chapter 4 considers the theory that, to avoid the 'tyranny of the majority', we should be given the liberty to act just as we wish, provided that we do no harm to others.

If citizens are to have liberty, should this include the liberty to acquire and dispose of property however they see fit? Or are there justified restrictions on economic activity in the name of liberty or justice? This is the topic of Chapter 5: distributive justice.

The five main chapters of this book take us through topics of enduring concern: the state of nature, the state, democracy, liberty, and property. The final chapter looks briefly at some questions that have come to greater attention in more recent decades, such as issues of gender, race, disability, sexual orientation, immigration, global justice, and justice to future generations. By this point, with two-and-a-half thousand years of hindsight, we may have some sort of answer to a question raised, yet not satisfactorily answered, in this Introduction—how do we do political philosophy? On this topic, as on all those discussed here, my aim is not to force an opinion on you; I hope instead to present some materials that will help you form your own view. Of course, it will be possible to read this book and end up as uncertain as before. But we must not underestimate the progress made by advancing from muddled ignorance to informed bemusement.

1

THE STATE OF NATURE

Introduction

> 'I should have thought that a pack of British boys—you're all
> British aren't you?—would have been able to put up a better show
> than that—I mean—'
> 'It was like that at first,' said Ralph, 'before things—'
> He stopped.
> 'We were together then—'
> The officer nodded helpfully.
> 'I know. Jolly good show. Like the Coral Island.'
>
> William Golding, *Lord of the Flies*
> (Harmondsworth: Penguin, 1954), 192

R. M. Ballantyne's *Coral Island* (1858) is a story in which three English
boys are marooned on a desert island. Through courage, intelligence,
and cooperation they repel pirates and native savages to enjoy an idyllic life in the South Seas. William Golding's characters also find themselves on a bountiful coral island, but soon fall first into dispute, and
then into desperate tribal warfare. In telling their stories as they do,
Ballantyne and Golding suggest opposing pictures in answer to our first
question: what would life be like in a 'natural' state, a world without
government?

Why ask this question? What is its relevance for political philosophy?
We take for granted that we live in a world of political institutions: central government, local government, the police, the law courts. These institutions distribute and administer political power. They place people in
offices of responsibility, and these people then claim to have the right to
command us to act in various ways. And, if we disobey and are caught,

we will be punished. The life of each one of us is structured and controlled, in part, by the decisions of others. This level of interference in
our lives can seem intolerable. But what is the alternative?

A natural starting point for thinking about the state is to ask: what
would things be like without it? To understand why we have something,
it is often a good tactic to consider its absence. Of course, we could hardly
abolish the state just to find out what life would be like without it, so the
best we can do in practice is carry out a thought-experiment. We imagine
a 'state of nature'; a situation where no state exists and no one possesses
political power. Then we try to decide what it would be like to live under
those conditions. This way we can come to a view about life without the
state, and this, we hope, will help us to see just why we have a state.
Perhaps we will come to understand how the state is justified, if it is, and
also what form it should take.

Was there ever a state of nature? Many philosophers seem reluctant to
commit themselves on this topic. Jean-Jacques Rousseau (1712–78), for
example, thought that so much time would have been required to pass
from a state of nature to 'civil society' (a society governed by a formal
state) that it would be blasphemous to assume that modern societies had
arisen in this way. He argued that the amount of time needed for the
transition was longer than the age of the world, as recorded in the scrip-
tures. Yet, on the other hand, Rousseau also believed that there were
contemporary examples of peoples living in a state of nature, while John
Locke (1632–1704) thought this was true of many groups living in sev-
enteenth-century America.

But even if there never has been a true state of nature, we can still
consider the question of what it would be like if, hypothetically, we
found ourselves without a state. Thomas Hobbes (1588–1679), deeply
worried by the English Civil War, thought he saw his country falling into
a state of nature. In *Leviathan* (1651) he drew a picture of how unpleasant this would be, hoping to persuade his readers of the advantages of
government. Accordingly, for the purposes of this chapter we need not
spend much time discussing the question of whether, as a matter of fact,
human beings have ever lived in a state of nature. All we need to argue
is that it is possible.

Is it possible? Sometimes it is claimed that not only have human beings always lived under a state, but that it is the only way they possibly

could live. On this view, the state *exists naturally* in the sense of being *natural to human beings*. This is a view often associated with the ancient Greek philosopher Aristotle (384–322 BCE). Maybe we would not be human beings if we lived in a society without a state. Perhaps we would be a lower form of animal. If human beings exist, then so does the state. If this is true, then speculation about the state of nature is redundant.

In response, some theorists claim that we have plenty of evidence that human beings have been able to live without the state, and such claims have been vital to the case made by anarchist writers (we will return to these later in the chapter). But even if human beings have never actually lived for any length of time without a state, it is very hard to see how it could be established that it is absolutely impossible. And so, as a way of trying to work out why we have the state, we will assume that human beings could find themselves in a world without it. What would that world be like?

Hobbes

> In [the state of nature] there is no place for Industry; because the fruit thereof is uncertain: and consequently no Culture of the Earth; no Navigation, nor use of the commodities that may be imported by Sea; no commodious Building; no Instruments of moving, and removing of things as require much force; no Knowledge of the face of the Earth; no account of Time; no Arts; no Letters; no Society; and which is worst of all, continuall feare, and danger of violent death; And the life of man, solitary, poore, nasty, brutish, and short.
>
> Thomas Hobbes, *Leviathan*, ed. C. B. MacPherson, ([1651],
> Harmondsworth: Penguin, 1968), 186

Hobbes's greatest work, *Leviathan*, pursues a theme that had obsessed him for more than twenty years: the evils of civil war and the anarchy by which it would be accompanied. Nothing could be worse than life without the protection of the state, Hobbes argued, and therefore strong government is essential to ensure that we do not lapse into the war of all against all.

But why did Hobbes believe that the state of nature would be so desperate, a state of war, a state of constant fear and danger of a violent death? The essence of Hobbes's view is that, in the absence of government, human nature will inevitably bring us into severe conflict. For Hobbes, then, political philosophy begins with the study of human nature.

Hobbes suggests that there are two keys to the understanding of human nature. One is self-knowledge. Honest introspection tells us a great deal about what human beings are like: the nature of our thoughts, hopes, and fears. The other is knowledge of the general principles of physics. Just as to understand the citizen (the individual in political society) you have to understand human nature, Hobbes believed, as a philosophical materialist, that to understand human nature you must first understand 'body' or matter, of which, he urged, we are entirely composed.

For our purposes, the most important aspect of Hobbes's account of matter is his adoption of Galileo's principle of the conservation of motion. Prior to Galileo, philosophers and scientists had been puzzled by the question of what kept objects in motion. By what mechanism, for example, does a cannon ball remain in flight once it has been fired? Galileo's revolutionary answer was to say that this was the wrong question. We should assume that objects will continue to travel at a constant motion and direction until acted on by another force. What must be explained is not why things keep going, but why they change direction and why they stop. In Hobbes's lifetime this view was still a novelty, and, he pointed out, defied the common-sense thought that, just as we tire and seek rest after moving, objects will naturally slow down too. But the truth, he claims, is that 'when a thing is in motion, it will eternally be in motion, unless somewhat els stay it' (*Leviathan*, 87). This, he thought, was true for us too. Becoming tired and desiring rest is simply to have a different motion act upon us.

So Hobbes used the principle of the conservation of motion in developing a materialist, mechanist view of human beings. The broad outlines of this account are laid out in the introduction to *Leviathan*: 'What is the *Heart*, but a *Spring*; and the *Nerves* but so many *Strings*; and the *Joynts*, but so many *Wheeles*, giving motion to the whole Body . . . ?' (81). Thus human beings are animated through motion. Sensation, for example, is a 'pressing' on an organ. Imagination is a 'decaying relic' of sensation.

A desire is an 'internal motion towards an object'. All of this is meant quite literally.

The importance of the theory of the conservation of motion is that with it Hobbes paints a picture of human beings as always searching for something, never at rest. 'There is no such thing as perpetuall Tranquillity of mind while we live here; because Life it selfe is but Motion, and can never be without Desire' (*Leviathan*, 129–30). Human beings, Hobbes argues, seek what he calls 'felicity', continual success in achieving the objects of desire. It is the search to secure felicity that will bring us to war in the state of nature. Ultimately, Hobbes argued, our fear of death would lead human beings to create a state. But without a state, in the state of nature, Hobbes thought that the search for felicity would lead to a war of all against all. Why did he think this?

One clue can be found in Hobbes's definition of power: one's 'present means to obtain some future apparent Good' (*Leviathan*, 150). To be assured of achieving felicity one must become powerful. Sources of power, Hobbes claims, include riches, reputations, and friends, and human beings have 'a restlesse desire of Power after power, that ceaseth onely in Death' (*Leviathan*, 161). This is not only because humans can never reach a state of complete satisfaction, but also because a person 'cannot assure the power and means to live well, which he hath present, without the acquisition of more' (*Leviathan*, 161). Others will also seek to increase their power, and so the search for power is, by its nature, competitive.

Everyone's natural, continual, attempt to increase power—to have riches and people under their command—will lead to competition. But competition is not war. So why should competition in the state of nature lead to war? An important further step is Hobbes's assumption that human beings are by nature 'equal'. An assumption of natural equality is often used in political and moral philosophy as a basis for the argument that we should respect other people, treating one another with care and concern. But for Hobbes the assumption is put to quite a different use, as we might suspect when we see how he states the point: we are equal in that all humans possess roughly the same level of strength and skill, and so any human being has the capacity to kill any other. 'The weakest has strength enough to kill the strongest, either by secret machination or by confederacy with others' (*Leviathan*, 183).

To this Hobbes adds the reasonable assumption that in the state of nature there is a scarcity of goods, so that two people who desire the same *kind* of thing will often desire to possess the same thing. Finally, Hobbes points out that no one in the state of nature can become invulnerable against the possibility of attack. Whatever I possess, others may desire, and so I must constantly be on my guard. Yet even if I possess nothing, I cannot be free from fear. Others may take me to be a threat and so I could easily end up the victim of a pre-emptive strike. From these assumptions of equality, scarcity, and uncertainty, it follows, thinks Hobbes, that the state of nature will be a state of war:

> From this equality of ability, ariseth equality of hope in the attaining of our Ends. And therefore if any two men desire the same thing, which neverthelesse they cannot both enjoy, they become enemies; and in the way to their End, (which is principally their owne conservation, and sometimes their delectation only) endeavour to destroy, or subdue one another. And from hence it comes to pass, that where an Invader hath no more to feare than another mans single power; if one plant, sow, build, or possesse a convenient Seat, others may probably be expected to come prepared with forces united, to dispossesse, and deprive him, not only of the fruit of his labour, but also of his life or liberty. And the Invader again is in the like danger of another. (*Leviathan*, 184)

Worse still, Hobbes argues, people seek not only the means of immediate satisfaction, but also power in order to satisfy whatever future desires they will have. Now, as reputation of power is power, some people will attack others, even those who pose no threat, purely to gain a reputation of strength as a means of future protection. As in the school playground, those with a reputation for winning fights are least likely to be attacked for their goods, and may even have goods surrendered to them by others who feel unable to defend themselves. (Of course, those with a reputation for strength cannot relax either: they are the most likely victims of those seeking to enhance their own reputations.)

In sum, Hobbes sees three principal reasons for attack in the state of nature: for gain, for safety (to pre-empt invaders), and for glory or reputation. At bottom, Hobbes relies on the idea that human beings, in the search for felicity, constantly try to increase their power (their present means to obtain future goods). When we add that human beings are roughly equal in strength and ability; that desired goods are scarce; and that no one can be sure that they will not be invaded by others, it seems reasonable to conclude that rational human action will make the state of nature a battlefield. No one is strong enough to ward off all possible attackers, nor so weak that attacking others, with accomplices if need be, is never a possibility. The motive to attack falls into place when we also recognize that attacking others in the state of nature is often the surest way of getting (or keeping) what you want.

Should it be objected that this depiction of our likely plight in the state of nature relies on an assumption that human beings are unrealistically cruel, or unrealistically selfish? But Hobbes would reply that both objections miss the point. Human beings, Hobbes argues, are not cruel: 'that any man should take pleasure in other mens great harms, without other end of his own, I do not conceive it possible' (Leviathan, 126). As for selfishness, he would agree that human beings do generally, if not always, seek to satisfy their self-centred desires. But of equal or greater importance as a source of war is fear: the fear that others around you may try to take from you what you have. This can lead you to attack, not for gain, but for safety or perhaps even reputation. Thus we come close to the idea of a war in which everyone is fighting everyone else in self-defence.

Still, it might be said, it is unreasonable to suppose that everyone will be so suspicious of each other that they will always be at each other's throats. But Hobbes accepts that there will be periods of time without actual conflict. He defines the state of war not as constant fighting, but as a constant readiness to fight, so that no one can relax and let down their guard. Is he right that we should be so suspicious? Why not assume that people in the state of nature will adopt the motto 'Live and let live'? But consider, says Hobbes, how we live even under the authority of the state. What opinion of your neighbours do you express when you lock your doors against them? And of other members of your household when you lock your chests and drawers? If we are so suspicious when we live with the protection of law, just think how afraid we would be in the state of nature.

At this point, it might be argued that, while Hobbes has told us an amusing story, he has overlooked one thing: morality. Although creatures with no moral sense might behave as Hobbes outlines, we are different. The great majority of us accept that we should not attack other people or take their property. Of course, in a state of nature a minority would steal and kill, as they do now, but there would be enough people with a moral sense to stop the rot spreading and prevent the immoral minority from bringing us to a general war.

This objection raises two central questions. First, does Hobbes believe that we can make sense of the ideas of morality in a state of nature? Second, if we can, would he allow that the recognition of moral duty, in the absence of the state, is sufficient motivation to override the temptation to invade others for their goods? Let us consider Hobbes's position on the first of these questions.

Hobbes seems to deny that there can be a morality in the state of nature: 'To this warre of every man against every man . . . nothing can be Unjust. The notions of Right and Wrong, Justice and Injustice, have no place' (*Leviathan*, 188). The argument Hobbes uses at this point is that injustice consists of the breach of some law, but for a law to exist there must be a lawgiver, a common power, able to enforce that law. In the state of nature there is no common power, so no law, so no breach of law, and so no injustice. Each person has 'the Liberty . . . to use his own power . . . for the preservation of his own Nature; that is to say of his own Life; and consequently, of doing any thing, which in his Judgement, and Reason, he shall conceive to be the aptest means thereunto' (*Leviathan*, 189). One of the consequences of this, claims Hobbes, is that 'in such a condition every man has a Right to every thing; even to one anothers body' (*Leviathan*, 190). Hobbes calls the liberty to act as you think fit to preserve yourself the 'right of nature': its consequence seems to be that, in the state of nature, you are permitted to do anything, even take another's life, if you believe that this will help you survive.

Why does Hobbes take such an extreme position, granting everyone liberty to do anything they think fit in the state of nature? Perhaps his position is not so extreme. We would find it hard to disagree that people in the state of nature have the right to defend themselves. That said, it also seems evident that individuals must decide for themselves what reasonably counts as a threat, and further, what is the most appropriate action to take in the face of such a threat. No one, it would seem, could reasonably be criticized for any action they take to defend themselves. As pre-emption is a form of defence, invading others can often be seen as the most rational form of self-protection.

This, then, is the simple initial account of Hobbes's view. In the state of nature there is no justice or injustice, no right or wrong. Moral notions have no application. This is what Hobbes calls the 'Natural Right of Liberty'. But as we shall see, Hobbes's view does have further complications.

In addition to the Natural Right of Liberty, Hobbes argues that what he calls the 'Laws of Nature' also exist in the state of nature. The first 'fundamental law' is this: 'Every man ought to endeavour Peace, as farre as he has hope of obtaining it; and when he cannot obtain it, that he may seek, and use, all helps, and advantages of Warre' (*Leviathan*, 190). A second law instructs us to give up our right to all things, provided others are willing as well, and each should 'be contented with as much liberty against other men, as he would allow other men against himselfe' (*Leviathan*, 190). The third, which is particularly important for Hobbes's later social contract argument for the state, is to perform whatever covenants you make. In fact, Hobbes spells out a total of nineteen Laws of Nature, concerning justice, property, gratitude, arrogance, and other matters of moral conduct. All these laws, Hobbes supposes, can be deduced from the fundamental law, although he realizes that few people would be able to carry out the deduction, for most people 'are too busie getting food, and the rest too negligent to understand' (*Leviathan*, 214). But the Laws of Nature can be 'contracted into one easy sum . . . Do not that to another, which thou wouldest not have done to thy selfe', a negative formulation of the biblical 'golden rule' ('Do unto others as you would have them do unto you').

The Laws of Nature, then, could easily be called a moral code. But if Hobbes intends these as a set of moral rules to govern the state of nature, then this seems to contradict his earlier statement that there is no right or wrong in such a condition. Furthermore, if people are motivated to obey the moral law, perhaps this will make the state of nature rather more peaceful than Hobbes expects. However, Hobbes does not describe the Laws of Nature as moral laws, but rather as theorems or conclusions of reason. That is, Hobbes believes that following these laws gives each person the best chance of preserving his or her own life.

This, however, seems to lead into a different problem. The fundamental Law of Nature tells us it is rational to seek peace. But Hobbes has already argued that the state of nature will be a state of war, because it is rational, in the state of nature, to invade others. How can Hobbes say that rationality requires both war and peace?

The answer, I think, is that we have to distinguish between *individual* and *collective* rationality. Collective rationality is what is best for each individual on the assumption that everyone else will act the same way. The Laws of Nature express what is collectively rational. We can illustrate this distinction with an example from Jean-Paul Sartre. Consider a group of peasants, who each farm their own plot on a steep hillside. One by one they realize that they could increase the usable part of their plot by cutting down their trees and growing more crops. So they all cut down their trees. But in the next heavy storm the rain washes the soil off the hill, ruining the land. Here we can say that the individually rational thing for each peasant is to cut down his or her trees, to increase the amount of land available for farming. (Cutting down the trees on just one plot will not make any significant difference to soil erosion.) But collectively this is a disaster, for if they all cut down their trees everyone's farm will be ruined. So the collectively rational thing to do is leave most, if not all, of the trees standing.

The interesting feature of cases of this nature (known in the literature as the 'prisoner's dilemma') is that, where individual and collective rationality diverge, it is very hard to achieve co-operation on the collectively rational outcome. Every individual has an incentive to 'defect' in favour of the individually rational behaviour. Suppose the peasants understand the structure of their situation, and so agree to refrain from cutting down trees. Then any individual peasant can reason that he or she will personally increase yield by felling trees. (Remember that clearing just one plot will not lead to significant soil erosion.) But what is true for one is true for all, and so they may each begin to clear their plots, to gain an individual advantage. Even if they make an agreement, everyone has good reason to break that agreement. Hence the collectively rational position is unstable, and individuals will tend to defect, even if they know the consequences if everyone were to act that way.

With this in mind, one way of thinking about Hobbes's argument is that, in the state of nature, the *individually* rational behaviour is to attack others (for reasons we have already seen) and this will lead to the state of war. However, the Laws of Nature tell us that the state of war is not the inevitable situation for human beings because another level of behaviour—*collective* rationality—may also be available. If only we could somehow ascend to the level of collective rationality and obey the Laws of Nature, we can live in peace, without fear.

The question now is whether Hobbes believed that each person in the state of nature has a duty to obey the Laws of Nature, and if so whether the recognition of their duty should be sufficient to motivate people to obey the Laws. Hobbes's answer here is subtle. He says that the Laws bind '*in foro interno*' (in the internal forum), but not always '*in foro externo*' (in the external forum). What he means is that we should all desire that the Laws take effect, and take them into account in our deliberations, but this does not mean that we should always obey them under all circumstances. If other people around me are disobeying the Laws, or, as will often be the case in the state of nature, I have reasonable suspicion that they will break the Laws, then it is simply stupid and self-defeating for me to obey. Anyone obeying in these circumstances will 'make himselfe a prey to others, and procure his certain ruine' (*Leviathan*, 215). (In the technical language of contemporary game theory, anyone acting this way is a 'sucker'!)

In sum, then, Hobbes's position is that we have a duty to obey the Laws of Nature when others around us are known (or can reasonably be expected) to be obeying them too, for then our compliance will not be exploited. But if we are in a position of insecurity, the attempt to seek peace and act with moral virtue will lead to an individual's certain ruin and so we are permitted to 'use all the advantages of war'. The real point, then, seems to be not exactly that moral notions have no application in the state of nature, but that the level of mutual suspicion and fear in the state of nature is so high that we can generally be excused for not obeying the law. We should only act morally when we can be assured that those around us are doing so too, but this is so rare in the state of nature that the Laws of Nature will, in effect, almost never come into play.

Hobbes sees the way out of this predicament as being the creation of a ruler or 'sovereign' who will severely punish those who disobey the Laws. If the sovereign is effective in keeping people to the Laws, then, and only then, can no one have reasonable suspicion that others will attack. In that case there is no longer an excuse to start an invasion. The great advantage of the state, argues Hobbes, is that it creates conditions under which people can securely follow the Laws of Nature.

We should conclude this section by recalling Hobbes's account of the state of nature. It is a state where everyone is rightly suspicious of everyone else, and this suspicion, not mere egoism or sadism, leads to a war, where people will attack for gain, safety, and reputation. The war is self-fuelling and self-perpetuating, as reasonable suspicion of violent behaviour leads to an ever-increasing spiral of violence. In such a situation life is truly miserable, not only racked by fear, but lacking material comforts and sources of well-being. As no one can be sure of retaining any possessions, few will plant or cultivate, or engage in any long-term enterprise or plan. People will spend all their time grubbing for subsistence and fighting battles. Under such circumstances there is absolutely no chance that the arts or sciences could flourish. Our short lives would be lived without anything to make them worthwhile.

Locke

> The State of Nature, and the State of War, which however some Men have confounded, are as far distant as a State of Peace, Good Will, Mutual Assistance, and Preservation, and a State of Enmity, Malice, Violence, and Mutual Destruction are from one another.
>
> John Locke, *Second Treatise of Civil Government*, ed. Peter Laslett ([1689], student edn, Cambridge: Cambridge University Press, 1988), s. 19, 280

It is a matter of scholarly debate whether Locke had Hobbes explicitly in mind when he wrote this passage. His official target was the view of Sir Robert Filmer (1588–1653), a defender of the doctrine of the Divine Right of Kings: that the king ruled with authority granted by God. Nevertheless, it is hard to deny that, at a number of points, Locke seems to be arguing with Hobbes, whose work must have been well known to him. As we shall see, comparing the two accounts of the state of nature casts light on them both.

While, as we saw, Hobbes identified the state of nature with a state of war, Locke is keen to emphasize that this is a mistake. Locke supposed that it would generally be possible to live an acceptable life even in the absence of government. Our question must be how Locke managed to draw this conclusion. Or, in other words, where, according to Locke, does Hobbes go wrong?

Let us start at the beginning. The state of nature, says Locke, is first, a state of perfect freedom; second, a state of equality; and third, bound by a Law of Nature. Verbally, of course, this sounds just like Hobbes's view, but each of these three elements is given quite a different interpretation by Locke. Hobbes's principle of equality was a claim about the mental and physical capabilities of all people. For Locke, it is a moral claim about rights: no person has a natural right to subordinate any other. This assertion was explicitly aimed against those, including Filmer, who accepted the feudal view of a natural hierarchy, headed by a sovereign, ruling by divine appointment. Filmer argued that God had appointed Adam first sovereign, and contemporary sovereigns can trace their title back to God's initial grant. For Locke, it is self-evident that no one *naturally* has a right to rule, in the sense that no one has been appointed as ruler by God. Although Hobbes did not mean this by his assumption of equality, he would accept Locke's position here. Hobbes thought that whoever did, in fact, exercise power over the community was, for that reason, to be recognized as its sovereign.

There is, however, greater disagreement between the two on the nature and content of the Law of Nature. For Hobbes, the fundamental Law of Nature was to seek peace, if others are doing so, but otherwise to use the advantages of war. This, and Hobbes's other eighteen Laws, were said to be 'theorems of reason'. Locke, too, believes the Law of Nature to be discoverable by reason, but Locke's Law has a theological aspect absent in Hobbes's Laws. The Law, says Locke, is that no one ought to harm another in their life, health, liberty, or possessions. The reason for this, according to Locke, is that while we have no natural superiors on earth, we do have one in heaven. In other words, we are all creatures of God, his property, put on earth as his servants, 'made to last during his, not one anothers Pleasure'. Therefore 'Every one . . . is *bound to preserve himself*, and not to quit his station wilfully; so by the like reason when his own Preservation comes not in competition, ought he, as much as he can, *to preserve the rest of Mankind*' (*Second Treatise*, s. 6, 271). The Law of Nature, for Locke, is simply the idea that mankind is to be preserved as much as possible. So, Locke argues, we have a clear duty not to harm others in the state of nature (except for limited purposes of self-defence), and we even have a duty to help others if we can do so without damage to ourselves.

Clearly, then, Hobbes and Locke have significantly different views of the nature and content of the Laws of Nature. A still greater difference lies in their use of the term 'natural liberty'. For Hobbes, we saw, to say that we have natural liberty is to say that it can often be entirely rational, and beyond moral criticism, to do whatever is appropriate to help secure our own survival, even if this means attacking the innocent. Locke's understanding is very different, claiming that although the state of nature 'be a *state of Liberty*, yet it is *not a state of Licence* . . . The *state of Nature* has a Law of Nature to govern it, which obliges every one' (*Second Treatise*, s. 6, 270–1).

Natural liberty, on Locke's view, is no more than the liberty to do what the Law of Nature allows. That is, we are given the liberty to do only what is morally permitted. So, for example, although Locke's Law of Nature prevents me from invading the property of others, this is in no sense a limitation of my liberty. Locke would certainly disagree with Hobbes's claim that in the state of nature everyone has a right to everything, even each others' bodies (although he does accept that we have considerable rights of self-defence).

Do these disagreements between Hobbes and Locke add up to enough to establish Locke's conclusion that the state of nature need not be a state of war? Clearly it is important for Locke that even in the state of nature we have a moral duty to restrict our behaviour. Yet this, on its own, does not seem enough to show that in the state of nature fear and suspicion would not exist. And, as Hobbes argues, it is fear and suspicion that causes the state of nature to tumble into war. To avoid this, Locke requires not only that the state of nature be subject to moral assessment but that somehow or other people will be motivated to act as the Law of Nature instructs.

This suggests a strategy for resisting Hobbes's pessimistic conclusion. Hobbes argued that human beings would be driven by the search for felicity (the continued satisfaction of their desires), and this, at least initially, leads them into conflict. If Hobbes has misdescribed human motivation—if human beings, say, really are strongly altruistic—then peace might easily be achieved. That would be one route to Locke's conclusion. Is it the route Locke takes? Locke does not explicitly put forward a theory of human motivation in the *Two Treatises*, but it seems clear that he did not think that human beings would automatically be motivated to follow the moral law. Indeed he comes very close to sounding like Hobbes: 'For the *Law of Nature* would, as all other Laws that concern Men in this World, be in vain, if there were no body that in the State of Nature, had a *Power to Execute* the Law and thereby preserve the innocent and restrain offenders' (*Second Treatise*, s. 7, 271). In other words, the Law of Nature, like all laws, needs a law-enforcer. Without such an enforcer it would be empty.

Hobbes is perfectly prepared to accept that in the state of nature his Laws of Nature are ineffective. Unlike Hobbes, however, Locke cannot accept that the Law of Nature could be in vain: it is, after all, in Locke's view the law of God, who presumably does nothing in vain. Therefore there must be a way of enforcing the law: somebody who has the power to enforce it. But we are all equal in the state of nature, so if anyone has such power then everyone must have it. Therefore, Locke concludes, there must be a natural right, held by each person, to punish those who offend against the Law of Nature. Each of us has the right to punish those who harm another's life, liberty, or property.

The right to punish is not the same thing as the right of self-defence. It is the right not simply to try to prevent or ward off a particular episode of harm or damage, but to make anyone who has overstepped the Law of Nature pay for their transgression. This 'strange doctrine' as Locke calls it, plays a very important role in the derivation of his view of the state of nature. If the Law of Nature can be enforced, then we have good reason to hope that life could be relatively peaceful. Offenders can be punished to make reparation, and to restrain and deter them, and others, from similar acts in the future: 'Each Transgression may be *punished* to that *degree*, and with so much *Severity* as will suffice to make it an ill bargain to the Offender, give him cause to repent, and terrifie others from doing the like' (*Second Treatise*, s. 12, 275). It is important that this natural right to punish is not restricted solely to the individual who suffers the wrong. If that were so, then, disastrously, those who commit murders would have to go unpunished. But, more importantly, the victim may not have sufficient strength or power to subdue, and exact retribution from, the offender. Locke therefore argues that those who break the law are a threat to us all, as they will tend to undermine our peace and safety, and so every person in the state of nature is given what Locke calls the 'Executive Power of the Law of Nature'. Locke has in mind the idea that law-abiding citizens, outraged by the offence, will band together with the victim to bring the villain to justice, and together they will have the necessary power to do so.

Locke realizes that the claim that we all have a natural right to punish offenders may seem surprising. However, in support of his view he claims that, without it, it is hard to see how the sovereign of any state can have the right to punish an alien who has not consented to the laws. If the foreigner has not consented to the sovereign's laws, then he has not accepted that he is liable to punishment for breaching them. Therefore such a person cannot justly be punished, unless there is some sort of natural right to punish. In effect, the sovereign is in the state of nature with the alien, and so the sovereign's behaviour is sanctioned not by the laws of the land, but by the Executive Power of the Law of Nature. (In fact, we will see in Chapter 2 that Locke has a more obvious strategy to explain the sovereign's right: that the alien *tacitly consents* to the law.)

If the Law of Nature is enforceable, then a number of other rights can be secured, even in the state of nature. For Locke, the most important of these is the right to private property. We can already see what the basic form of the argument must be. God put us on earth, and it would be absurd to think that he put us here to starve. But we will starve unless we can rightfully consume objects such as apples and acorns; furthermore, we will do better still if individuals can securely possess plots of land and rightfully exclude others. For then we can cultivate the land, and be secure in our enjoyment of its products. (We will look at this argument in more detail in Chapter 5.)

To the modern reader, Locke's continual invocation of God and God's purposes may seem an embarrassment. Surely it should be possible to consider questions of political philosophy outside a theological framework? However, Locke also appeals to 'natural reason' in establishing the premisses of his arguments, even if he gives it a lesser role. So, for example, he thinks it absurd, and against natural reason, to suppose that human beings may not make use of the earth without the permission of all others, for if this were the case we should starve. This alternative argument certainly seems plausible, and so some followers of Locke have been prepared to drop the theological underpinnings of his view in favour of this 'natural reason' approach.

To return to the main argument, so far the central difference between Hobbes and Locke seems to be that Locke thinks that, even in the state of nature, there is an enforceable and effective moral law, backed by the natural right of punishment, while Hobbes would be highly sceptical of this claim. We can imagine how Hobbes would reply to Locke. According to Hobbes, the only way of subduing any power is through the exercise of a greater power. So we might all gang up on a villain to exact reparation and deter future such acts. But then the villain—who may well be an unreasonable person with like-minded friends—might return, armed, with forces united, to gain revenge. Such thoughts could act as a powerful disincentive to those thinking of exercising their executive power of the law of nature. If you want to avoid unpleasantness in the future, don't get involved now. So Hobbes would probably argue that even if people did have a natural right to punish offenders, this would rarely be used with any effect unless a single, stable, authority existed: for example, within a tribe or group an acknowledged leader to adjudicate disputes and enforce judgements. But that would already be a fledgling state. So in the state of nature, even if there were a right to punish, it would be ineffective as a means to peace.

However, there is still one seemingly vital difference between Hobbes and Locke that I have not yet mentioned. Remember that for Hobbes, one of the key factors that brought people into conflict was a natural scarcity of goods. Two people will often desire the same thing, and this will make them enemies. Locke, on the other hand, appears to make a very different assumption: nature has given things richly. There is a natural abundance of land, and plenty of room for everyone, particularly 'in the first Ages of the World, when Men were more in danger to be lost, by wandering from their Company, in the then vast Wilderness of the Earth, than to be straitened for want of room to plant in' (*Second Treatise*, s. 36, 293). Hence, Locke implies, under these conditions there is very little reason for conflict and dispute. Most people, presumably, would rather cultivate their own plot than invade their neighbour's, and so we can expect a relatively peaceful climate and few sources of quarrel. If this is right, then peace in the state of nature is secured not only by the natural right to punish, but—equally importantly—also by the fact that it would rarely have to be used.

How plausible is this? Hobbes no doubt would point out that abundance of land does not rule out scarcity of finished and consumable goods. It will often be far less trouble to take another's product by stealth than to go to the effort of ploughing, sowing, and harvesting. Furthermore, if others have similar thoughts then I am wasting my energy by cultivating my own land, for, as Hobbes argued, whatever I produce will end up in the hands of others. For Locke to refute this he must either show that the natural right to punish can be used effectively or that human beings have some fairly strong motivation to obey the moral law. Otherwise a few highly anti-social individuals could ruin things for everyone.

Locke, indeed, comes close to admitting that the state of nature may not be as peaceful as he first supposed. After all, he has to be careful not to paint it in too idyllic tones, for then it would be very difficult to explain why we ever left it and created the state. The primary fault, Locke sees, is with the administration of justice. It is not so much that we will squabble over goods, but that we will squabble over what justice requires. We will, in other words, disagree about the interpretation of the Law of Nature. People will disagree about whether an offence has taken place. They will disagree about its proper punishment and compensation. And they might not have the power to exact what they believe to be its proper punishment. So the attempt to administer justice, even between the would-be law-abiding, is itself a powerful source of dispute. This Locke sees as the primary 'inconvenience' of the state of nature. The only thing that prevents serious trouble is the thought that, given initial abundance of land, disputes would be few.

But Locke sees the initial abundance of land eventually turning to scarcity: not through massive population growth, but through greed and the 'invention' of money. Prior to the existence of money no one would have any reason to take more land than was necessary for their own family's survival. If you grew more than you could use, it would simply go to waste, unless you could exchange it for something more permanent. But once money exists then such exchanges become easy, and it is possible to hoard up enormous amounts of money without the risk that it will spoil. This gives people a reason to cultivate more land to produce goods for sale. In turn, this leads to pressure on land which then—and for this reason only, thinks Locke—becomes scarce. Now Locke does not say that such scarcity introduces the Hobbesian state of war, but he recognizes that once land is in short supply and under dispute the inconveniences of the state of nature multiply and multiply. It becomes imperative to establish civil government. So although it is initially peaceful, eventually, even for Locke, the state of nature becomes almost unbearable.

Rousseau

> The Philosophers who have examined the foundations of society have all felt the necessity of going back as far as a state of Nature, but none of them has reached it. . . . all of them, continually speaking of need, greed, oppression, desires, and pride transferred to the state of Nature ideas they had taken from society; They spoke of Savage Man and depicted Civil Man.
>
> Rousseau, *Discourse on the Origin of Inequality* ([1755],
> Cambridge: Cambridge University Press, 1997), 132

One way to avoid Hobbes's pessimistic conclusions about the state of nature is to start from different premises. In particular, life without the state might seem a much more attractive possibility if we adopted a different theory of human nature and motivation. Hobbes argues that people continually seek felicity: the power to satisfy whatever future desires they may have. This, together with fear and suspicion of fellow human beings, in a condition of scarcity, drives the argument for the state of war. But suppose Hobbes was quite wrong. Suppose people naturally and spontaneously desire to help each other whenever they can. Perhaps, instead of competing in a struggle for existence, humans offer mutual aid, and act for the sake of each other's comfort. If so, then the state of nature will look very different.

Although Rousseau does not make these optimistic assumptions about the natural goodness of human beings, his view takes a substantial step in this direction. Like Hobbes and Locke, he assumes that human beings are primarily motivated by the desire for self-preservation. Yet he also believes that this is not the end of the story. Hobbes and Locke overlooked a central aspect of human motivation—pity or compassion—and so overestimated the likelihood of conflict in the state of nature. Rousseau believes that everyone has 'an innate repugnance to see his kind suffer' (*Discourse on the Origin of Inequality*, 152). This, he adds, is 'so Natural that even the Beasts sometimes show evident signs of it'.

Compassion, or pity, argues Rousseau, acts as a powerful restraint on the drives that might lead to attack and war.

> It is pity that carries us without reflection to the assistance of those who we see suffer; pity that, in the state of Nature, takes the place of Laws, morals, and virtue, with the advantage that no one is tempted to disobey its gentle voice: pity that will keep any Sturdy savage from robbing a weak child or an infirm old man of his hard-won subsistence if he can hope to find his own elsewhere. (*Discourse on the Origin of Inequality*, 154)

Rousseau does not doubt that if modern citizens, moulded and corrupted by society, were placed in a state of nature, they would act just as Hobbes depicted them. But both Hobbes and Locke have projected the qualities of human-in-society (or even human-in-bourgeois-society) on to savage human. That is, they have depicted socialized traits as if they were natural.

Rousseau follows this with a second claim. When we understand how 'the savage' behaves—motivated by both self-preservation and pity—the state of nature would be far from the Hobbesian state of war, and even in some respects preferable to a more civilized condition. This does not mean that Rousseau is advocating a *return* to the state of nature, for that would be impossible for us, tainted and softened by society. Still, for Rousseau, it is something of a matter of regret that we have grown civilized. For Rousseau took an extreme, and extremely dismal, view of human progress. His treatise on education, *Émile* (1762), begins: 'God makes all things good; man meddles with them and they become evil.' And his early essay, the *Discourse on the Arts and Sciences* (1750), argues that the development of the arts and sciences has done more to corrupt than to purify morality.

However, it is important to make clear that Rousseau's claim that human beings are naturally motivated by pity or compassion is very different from the point we attributed to Locke in the previous section: that human beings in the state of nature will often respect each other's *rights*. Like Hobbes, Rousseau argues that notions of law, right, and morality have no place in the state of nature, and so, clearly, he cannot mean that we have a natural impulse to follow a moral law. But unlike Hobbes and Locke he claims that we generally try to avoid harming others, not because we recognize that harm is immoral, but because we have an aversion to harm, even when it is not our own. We are naturally sympathetic to others, and are upset by their suffering. So we take steps to avoid it if we can.

It is surely very plausible that by nature human beings often have sympathy for one another. But is this enough to prevent war in the absence of government? The trouble is that Rousseau has given natural man two drives—self-preservation and compassion—and it seems more than possible that the two could come into conflict. If another has what I believe to be essential for my preservation, but I can take it only by causing harm, what would I—or rather the savage—do? It would surely be rare for any creature to put a stranger's well-being before their own survival, and consequently if goods are scarce the influence of pity must fade. Rousseau more or less admits this. Pity stops the savage robbing the weak or sick, provided there is hope of gaining sustenance elsewhere. But what if there is little or small hope of this? Perhaps, then, in a condition of scarcity we would suffer doubly. Not only would we be in a state of war, but we would also feel terrible about all the harm we were doing to our fellow human beings. But the main point is that in a condition of scarcity, natural compassion does not seem enough to hold off the threat of war.

Rousseau tries to avoid this type of problem by supposing that the savage has few desires, and, relative to those desires, goods are more likely to be obtained by hunting and gathering than by taking them from others. This is not because of nature's munificence, but because the savage, claims Rousseau, is a solitary being, rarely coming into contact with others. Indeed there would not even be families. Rousseau speculates that children would leave their mothers as soon as they could survive on their own, and that among savages there would be no permanent union of man and woman. Compassion is not a strong enough sentiment to create a family bond.

Part of Rousseau's explanation of the solitary life of the savage is that nature has equipped the savage to survive alone. Strong and fleet of foot, not only a match for wild beasts but generally free from disease (which Rousseau claims to be a consequence of indulgence and unhealthy habits), the savage desires only food, sexual satisfaction, and sleep, and fears only hunger and pain.

Natural solitude rules out any desire for 'glory' or reputation, for the savage takes no interest in others' opinions. Indeed, as Rousseau argues that at this stage the savage has not yet developed language, the opportunities for forming and expressing opinions seem greatly restricted. Equally, the savage has no desire for power. Hobbes, we saw, defined power as 'the present means to satisfy future desires'. But, Rousseau argues, the savage has little foresight, and barely even anticipates future desires, let alone seeks the means to satisfy them. Rousseau likens the savage to the contemporary Caribbean, who, according to Rousseau, 'sells his Cotton bed in the morning, and comes weeping to buy it back in the evening, for not having foreseen he would need it for the coming night' (*Discourse on the Origin of Inequality*, 143). Consequently all of Hobbes's drives to war—desires for gain, safety, and reputation—are either defused or absent in Rousseau's state of nature.

Still, despite its relatively peaceful character, Rousseau's state of nature hardly seems a welcoming prospect. Rousseau's savage may well be king of the beasts, but nevertheless, as portrayed, seems barely distinguishable from the other wild animals. The savage, says Rousseau, is 'an animal less strong than some, less agile than others; but, all things considered, the most advantageously organized of all' (*Discourse on the Origin of Inequality*, 134). Given that this is all we would have to boast of in the state of nature, why should Rousseau regret that we have now passed to a more civilized era? Furthermore, it is hard to see how such a transition would even be possible. What dynamic is there for change in Rousseau's picture? It is far from clear how, even hypothetically, we could have got here, from there.

Rousseau himself admits that what he says is no more than 'probable conjecture', for the transition could have happened in many ways. And it has to be admitted that it is not always easy to fit together everything Rousseau says on this topic. However, the key is the thought that human beings, unlike brutes, have two special attributes: free will and the capacity for self-improvement. As we shall see, this latter capacity, Rousseau supposes, is the source of all human progress and all human misfortune.

The state of nature as set out so far lies deep in human prehistory: the condition of 'infant man', who spends time 'wandering in the forests, without industry, without speech, without settled abode, without war and without tie, without any need of others of his kind and without any desire to hurt them, perhaps even without ever recognizing any one of them individually' (*Discourse on the Origin of Inequality*, 157). We begin the path to civilization through the first exercise of the capacity of self-improvement: the development of tools in the struggle for subsistence, a struggle brought about, Rousseau speculates, by an increase in population. It is interesting that Rousseau sees innovation, and not Hobbesian competition, as the primary response to scarcity. Here Rousseau is probably relying on the idea that, as the savage has a natural aversion to harming others, most will prefer to get what they need by working for it, rather than taking things from others. And it is innovation to make work easier—tool-making—that first awakens man's pride and intelligence.

Another innovation is the idea of co-operation: mutuality of interest spurs collective pursuits as, for example, in the formation of hunting parties. Over time the advantages of living in groups, and making common huts and shelters, become apparent, and the habit of living in these new conditions 'gave rise to the sweetest feelings known to man, conjugal love and Paternal love' (*Discourse on the Origin of Inequality*, 164).

In this condition another novelty arises: leisure time. Co-operation and tool-making conquer scarcity sufficiently well to give the opportunity to create goods which go beyond bare survival needs. The savage now starts to create convenience or luxury goods, unknown to former generations. However, 'This was the first yoke which, without thinking of it, they imposed on themselves, and the first source of the evils they prepared for their Descendants' (*Discourse on the Origin of Inequality*, 164). Why? Because man now develops what we could call 'corrupted needs'. Rousseau tells what is now a familiar and plausible story. We become dependent on what were at first considered luxuries. After the novelty wears off, having them gives us little or no pleasure, but losing them is devastating—even though we once managed perfectly well without them.

From here a number of other negative elements are introduced: as societies develop, so do languages, and the opportunity for comparison of talents. This gives rise to pride, shame, and envy. For the first time an injury is treated as an affront, a sign of contempt rather than simply as damage, and those so injured begin to seek their revenge. As the state of nature begins to transform itself, causes of dissension and strife break out. But, even so, Rousseau says of this stage that it must have been the happiest and most stable of epochs, 'the genuine youth of the World' (*Discourse on the Origin of Inequality*, 167): halfway between the savage's natural indolence and stupidity, and the civilized being's inflamed pride.

Though this is a stable period it cannot last forever, and the real rot sets in with the long and difficult development of agriculture and metallurgy. From here it is a short step to claims of private property and rules of justice. But private property leads to mutual dependence, jealousy, inequality, and the slavery of the poor. Eventually:

> The breakdown of equality was followed by the most frightful disorder: thus the usurpations of the rich, the Banditry of the Poor, the unbridled passions of all, stifling natural pity and the still weak voice of justice, made men greedy, ambitious, and wicked. A perpetual conflict arose between the right of the stronger and the right of the first occupant, which only led to fights and murders. Nascent society gave way to the most horrible state of war. (*Discourse on the Origin of Inequality*, 171–2)

And so eventually we arrive at war: not as part of the initial state of innocence but as a result of the creation of the first rudimentary societies. At this point, 'The rich under the pressure of necessity, at last conceived the most well-considered project ever to enter the human mind; to use even his attackers' forces in his favor' (*Discourse on the Origin of Inequality*, 172). This was a plan, of course, to institute social rules of justice to ensure peace: rules that bind all equally, but which are greatly advantageous to the rich, for they, after all, are the ones with property to secure. Finally, the first civil societies—societies with laws and governments— are born. (We will see in Chapter 3 how far from ideal Rousseau takes these first societies to have been.) And once more we see the emergence of civil society taken to be a response to a situation of war or near-war in the state of nature.

Anarchism

> No more laws! No more judges! Liberty, equality and practical human sympathy are the only effective barriers we can oppose to the anti-social instincts of certain among us.
>
> Peter Kropotkin, *Law and Authority* ([1886],
> repr. in *The Anarchist Reader*, 1977), 117

Even Rousseau, who believed in man's natural innocence, thought that ultimately life without government would be intolerable. Many anarchist thinkers, however, have tried to resist this conclusion. William Godwin (1756–1836), husband of Mary Wollstonecraft (1759–97) (see Chapter 3), differed from Rousseau on two counts. First, human beings, when 'perfected', could become not only non-aggressive but also highly co-operative. Second, this preferred state for human beings was not buried in the distant past, but an inevitable future in which the state would no longer be necessary. The Russian anarchist, Peter Kropotkin, held a somewhat similar view that all animal species, including human beings, profited through natural 'mutual aid'. This he put forward as an alternative to Darwin's theory of evolution through competition. The fittest, suggests Kropotkin, are those species best able to achieve co-operation.

Kropotkin was able to marshal impressive evidence of co-operation within the animal kingdom, and other anarchists have argued—surely correctly—that there are endless examples of uncoerced co-operation among human beings. Many philosophers and social scientists have accepted that even highly selfish agents will tend to evolve patterns of co-operative behaviour, even for purely selfish reasons. In the long run co-operation is better for each one of us. If the state of war is damaging for all, then rational, self-interested creatures will eventually learn to co-operate.

But, as Hobbes would have been quick to point out, however much evidence there is of co-operation, and however rational co-operation can be, there is still plenty of evidence of competition and exploitation, and this will often seem rational too. And, like the rotten apple, a small measure of anti-social behaviour can spread its evil effects through everything it touches. Fear and suspicion will corrode and wear away a great deal of spontaneous or evolved co-operation.

One response open to the anarchist is to insist that there are no rotten apples. Or at least, insofar as there are, that this is a creation of governments: as Rousseau suggests, we have become softened and corrupted. Anarchists argue that we propose government as the remedy to anti-social behaviour, but, in general, governments are its cause. Nevertheless the thought that the state is the source of all forms of strife among human beings seems impossibly hopeful. In fact, the thesis appears to undermine itself. If we are all naturally good, why has such an oppressive and corrupting state come into existence? The most obvious answer is that a few greedy and cunning individuals, through various disreputable means, have managed to seize power. But then, if such people existed before the state came into being, as they must have done on this theory, it cannot be the case that we are *all* naturally good. Therefore to rely on the natural goodness of human beings to such an extent seems utopian in the extreme.

Hence most thoughtful anarchists have made a different response. The absence of governments does not mean that there can be no forms of social control over individual behaviour. Social pressure, public opinion, fear of a poor reputation, even gossip, can all exert their effects on individual behaviour. Those who behave anti-socially will be ostracized.

Furthermore many anarchists have accepted the need for the authority of experts within society. Some people know how best to cultivate food, for instance, and it is sensible to defer to their judgement. And within any sizeable group political structures are necessary to co-ordinate behaviour on the medium and large scale. For example, in times of international conflict even an anarchist society needs generals and military discipline. Deference to the opinions of experts and obedience to social rules may also be essential in peacetime too.

Such rules and structures are said not to amount to states as they allow the individual to opt out: hence they are voluntary in a way no state is. As we shall see in Chapter 2, the state claims a monopoly of legitimate political power. No 'voluntarist', anarchist social system would do this. However, the existence of anti-social people who refuse to join in the voluntary society places the anarchist in a dilemma. If the anarchist society refuses to attempt to restrain the behaviour of troublesome people, then it is in danger of falling into severe conflict. But if it enforces social rules against such people, then, in effect, it has become indistinguishable from a state. In sum, as the anarchist picture of society becomes increasingly realistic and less utopian, it also becomes increasingly difficult to tell it apart from a liberal, democratic, state. In the end, perhaps we simply lack an account of what a peaceful, stable, desirable situation would be in the absence of something very like a state (with the exception of anthropological accounts of small agrarian societies).

Yet, as we shall see in Chapter 2, anarchism should not be dismissed so quickly. We have seen some of the disadvantages of the state of nature. What about the disadvantages of the state? How rational is it to centralize power in the hands of the few? We are yet to examine the arguments that have been given to justify the state. If it turns out that these attempts to justify the state do not work, then we will have to take a fresh look at anarchism. And in fact, for just this reason, we will need to raise the subject again.

Conclusion

I began this chapter with Hobbes's famous depiction of the state of nature as a miserable state of war of all against all. The basic argument is that individuals, motivated by the drive for 'felicity', will inevitably come into conflict over scarce goods, and, in the absence of a sovereign, this conflict will escalate into full-scale war. A number of counter-arguments were made in response. Locke suggested that the state of nature is governed by a moral law that could be enforced by every individual. He supplemented this with the claim that we are initially in a condition of abundance, not scarcity, and with an implicit assumption that people will often be directly motivated to follow the moral law.

While Rousseau agrees with Locke that Hobbes was wrong to suggest that our natural condition is one of extreme scarcity, he denies that ideas of morality and moral motivation have any place in a state of nature. Instead he proposes that natural pity or compassion will prevent war from breaking out, pointedly remarking that we cannot tell how 'natural man' would behave on the basis of our observations of 'civilized man'. But whatever the force of these responses to Hobbes, both Locke and Rousseau admit that the counteracting causes to war they have identified can only serve to delay the onset of severe conflict, and will not avoid it forever.

The anarchists are more optimistic in their attempts to avoid this conclusion. We considered three main strategies to defend the anarchist position. The first was to argue that co-operation will evolve in the state of nature, even among self-interested creatures. The second was to claim that human beings are naturally good. The third, and most plausible, is the argument that political and social structures and rules, short of the state, can be devised to remedy the defects of the state of nature. Yet, as I suggested, the gap between rational anarchism and the defence of the state becomes vanishingly small. In the end, I think, we must agree with Hobbes, Locke, and Rousseau. Nothing genuinely worthy of being called a state of nature will, at least in the long term, be a condition in which human beings can flourish. But whether this turns out to be a 'refutation' of anarchism remains to be seen.

2

JUSTIFYING THE STATE

Introduction

> All that makes existence valuable to any one depends on the enforcement of restraints upon the actions of other people.
>
> John Stuart Mill, *'On Liberty'*, in *Utilitarianism and Other Writings*, ed. Mary Warnock ([1859], 2nd edn, Oxford: Blackwell, 2003), 91

If the arguments of Chapter 1 are correct, sooner or later, among any fairly sizeable group of people, life in the state of nature will become intolerable. Reason enough, it may be said, to accept that the state is justified, without the need of further argument. After all, what real alternative to the state do we have? If we agree with the claim of John Stuart Mill (1806–73), that life without restraints on the behaviour of others would be of little or no worth, and also believe that the idea of 'enforceable restraints' without the state is mere wishful thinking, then any further argument about its justification seems idle.

That we have no real alternative to the state acts as a negative justification: we cannot think of anything better. Still, this does not end the philosophical discussion. The defender of the state should hope to find something more positive to say, in order to provide an argument to show that we have a moral *duty* to obey the state. Such an argument will also enable us to understand when the state might lose its legitimacy, as was widely believed to have happened, for example, during the so-called 'Arab Spring' between 2010 and 2012, in which many Arab states were challenged by serious protests, and in some cases the people even attempted revolutions. How we might give a positive justification of the state should become clearer as this chapter progresses. But first we should remind ourselves why it is far from obvious that we do have a moral duty to obey the state.

As we saw, Locke assumed that human beings are naturally free, equal, and independent. This means that they are not naturally under the authority of any other person. Hence legitimate power relations must be, in some sense, artificial, a human creation or construction. Accordingly, Locke went on to conclude that the only way of coming under another person's authority was to give that person your consent (except in the case of justified punishment). This holds, for Locke, whether the person claiming authority is another private individual or the sovereign. As a result the sovereign, who claims authority over you, has no right to that authority unless you have voluntarily put yourself in this position through your own consent. So for Locke the problem of justifying the state is to show how its authority can be reconciled with the natural autonomy of the individual. His answer is to appeal to the idea of individual consent, and the device of the social contract. Essentially, for Locke and the social contract theorists, the state is justified if, but only if, every individual over whom it claims authority has consented.

Locke, then, belongs in a tradition of theorists who give great weight to the idea of personal autonomy or natural liberty. Our political institutions, according to these theorists, must be justified in terms of the will, choices, or decisions of those over whom they have authority. This is a very appealing view, as it accords great respect to each individual, giving them the responsibility and opportunity to control their own destiny through their own choices. But there are other important approaches to the defence of the state that downplay the importance that Locke gives to autonomy and put other values in its place. In the utilitarian theory of Jeremy Bentham (1748–1832), for example, the primary value is not autonomy but happiness. The utilitarian theory, in its crudest form, says that we should aim to maximize the sum total of happiness in society. On this account the state is justified if, and only if, it produces more happiness than any alternative. Whether we consent to the state is irrelevant. What matters is whether it makes the members of society, in total, happier than they would be without it. This chapter will examine consent theory and the utilitarian theory, together with some other approaches to the moral defence of the state.

The state

Before deciding how best to justify the state, we had better be sure what it is. As we know from history and contemporary politics, there are many different types of state. Probably most people reading these words live in modern liberal democracies. Others live under dictatorships, benign or tyrannical, based on military rule, a monarchical family line, party membership, or something else again. Some states promote the free market, while others attempt collective forms of production and distribution. When we add to these actual states the theoretical models of the state, especially from communist and utopian writings, it might seem that different real and possible states have so little in common that trying to 'define' the state is a hopeless task.

Nevertheless, it has often been noted that there are some things that all states seem to have in common. First of all it is common to distinguish the state as a political entity from the 'nation', which is more of a cultural concept, based on language or historical traditions. Often the two will come together in the 'nation-state', but sometimes within a single state there are separate nations. This becomes most obvious and politically important when part of a state that regards itself as a separate nation seeks independence. Recently, for example, the Scottish National Party has sought political independence from the United Kingdom, as have Basque nationalists in Spain. States, then, are political entities that may or may not have a single national identity.

States clearly possess, or at least claim to possess, political power. We have seen that Locke defined political power as the right to make laws, with the right too to punish those who fail to obey them. The sociologist Max Weber (1864–1920) made a similar point, if in more startling language: states possess a monopoly of legitimate physical force within a given territory. Within any state, force, violence, or coercion is seen as primarily the state's business, either directly, through its agents—the police and law courts—or indirectly, through the permissions it gives citizens to use force against each other on occasion: in self-defence, for example. All legitimate force or coercion is undertaken or supervised by the state.

The other side to this is that the state accepts the responsibility of protecting everyone who resides within its borders from illegitimate force. Surely it is only for this reason that we are prepared to grant the state its monopoly of force. We forfeit the right to protect ourselves only on the understanding that we do not need self-protection: the state will do what is necessary for us.

Accordingly it is often claimed that the state possesses two essential features: it maintains a monopoly of legitimate coercion or force and it offers to protect everyone within its territory. Is this a 'definition' of 'the state'? One common objection to such a claim is that it is perfectly obvious in practice that no actual state can live up to the ideal. No state can really monopolize force, nor can it protect everyone within its territory. We need only think of the murder rate in any large city, and the precautions ordinary citizens feel they have to take in order to ensure their personal safety. What we say about such cases is that certain states do not manage to monopolize force, and, sadly, fail to protect all their citizens: we would not say that such societies do not have states at all. But it would seem that this would be forced upon us if we treated the two 'essential features' of the state as providing a definition.

In answer to this it should be re-emphasized that the proposed definition claims only that the state maintains a monopoly of *legitimate* violence. The existence, then, of illegitimate violence is irrelevant. And the state *offers* protection to all, even if it also often fails to deliver. But both of these replies are problematic. Many people in the United States claim a right to arm themselves in self-defence. Not only do they believe that they should have this right, but they also argue that the government has no authority over them in this matter. For the very reason they have the right to bear arms, so it is sometimes said, is to defend themselves against the state should it ever become necessary. So, in effect, these people claim, with a great deal of conviction, that the state or government has no business trying to monopolize the means of force. And the argument that the state offers protection to all hardly seems universally true. Many states simply ignore the plight of unfavoured minorities, particularly those belonging to certain ethnic groups. Worse, in extreme cases, these minorities even suffer illegitimate violence from the state itself, in the form of persecution, purges, or 'ethnic cleansing'. Such states fail to possess one of the features all states are said to have, but it would be absurd to deny that they are states.

Both defining qualities of the state, then, are problematic. At this point we have done no more than indicate an ideal type of state, one which does indeed possess the two features we indicated. Let us leave the issue of definition aside and move on to our central question: how can we justify a state, whether or not it lives up to the ideal?

The goal of justification

At this point it will be helpful to introduce some terminology. The task of justifying the state is often said to be the task of showing that there are *universal political obligations*. To say that someone has political obligations is to say, at least, that they have the duty, in normal circumstances, to obey the law of the land, including paying taxes where these are due. Other duties may also be implied: to fight, if called for, in defence of the state; perhaps to behave patriotically; even to seek out and expose the enemies of the state. But let us concentrate on the duty to obey the law.

Political obligation is the obligation to obey each law because it is the law, and not necessarily because we think it has some independent moral justification. Most of us obey the laws against murder without a second thought. If we were asked why we refrain from killing people most of us would surely answer that the idea of killing someone has never entered our heads as a serious option. If called on for a further reason we would probably say that killing is wrong, or immoral. It would cause us great concern, surely, to be told that someone's primary reason for not killing others is that doing so is illegal. Few people, then, need the law to stop them from committing murder. Thus here we have a law which coincides with what morality independently also requires.

But there also exist laws that seem to have little grounding in morality. Take traffic laws, for example. You may believe that you have a moral obligation to stop at a red light at a deserted crossroads, but only because this is what the law tells you to do. Of course, people occasionally think that what the law requires them to do is morally wrong. For example, some of our taxes are used to fund military operations overseas, and many taxpayers think that such a policy is morally reprehensible. But even in this case the 'good citizen' may well feel an obligation to obey the tax laws, and thus reluctantly continue to contribute to this and other projects, simply because it is what the law requires. Any protest, such a citizen might suppose, must be carried out by other means. Breaking the law, many people think, would only be appropriate in the most urgent and serious cases.

'Justifying the state' is normally thought to mean showing that there are universal obligations to obey the law. A 'universal' obligation, in this context, does not mean the duty to obey all laws at all times. Only a certain rather unpleasant kind of fanatic could believe that we are always morally obliged to obey the law whatever it tells us to do; that for example, I ought to stop at a red light even if I am driving a dying person to hospital. Rather, the idea is that political obligations are universal in the sense that they apply to all people who reside within the borders of the state. It may be that the state is prepared to exempt certain people from certain laws (although this is often a sign of corruption), but the point is that the goal of justification of the state is to show that, in principle, everyone within its territories is morally bound to follow its laws and edicts. We should turn now to see whether such justification can be achieved.

The social contract

> I moreover affirm, That all Men are naturally in [the state of nature], and remain so, till by their own Consents they make themselves Members of some Politick Society; And I doubt not in the Sequel of this Discourse, to make it very clear.
>
> John Locke, *Second Treatise of Civil Government*, ed. Peter Laslett ([1689], student edn, Cambridge: Cambridge University Press, 1988), s. 15, 278

Voluntaristic obligation

Let us use the term 'voluntarism' for the view, mentioned earlier, defended by Locke: political power over me can be created only as a consequence of my voluntary acts. Another person can have political power over me only if I have granted them that power.

This view is sometimes expressed in terms of the so-called 'self-assumption' principle: that no one has any duties whatsoever unless they have 'assumed' those duties, that is, they have voluntarily undertaken them. Taken literally, this is a view of little plausibility and should be dismissed. My duty not to attack the innocent seems not in any way to be conditional on my prior 'assumption' of that duty. We must, it seems, accept that we have some moral duties, whether or not we have agreed to them. But this is not enough to show that anyone has the right to make laws and compel me to obey them. And that, of course, is what the state does.

On this account it becomes obvious that the problem of political obligation, at least for Locke, is to show how the existence of the state can be explained in voluntaristic terms. It needs to be shown that somehow or other, every last individual—or at least every adult capable of doing so—has given the state its authority over them. On this view, in order to justify the state it is not enough simply to point out how much better off we would be under the authority of the state than in the state of nature. We would also have to show that each person has voluntarily consented to the state.

To put this in another way, even if it is true that the state is to my advantage, it does not follow, for Locke, that the state is justified. For I have a natural right to freedom, and therefore political power over me can be brought into existence only through my own consent. Accordingly, a state which purports to exercise political power over me, but which does not have my consent, has no right to govern and hence is illegitimate. This remains so even if life in civil society is far superior to life in the state of nature.

The project of showing that individuals consent to the state lies behind the idea of social contract theory. If, somehow or other, it can be shown that every individual has consented to the state, or formed a contract with the state, or made a contract with each other to create a state, then the problem appears to be solved. We would have shown how the state comes to have universal authority—authority over each one of us—by showing that everyone has consented to that authority. In the abstract, then, social contract theory is an obvious, elegant solution to the problem of political obligation. It satisfies the twin demands of universalism—every person must be obligated—and voluntarism—political obligations can come into existence only through consent.

This is all very well in theory, but where can we look for a social contract in practice? Could the social contract be an 'original contract', that is, a real historical event? On such a view it was the moment, and mechanism, which took our ancestors from the state of nature to civil society. This view is commonly—and probably rightly—met with blank incredulity. Even if we accept that there was a real, historical, state of nature (and we saw in Chapter 1 some reasons to question this), could there have been such a contract? What is the evidence? Which museum is it in? Such a momentous event should have left some trace on the historical record. Furthermore, how could such a contract have happened? Aside from the obvious practical problems of communication and co-ordination, critics inspired by Rousseau have pointed out that it is absurd to think that savages in the state of nature could have the conceptual sophistication to create and respect any sort of legal agreement.

But much more importantly, even if there had been such a contract, what would it prove? We could hardly maintain that it explains the political obligations of existing citizens. After all, no reasonable legal system allows one generation to make a contract that binds succeeding generations. Yet this is exactly what the doctrine of the original contract seems to presume.

If social contract theory depends on a doctrine of the original contract, then surely it is doomed. Fortunately there are other ideas that may play a more suitable role. If the goal of constructing a voluntaristic account of the state is to be achieved, then it is important that all those presently said to be bound by the state should have been able to consent to it. This seems to require some sort of on-going consent, given by every individual.

Could it be that every one of us has knowingly, and voluntarily, given our consent to the state? It is hard to see how. I cannot remember ever having been asked whether I agreed to be governed, or at least not by anyone with any official status. It is true that boy scouts and schoolchildren are often required to pledge their allegiance to the flag or to 'God and the Queen', but they are given no real choice, and, in any case, are not old enough for their pledge to have legal standing. There are few, if any, states in which literally everyone is required to pledge. As is often observed, the only people in modern states who explicitly give their consent are those who gain citizenship through naturalization. The vast majority of ordinary citizens are left untouched.

Here it might be replied that consent is given in a less obvious or explicit fashion. One thought is that consent is communicated via the ballot box. In voting for the government, we give it our consent. And it is not wholly implausible that even those who vote against the government nevertheless indicate their consent to the system as a whole through voting. But this leaves us with two problems. Some of those who vote against the government might claim to be expressing their dissent to the system as a whole. Further, what can be said about those who abstain? Refusing to vote can hardly be treated as a way of expressing consent to the government. The situation is not improved by making abstention illegal and forcing everyone to vote. As voting would no longer be voluntary, it could not possibly be represented as an act or sign of consent.

However, a much more interesting development of this line of thought is the claim that political obligations arise only where society is arranged as a 'participatory democracy'. A participatory democracy is one in which all citizens take an active role in government, far more extensive than anything we have encountered in modern democracies. An important consequence of this view is that, as contemporary democracies fail to match the ideal, citizens in such states have no political obligations. The theory of participatory democracy deserves proper attention, and we will return to it in Chapter 3. In the meantime, let us return to other interpretations of the social contract.

Tacit consent

So far we have not been able to see how to develop a plausible theory of explicit or express consent. We have already considered the idea that voting is a way of *tacitly* consenting, but perhaps the idea of tacit consent can be developed in a more promising form. In fact all the major social contract theorists—Hobbes, Locke, and Rousseau—rely in different ways on arguments based on tacit consent. Here the central thought is that by quietly enjoying the protection of the state you are giving it your tacit consent. And this is enough to bind each individual to the state. Although Locke believed that only express consent could make you a full member of your political society, he famously argued that, nevertheless, political obligations can be created through tacit consent:

> Every Man that hath any Possession, or Enjoyment, of any part of the Dominions of any Government, doth thereby give his *tacit Consent*, and is as far forth obliged to obedience to the laws of that Government, during such Enjoyment as any one under it; whether this Possession be of Land to him and his Heirs for ever, or a Lodging only for a Week; or whether it be barely travelling freely on the Highway. (*Second Treatise*, s. 119, 348)

Perhaps this seems plausible. I tacitly consent to the state by accepting its protection and other benefits. Now it might be that the mere receipt of benefits is alone enough to bind you to the state, and we shall look at such an argument later in this chapter. But the current proposal is subtly different, for it adds a further step in the argument: receiving benefits is a way of tacitly consenting to the state, and it is the *consent* that binds. Should we accept this claim?

It is likely that behind the argument is the thought that those who do not like the package of benefits and burdens offered by the state can get up and go. But if the doctrine depends on this, then many would claim that it has been decisively refuted by David Hume (1711–76):

> Can we seriously say, that a poor peasant or artizan has a free choice to leave his country, when he knows no foreign language or manners, and lives from day to day by the small wages he acquires? We may as well assert, that a man, by remaining in a vessel, freely consents to the dominion of the master; though he was carried on board while asleep, and must leap into the ocean, and perish, the moment he leaves her. ('Of The Original Contract', *Essays Moral Political and Literary*, ed. E. F. Miller ([1748], Indianapolis: Liberty Press, 1985) 475)

What does this objection show? Hume's idea is that residence alone cannot be construed as consent. Why not? Simply because nothing could count as dissent, except leaving the country. But that is surely too onerous a condition to allow us to conclude that those who stay consent.

This is often taken as a convincing refutation. But on the other hand there might be cases that meet even these demanding conditions. Rousseau, for example, supposes that residence constitutes consent, but only within a 'free' state, 'for elsewhere family, goods, lack of asylum, necessity, violence may keep the inhabitant in the country in spite of himself, and then his mere residence no longer implies his consent to the contract or to its violation' (*The Social Contract*, [1762], bk. IV, ch. 2, 124n). It is peculiar, if typical, of Rousseau to think that family or goods render you unfree. But we can see his point, even if we would wish to amend his account. In a free state, Rousseau implies, the act of dissenting—leaving the territories of the state—is simple enough.

The idea that any dissenter can leave might be plausible if we think of a world of walled city-states, which one may leave simply by walking through the gates (as Rousseau, almost by accident, left Geneva in his youth). Hume clearly has in mind something much more like Great Britain, where leaving is no simple matter, as his image of the state as a vessel on the high seas suggests. In the contemporary world, a world of nation-states, the doctrine of tacit consent seems far less appropriate than it did for Rousseau; not so much for the reason that states are surrounded by seas, but because even those who want to leave often find that there is simply nowhere to go. No other country will have them, and in any case what is the point of swapping one objectionable regime for another? We should, in the end, agree with Hume. The conditions for tacit consent are not met in the modern world. The state cannot be justified in these terms.

Hypothetical consent

Perhaps it is a mistake to think that the social contract theorist needs to appeal to some form of actual consent, be it historical, express, or tacit. Rather, it could be argued that the social contract is purely hypothetical: it merely tells us what we *would do*, or *would have done* in the state of nature. According to this view, the thought that if we were in the state of nature we would have contracted to bring about the state is itself enough to show that the state is justified.

How should we understand this sort of argument? As a first step, it is worth reminding ourselves of a point mentioned in Chapter 1: perhaps the best way of getting clear about your relation to something is to imagine its absence. This is a tactic often used, for example, by parents to persuade their children to eat unappetizing food: you would be grateful for it if you were starving. Accordingly, then, the hypothetical contract argument tells us that if, somehow or other, we found ourselves without a state, we would find it rational to try to bring one into existence as soon as we appreciated the nature of our plight.

We can understand the hypothetical contract argument as running like this: even if you were not under the authority of the state, and somehow found yourself in the state of nature, then, if you were rational, you would do everything in your power to recreate the state. In particular, you would rationally and freely join in a contract to bring about the state. The hypothetical contract theorist will now plausibly ask: how can this argument *fail* to justify the state?

If it really is true that all rational individuals in the state of nature would freely make this choice, then we do seem to have a good argument here to justify the state. But we should still ask how this relates to the 'voluntaristic' assumptions of social contract theory. For if we assume that we can only acquire political obligations by our own voluntary acts of consent, and recognize that *hypothetical* acts of consent are *not* acts, it seems to follow that the hypothetical contract argument will not satisfy the demands of social contract theory.

This observation puts us in an interpretative quandary. If the hypothetical contract argument is not the sort of argument that could satisfy the social contract theorist, then what sort of argument is it? One possibility is to say that it is a way of showing that certain sorts of state are *worthy* of our consent. That is, the state has a number of desirable features—essentially that it is our best hope of peace and security—and the fact that we would consent to bring it into existence from the state of nature simply confirms that it has those features. On this interpretation it is the features of the state, and not our consent, which provide the main basis of its justification. Consent simply drops out of the picture. Ultimately, then, according to this line of argument, the hypothetical contract argument is not a form of voluntaristic defence of the state. It is much closer to the utilitarian theories that we will encounter shortly. The state is justified through its contribution to human well-being.

On the other hand, there is a way in which we might try to reconstruct hypothetical contract theory in voluntaristic terms. Consider the argument that hypothetical consent somehow indicates the presence of real consent. We should start from the thought that although almost no one ever formally expresses their consent to the state, there is nevertheless a sense in which all, or most, of us can be said to consent. Perhaps if we were asked, and required to think about the matter seriously and hard, we would each express our consent. So it would seem fair to say that anyone of whom this is true has a *disposition* to consent to the state. But this seems the same as saying that such people consent to the state, even if they do not realize it. Just as we can have beliefs we have never brought to consciousness (for example, for many years I must have believed that giraffes do not have nine legs, although before first writing these words I had never consciously formed this thought), we can consent to the state without realizing that we do so.

The device of the hypothetical contract can now be thought of as a way of getting us to realize what we really think. By reflecting on how I would behave in the state of nature—run headlong into civil society if I could—I come to realize that I do consent to the state. The point is not that, after going through the thought-experiment, I come to consent for the first time. Rather, the idea is that, after going through the process, I come to realize that I have consented all along. On this interpretation the point of the hypothetical contract argument is to reveal dispositional consent: an as-yet-unexpressed attitude of consent.

How much can be achieved with such an argument? One difficulty is that the sense in which consent is used here is very weak. Unexpressed, even unacknowledged, dispositions to consent are rarely considered binding in other moral or legal contexts. Furthermore, there may well be people who go through the hypothetical contract reasoning, and then, after deep reflection, come to believe that they would be better off in the state of nature, and so prefer it to the state. Perhaps they distrust centralized power. Perhaps they are more optimistic about the state of nature than I have been here. Are there such people? It certainly seems that there are: the anarchists and their followers discussed in Chapter 1 would be good examples. Such people cannot possibly be said to have the disposition to consent to the state: they actively and explicitly dissent.

We might be tempted to suppose that such people are irrational. But what is so irrational about them? In any case, even if they are irrational, this is hardly a way of showing that they have consented. So even this weakest form of consent theory cannot deliver what we are looking for: a universal ground of political obligation. And if we insist that political obligations must be undertaken voluntarily, this is a risk we always run. The whole apple cart can be upset by a single dissenter. As contract theory is voluntarism *par excellence* it seems that universalism—the thesis that everyone has political obligations—simply cannot be delivered by contract or consent theory in any of the forms discussed here.

Anarchism revisited

Perhaps the answer is to accept that it is impossible to show that everyone has political obligations. The insistence on a voluntaristic foundation of the state is highly plausible, and if its cost is that we have to accept that some individuals escape the authority of the state, then perhaps we should bite the bullet.

The argument gives renewed support to the anarchist case briefly explored in Chapter 1. If we cannot find a way of justifying the state from acceptable premises, then some sort of anarchy seems forced upon us, morally speaking at least. This critical strategy seems the anarchist's strongest weapon. No one *asked* me whether we should have a state, and the police do not request my permission to act as they do. Therefore, the anarchist argues, the state and the police act illegitimately, at least in respect to their dealings with me.

The implications of this view may be far-reaching. Most radically it could be argued that once we accept the anarchists' argument, then the only reason we have for obedience to the state is prudence, especially fear of punishment. The strong person should resist this cowardly attitude, and take no notice of the state and its agents. Or, to put this in a somewhat more moderate form, we can admit that, as we have seen, what the law requires is often independently required by morality. We ought to do some things that the state decrees—refrain from murder, rape, or injuring others—but not because the state decrees it. Furthermore, the police often act in ways in which any citizen might: to protect the innocent, to detain and bring to justice anyone who wrongs another, and so on. So we can be grateful to the police for doing the dirty work for us. However, on this view, you should support the state and the police only in those cases where you independently agree with the reasons for which they act. The fact that a law is a law, or the police are the police, provides no reason at all for obedience. Hence the 'philosophical anarchist' recommends that we adopt a highly critical stance towards the activities of the police and the state. Sometimes they act with moral authority, but where they do not we are right to disobey, obstruct, or ignore them.

In some respects this seems a highly enlightened picture. The responsible citizen should not blindly follow the law, but always use his or her private judgement about whether the law is justified. If it is not, then there is no moral reason to obey.

This picture has to be correct—up to a point. To argue that one should never question or disobey a law would lead one, say, to defend the persecution of Jews in Nazi Germany or to defend the laws that punish homosexuality with death, which is still the case in some Middle Eastern and African countries. There must be some moral limit to the obligation to obey the law. However, it is not so easy to say what this moral limit should be. At the extreme, suppose you held the view that you should not obey the law unless it accords perfectly with your own moral judgement. Now, many people (wealthy people in particular) believe that taxation of income purely for purposes of redistribution of wealth has no moral justification. On the view about the justification of the state just canvassed, such people would be entitled to stop paying a portion of their tax. At the same time, a number of people, from a variety of social and economic backgrounds, believe that the inheritance of wealth is unjust. Who inherits and who does not is completely 'arbitrary from a moral point of view', to use the terminology of John Rawls (see Chapter 5). Many people think it is quite unfair that some individuals inherit vast fortunes, while the equally deserving get nothing. Now, if you think that there is no moral justification to inherited property, then you think that the Duke of Westminster has no more right to have you turned off 'his' inherited property than you have to exclude him, as it is not truly his. If you then add to this that you should obey the law only if it accords with your moral outlook, then you no longer have any reason (save fear of punishment) to respect much of other people's (claimed) property.

Clearly cases can be multiplied. The point is, if we accept the anarchist view just discussed, we have returned to the chaotic situation where people may follow their individual private judgement in all matters, even those of public concern. But it was for exactly this reason that Locke argued that we should move away from the state of nature. From such a perspective, the philosophical anarchist position begins to look like a very dangerous example of moral self-indulgence. Surely it is far better that we generally accept some publicly laid down and accepted set of laws, to guide our dealings with each other, than leave people to act on the basis of their own conflicting codes. In other words, having a *shared* set of laws is, within reason, much more important than anyone's private judgement about what the best laws should be.

In response, the anarchist may well argue that there is no reason to expect such a proliferation of conflicting moral views. After all, a particular moral perspective may well be the correct one, and so individuals might all be brought to share the same set of basic moral principles. It is the second of these claims that carries the weight in the argument, but how plausible is it? Even if there is a single set of true moral principles, how can we ensure that everyone comes to see that truth? For those who doubt that there is any such method the anarchist position remains unattractive in practice, whatever its merits in theory.

Utilitarianism

> Subjects should obey Kings ... *so long as the probable mischiefs of obedience are less than the probable mischiefs of resistance.*
>
> Jeremy Bentham, *A Fragment on Government,* ed.
> Ross Hamilton ([1776], Cambridge: Cambridge
> University Press, 1988) 56

The failure of the contract arguments, combined with the unattractiveness of anarchism, makes the examination of utilitarian theory all the more pressing. The fundamental idea of utilitarianism is that the morally correct action in any situation is that which brings about the highest possible total sum of utility. Utility is variously understood as happiness, pleasure, or the satisfaction of desires or preferences. For the purposes of our discussion it does not much matter which of these options we choose, so let us speak of maximization of happiness, for convenience. Put crudely, utilitarianism requires you to perform the action that will create more happiness (or less unhappiness) in the world than any other action available at the time.

Notice that if we are to take utilitarianism seriously we need to be able to measure and quantify happiness, so that we can determine which of several possible actions creates the most. This is often thought to be a grave difficulty. After all, if we are to compare situations we seem to need some scale by which we can measure: units of happiness, perhaps. How can we do this? Not only does the theory require us to compare one person's happiness with another's, and say who has more, but to say *how much more*. We would have to be able to make sense, it seems, of statements like: 'Fred is twice as happy as Charlie today, although yesterday he was three times as happy.' Many will think this is absurd. Trying to quantify happiness this way often seems just childish.

The problem of finding a way of comparing happiness is known as the problem of 'interpersonal comparisons of utility'. Strangely, none of the nineteenth-century founders of utilitarianism seemed to see the force of this problem, although in the past few decades a number of ingenious technical solutions have been proposed. No solution has been universally accepted and it would take us too far afield to give the issue proper consideration here. However, we should not be blind to the point that we are never at a complete loss when we are called on to make comparisons. We know of other people, say, who seem to enjoy certain foods, or forms of entertainment, far more or less than we do ourselves. More seriously, every day we see people who live in misery, while others, we know, lead wonderfully enjoyable lives. We do believe that comparisons can be made, even if we do not know exactly how we do it. For present purposes we will simply assume that interpersonal comparisons of utility can be made, while remembering that the utilitarian owes us an account of how, precisely, this can be done.

Returning to the main issue, we now need to ask what a utilitarian theory of political obligation would look like. According to Jeremy Bentham, as we saw above, we should obey our rulers as long as the benefits of doing so outweigh the costs. This, then, sounds like the theory that I should obey the law if, but only if, my obedience will lead to the greater happiness of society than my disobedience.

But if this is Bentham's doctrine, then a moment's thought reveals that it is a law-breaker's charter. For my happiness is, after all, part of the general happiness. So if breaking a law—say by stealing a book from a large bookshop—would increase my happiness, and I can be sure that no one would find out or suffer any noticeable loss or harm, it seems that utilitarianism would not only permit me, but require me, to carry out the theft. The more general message is that this utilitarian theory would very often sanction law-breaking.

Can this be what the utilitarian wants? It seems unlikely, and in fact there is a ready response. Consider what would happen if we all broke laws whenever we thought that doing so would lead to an increase in general happiness. In that case you could take any of my possessions whenever doing so would increase your happiness more than it would decrease mine. Possession would be extremely insecure, perhaps so uncertain that ultimately no one would work to produce anything if another could take it whenever the utilitarian calculation worked in their favour. This insecurity would lead to great overall unhappiness, rather like the insecurity in the state of nature. Paradoxically, when each of us tries to increase the general happiness individually, together we eventually bring about general misery. This is another example of the prisoner's dilemma discussed in Chapter 1: action that individually increases happiness collectively diminishes it.

Consequently, the utilitarian can argue that we need a body of laws that will be respected, even when breaking one of these on a particular occasion would, if it were permitted, lead to an increase in happiness. This can be called *indirect* utilitarianism. The idea is that if we all reason directly in utilitarian terms things will go very badly. Hence we need to follow non-utilitarian reasoning—obey the laws—to maximize happiness.

It will help illustrate the point to make an analogy with an individual's search for happiness. A discovery made over and over again by lotus-eaters everywhere is that if you personally set out with the single goal of becoming happy, and do everything you can to become happy, more likely than not you will fail. But if you aim at something else—form and pursue an ambition, get a hobby, make some good friends—you may well find happiness as a side-effect or indirect consequence. So, it is claimed, the direct search for happiness, both individually and socially, can be self-defeating. The best we can do is set ourselves other goals, or follow other rules, in the hope or expectation that happiness will follow as a consequence. The utilitarian political philosopher should recommend a system of laws for each person to follow, at least under normal circumstances. It is not, then, for the individual to consider the effect of following the law on the level of happiness within society.

This is probably Bentham's own real view: 'taking the whole body [of people] together, it is their duty to obey only when it is their interest' (*Fragment on Government*, 56). An extension of this passage provides several ideas:

1. Laws should be passed if, and only if, they contribute more to human happiness than any competing law (or the absence of law) would do.
2. Laws should be obeyed because they are laws (and will be obeyed because disobedience means punishment), and should only be disobeyed to avoid disaster.

3. Laws should be repealed and replaced if they fail to serve the proper utilitarian function.

The utilitarian message for political obligation now seems clear. The state, as provider and enforcer of a body of law, is justified if, and only if, it contributes more to human happiness than any feasible competing arrangement. If we think in terms of a basic contrast between the state and the state of nature, and we accept the arguments—particularly those of Hobbes—from Chapter 1, it seems that the utilitarian justification of the state looks very plausible. In terms of contributing to general happiness, the state seems greatly to outperform the state of nature. Thus, for the utilitarian, the justification of the state is complete.

However, despite this success, very few political philosophers seem entirely convinced by the utilitarian defence of the state. Many concede that the argument works very well in its own terms, but find fault with the argument's assumptions or premisses. The argument itself is very simple. In essence, it has just three premisses:

1. The morally best society is the one in which happiness is maximized.
2. The state promotes happiness better than the state of nature.
3. The state and the state of nature are the only alternatives we have.

Therefore:

4. We have a moral duty to bring about and support the state.

We saw in Chapter 1 that different sorts of anarchists will question premisses 2 and 3, but for the purposes of this argument, let us assume these premisses are true. The argument also seems valid in the formal sense that if the premisses are true, then the conclusion must also be true (assuming we have a moral duty to bring about and support the morally best society). Hence the only vulnerable part of the argument is the first premiss: the fundamental principle of utility.

And here lies the problem. Many philosophers reject utilitarian reasoning, for they think it has morally unacceptable consequences. In particular, it is often claimed that utilitarian morality permits, or even requires, grave injustices. A notorious difficulty, for example, is the 'scapegoat' objection: utilitarianism will permit enormous injustice in the pursuit of the general happiness.

The scapegoat objection is this. Suppose some hideous crime has been committed—perhaps a terrorist bombing in which several people are killed and many more injured. In such circumstances the police are under intense pressure to find the perpetrators. The population at large seeks vengeance, and reassurance that a similar attack will not happen again. The general happiness will certainly be served if the guilty parties are brought to justice. But opponents of utilitarianism have noticed that the general happiness will also be advanced if individuals *believed* by the population to be guilty are arrested and sentenced. As long as they are plausible suspects—have the accents, look the part, and so on—then at least the demand for vengeance will be satisfied, and we will all sleep more soundly in our beds (even if we do so only because of our false belief). Of course, the innocent will suffer. But it seems plausible that the increase in happiness (or decrease in misery) of the general population will outweigh the suffering of the innocent and so make the victimization pay off in utilitarian terms. It is claimed, therefore, that utilitarianism has the consequence that it can be morally correct to punish the innocent. Other examples of the same type—for instance, concerning the utilitarian justification of slavery—can easily be concocted.

The point is not that it is better to punish the innocent; surely it would be better still on the utilitarian calculus to find and punish the guilty. But when everything is taken into account it seems quite likely that some miscarriages of justice are defensible in utilitarian terms. Most of the philosophical discussion is based on fictional examples, but there are some real cases. The issue was brought to public attention in the United Kingdom in connection with the bombing of a pub by the IRA. The 'Birmingham Six' had been found guilty of murder in 1975, but claimed that their confessions had been beaten out of them by the police. They attempted to bring a civil action against the police for the injuries sustained in custody. Lord Denning, in his judgement at the Court of Appeal in 1980, was addressing the question of whether the civil action against the police should be allowed to go to trial. This is what he said:

> If the six men fail, it will mean that much time and money will have been expended by many people for no good purpose. If the six men win, it will mean that the police were guilty of perjury, that they were guilty of violence and threats, that the confessions were involuntary and were improperly admitted in evidence and that the convictions were erroneous. That would mean the

> Home Secretary would either have to recommend they be pardoned or he would have to remit the case to the Court of Appeal. This is such an appalling vista that every sensible person in the land would say: It cannot be right these actions should go any further. (Quoted in Chris Mullin, *Error of Judgement* (rev. edn, Dublin: Poolbeg Press, 1990) 216)

Eventually, in 1991, the conviction was quashed. Lord Denning later admitted that 'with the benefit of hindsight my comments can justly be criticised'. But the point is, so the critics of utilitarianism would say, his argument amounts to a perfect application of utilitarian reasoning. It would be better to let innocent men remain in jail than to admit that the police sometimes terrorize individuals into falsely confessing. And, it hardly needs to be said, so much the worse for utilitarian reasoning.

But in defence, it might seem that the utilitarian can avoid such problems by adopting the 'indirect utilitarianism' strategy outlined before. If we know that we live in the sort of society in which people can be victimized and made scapegoats, and kept in prison even if innocent, this will lead to such insecurity that it will greatly depress human happiness. After all, how do I know that I will not be the next utilitarian scapegoat? Accordingly the utilitarian must grant people the right not to be punished unless they are guilty. The scapegoat objection, and others like it, so it is often argued, can be avoided by this more subtle utilitarian approach. And, indeed, a utilitarian considering the Birmingham Six might well argue that—*contra* Denning's first argument—more good than harm has been done by their release. Discredit may have been brought upon the British judicial system, but, as a result of the case and its publicity, better procedures for recording confessions have been adopted, for the long-term benefit and security of all.

The success of the indirect utilitarian argument seems vital for the defence of utilitarianism. If utilitarian theory can accommodate a theory of individual rights—for example, rights against victimization—then many of the standard objections to it would disappear. We have seen a sketch of how utilitarianism might accomplish this task, but there are ways to develop the objection further. For example, it can be argued that general insecurity will only be a consequence of scapegoatism if the public realize what is going on. But if the public never discover the truth, then they will have nothing to worry about. (Or rather, they will have something to worry about, but as they don't know about it, they will not, in fact, worry. And so there will be no extra negative units to add to the utilitarian balance.) Thus scapegoatism is justified, on utilitarian grounds, provided it is highly efficient and secret. This, surely, is a troubling thought.

A deeper objection is that, even if the calculations work out as the utilitarian hopes, the correct result is achieved for the wrong reason. Perhaps a policy of secret victimization will not, in fact, maximize happiness. But opponents of utilitarianism argue that this is irrelevant: no one should be victimized, whatever the benefits in terms of general happiness. The Birmingham Six should be released whatever the consequences. Furthermore, if utilitarians are concerned only with maximizing happiness, why should they spend so much energy trying to produce a utilitarian theory of rights? This seems to reveal a lack of faith in their own theory.

For the purposes of the present discussion we will make the assumption—one that may be overturned later—that the utilitarian theory cannot, in the end, be rescued from such criticism. I do not want to say any more about the issue now, as I will return to it in detail in Chapter 4, where I will consider John Stuart Mill's *On Liberty*, which is often understood as providing a utilitarian theory of rights. The present point is simply that, although the indirect utilitarian justification of the state seems strong, utilitarianism itself is suspect, even in its indirect form. There are reasons to be dissatisfied with this approach to the defence of the state.

The principle of fairness

> Were you to preach, in most parts of the world, that political connexions are founded altogether on voluntary consent or a mutual promise, the magistrate would soon imprison you, as seditious, for loosening the ties of obedience; if your friends did not before shut you up as delirious, for advancing such absurdities.
>
> David Hume, 'Of the Original Contract', [1748], 470

Whether or not individuals consent to the state, it can seem unfair of them to enjoy its benefits without also accepting the necessary burdens that help produce those benefits. So, it has been argued, anyone who gains an advantage from the state has a duty of fairness to obey its laws, to contribute taxes, and so on.

The principle underlying this view was explicitly formulated by the legal theorist and philosopher H. L. A. Hart (1907–92), who stated it in these terms:

> When any number of persons conduct any joint enterprise according to rules, and thus restrict their liberty, those who have submitted to these restrictions when required have a right to similar submission from those who have benefited by their submission. ('Are There Any Natural Rights?', in J. Waldron, ed., *Theories of Rights* ([1955], Oxford: Oxford University Press, 1984) 85)

Hart's view is that this principle is the 'rational core' of the doctrine of tacit consent. Receiving benefits does bind you to the state, but not because it is a way of tacitly consenting. Rather, the force of the argument is that it is *unfair* to reap the benefits of the state, unless you are prepared to shoulder your share of the burdens too. The benefits, of course, are the security and stability of living in a society that operates a system of enforced laws. The corresponding burdens are political obligations. A more familiar application of the same principle concerns buying drinks in a bar. If three of your friends each buy a round for the four of you, they might rightly feel aggrieved if you decide to go home just when you finish your third drink.

If we accept Hart's principle, and concede that everyone receives benefits from the state, it would seem to follow that, in fairness to everyone else, each of us should obey the laws of our country. This relies on the plausible idea that if we benefit from the laws then it is unfair and exploitative to break them for our own convenience.

Can it really be shown that everyone really does benefit from the existence of the state? Perhaps Hobbes's arguments from Chapter 1 would be enough to convince most people. But another attempt to argue for this conclusion was made by Hume, although Hume was by no means a 'theorist of fairness' himself.

We can use some of his arguments to support the claim that we all do, indeed, benefit from the state. Hume's first step is to argue that each of us will profit if we live in a society governed by norms of justice, such as rules governing private property and personal security. We will, of course, have to make short-term sacrifices, but justice pays in the longer term. As justice will only flourish if we all obey the law, then it turns out that obedience to the law is, in fact, in each person's individual interest.

But is it really true that obedience to the law is in the interests of each of us? If so, then, as Hume himself points out, it seems extraordinary that we should need to be forced to obedience on pain of punishment. If it is in our interests to do what the law tells us, why do we need the law to force us to do it?

Hume's answer is, in effect, that human beings are not very good at acting rationally. Suppose we have a choice between acting in one way to get a small gain now, and acting in another way that will provide a greater benefit, but in the much longer term. While it is ultimately in our interests to take the second course, Hume believes that, left to ourselves, we will generally take the first:

> Tho' we may be fully convinc'd, that the latter object excels the former, we are not able to regulate our actions by this judgment; but yield to the sollicitations of our passions, which always plead in favour of whatever is near and contiguous.

> This is the reason why men so often act in contradiction to their known interest; and in particular why they prefer any trivial advantage, that is present, to the maintenance of order in society, which so much depends on the observance of justice. (*Treatise of Human Nature*, ed. L. A. Selby-Bigge, ([1739–40], 2nd edn, Oxford: Oxford University Press, 1978), 535)

In Hume's view, even though it is in our interests to obey the law, this interest is very remote and far off, and so we are likely to prefer the short-term, lesser benefit which will flow from disobedience. For, Hume supposes, if each of us follows our short-term interests, and acts unjustly, society will break down, to the great misfortune of us all. So reason tells us to seek the longer-term benefit and obey the law. However, Hume believes that although this is what our reason tells each of us, reason alone is insufficient to motivate us to act. Reason, Hume believes, is 'the slave of the passions'. And our irrational passions, our preference for immediate gratification, will swiftly overcome our rational deliberation.

So, Hume argues, as ''tis impossible to change or correct any thing material in our nature, the utmost we can do is to change our circumstances and situation, and render the observance of the laws of justice our nearest interest' (*Treatise of Human Nature*, 537). In other words, we need to find a way of making observance of the laws of justice contribute to our immediate interest. This is the only way in which we will be able to follow the laws, and thereby also bring about our long-term interests.

Accordingly, Hume argues that we should set up a system of civil magistrates, who have the power to make laws and enforce them through punishment. Obedience to the laws is already to our long-term advantage, while punishing people for disobedience makes obedience in our short-term interest too. It is necessary for us to be forced to obey the law—indeed, we should welcome this—because reason is too weak a source of human motivation. We need to be forced to act in our own rational self-interest.

Hume's purpose in making this argument was to explain the advantages of government, and to explain why we are generally prepared to accept the state, even though it is not founded on our consent. Arguing that we have any sort of moral obligation to obey is a further step, and one that Hume, strictly speaking, did not attempt. But theorists of fairness, like Hart, try to go further than Hume. We all benefit from the existence of the state, and it would be unfair to our fellow citizens to take those benefits without also accepting the burdens necessary to create them. These burdens are political obligations. Hence we have a duty of fairness to accept the duty to obey the state.

But do we really have any such duty? If we receive unsolicited benefits, must we pay for them? Reverting to the earlier example, need I buy my round, if I didn't ask for the drinks others bought me? Suppose I made clear at the start that I had no intention of buying a drink for anyone else. Can I then treat the drinks others have bought me as free gifts? Robert Nozick (1938–2002), in *Anarchy, State, and Utopia* (1974), claims that unsolicited benefits create no obligations to reciprocate. He presents an example in which the other members of your neighbourhood have discovered a public address system, and decide to institute a scheme for public entertainment. Each person is assigned a day on which to broadcast—play records, tell jokes, and so on—for the benefit of all. You have enjoyed 137 days of entertainment from others, but on day 138, when your turn comes, do you have a duty to give up a day to entertain the rest (*Anarchy, State, and Utopia*, 93)? Nozick thinks it obvious that you have no moral duty to do this, but it seems to follow from the principle of fairness as stated by Hart that you do. After all, you have reaped the benefits of the public address system, and so now it is your turn to shoulder the burdens, and do your bit for the rest. So, according to the principle of fairness, you should now contribute.

Why does Nozick argue that you have no such duty? Well, you did not ask for the benefit, and you were provided with it whether you liked it or not. Perhaps you would rather have had no benefits and no burdens. But whether you want them or not, if we say that you have a duty to comply in this case it gives others a licence to force even unwanted goods on you and then demand payment, which would hardly be just.

Perhaps this counter-example can be dealt with by spelling out the theory in more detail. It could be that you acquire a duty of fairness to contribute only if you *accept* (rather than merely receive) the benefits on the understanding of the costs. In the case of the public address system, you acquire a burden to tell jokes for a day only if you accept the scheme as a whole. Anyone who accepts the benefits but tries to avoid the burdens of contribution is being an exploiter or freerider, and so it is no injustice to make them pay. It seems reasonable to say that if the principle is amended to take this into account, then it generates enforceable obligations. It is unfair to accept benefits but refuse to pay.

However, once the principle is altered in this way a fresh difficulty arises. The problem now is that if the only benefits that give rise to obligations are those that are accepted, then this requires us to be able to distinguish accepted benefits from those that are merely received. But what would count as accepting the benefits of the state? After all, how can we reject them? We get them, or most of them, whether or not we want them. In other words, we have exactly the same problems as we found with the theory of tacit consent. How can we stop the acceptance of benefits becoming purely automatic? And if we can solve this difficulty, by giving a subtle account of what it is to accept the benefits, we then have to face the possibility that some people—the anarchists and perhaps others too—might refuse to accept the benefits. Even if they appreciate the arguments of Hume and others about the advantages of the state they still see other difficulties, and so prefer no benefits and no political obligations. And so they would acquire no duty of fairness to comply with the state. Consequently, on this understanding, like the consent-based arguments, the principle of fairness cannot deliver universal obligations to obey. It can only do so if we remain with Hart's original formulation in terms of 'receipt' of benefits. But as Nozick's example shows, this in itself leads to problematic consequences. So, on this brief examination, it seems that the principle of fairness, although it is an improvement on consent theory, does not solve the problem of political obligation.

Conclusion

We have looked at a number of defences of political obligation, but all seem wanting in one way or another. Voluntaristic defences within the contract tradition cannot explain the obligations of those who refuse to consent. Utilitarian arguments may well have unacceptable implications, as they seem to allow us—in principle at least—to sacrifice the innocent. The fairness argument can only succeed if everyone accepts the benefits of the state, and it is unlikely that this would be the case. Does this mean that we have no political obligations?

We should first be clear that, while these arguments, taken separately, fail to demonstrate a universal obligation to obey, some of them do nevertheless have some limited success. Some people expressly consent to the state: for example, those in special positions of responsibility, such as members of parliament, as well as naturalized citizens. Many more owe a duty of fairness, for most people willingly accept the benefits of the state, and it can be argued that they believe that an obligation to comply is a fair price. And if utilitarian reasoning is found acceptable then it may well be that the state is entirely justified. But even if utilitarianism is rejected, if any of the other arguments start from an acceptable moral basis, then a large proportion of members of most modern societies have political obligations. Only relatively few people will escape.

What are the consequences of this? No state will be happy with the idea that some people residing within its territory have no political obligations. For one thing, the task of trying to separate those who do and do not have political obligations will provide the officers of the state with immense practical difficulties, particularly when some will exploit these difficulties and try to pass themselves off as members of the groups that escape political obligation. It seems that even if the state is prepared to accept that, in theory, some people escape political obligations, in practice it would be forced to ignore this and act as if there were universal political obligations. No doubt it could make some exceptions, but probably only in special, well-defined, cases. Perhaps monks or groups that very clearly reject state assistance can be allowed to escape some taxes, or other groups can be excused compulsory military service. But no group will be able to avoid all political obligations.

However, suppose a state really did translate theory into practice, and accepted that it had no authority to interfere in the lives of some people living within its territory. Should this create difficulties for the rest of us? Not necessarily. The fact that some people avoid political obligations does not give them the right to harm anyone. These people still have a full set of moral obligations. Further, on Locke's view at least, all individuals have the right to enforce the moral law, even in the absence of government. So if governments do exist, then those of us who consider ourselves to be part of the state can call on the power of the state to protect us when threatened by independents. While the law of the land may have no special authority over independents who do not consider themselves part of the state, most moral views give us the right to self-protection by the most appropriate means: in this case, by the state. Therefore the existence of some independents does not mean we cannot use the state for protection against them. We can survive well enough in the presence of some independents. Consider the example of ambassadors, and others with diplomatic immunity. In one sense, the state in which they live has no authority over them. But this does not mean that the agents of the state must permit such diplomats to act however their whims take them. A diplomat swinging an axe in a shopping mall can rightfully be disarmed by the police, just as we can rightfully restrain each other. What we cannot do, in either case, is exercise legal punishment, or use force beyond what is needed for self-defence, at least not without further authority.

But, of course, no state would accept that people living within its territories can escape political obligations altogether. Diplomatic immunity is a very special case, regulated by international conventions. The law will be enforced against all, even if, in some cases, the state acts illegitimately. But in acting in such an illegitimate way, the state will act with the approval of the vast majority of its citizens.

3

WHO SHOULD RULE?

Introduction

> The English people thinks it is free; it is greatly mistaken, it is free
> only during the election of Members of Parliament; as soon as
> they are elected, it is enslaved, it is nothing. The use it makes of its
> freedom during the brief moments it has it fully warrants its losing it.
>
> Rousseau, *'The Social Contract'*, in *The Social Contract and other Later
> Political Writings* ([1762], Cambridge: Cambridge University Press,
> 1997), bk. III, ch. 15, 114

Whether or not we feel that the state is justified, the fact is that we have
one. And, from our current historical position, it is very hard to see how
this could ever really change. Everyone, then, even the philosophical
anarchist, has an interest in the question of what sort of state and government we should have. What should this government be like? Who
should rule? A common assumption is that only a democracy is ever
fully justifiable. Anything else—a tyranny, an aristocracy, an absolute
monarchy—lacks justification. But what is a democracy? Is it really so
attractive?

Democracy, we are told, is government 'of the people, by the people,
and for the people'. Government for the people is the idea that the government exists for the sake of its citizens, not for the benefit of the rulers.
Democratic governments rule 'in the interests of the governed', to use
Bentham's words. But then, so could other types of government. Vol-
taire argued in favour of 'benevolent dictatorship', where an enlightened despot, without the need to consult the people, would nevertheless
govern in their interest. In contrast, democracy is, most obviously,
a system in which the people rule: collective self-rule. This, then, is

an account of what it means to say that democracy is government 'for the people' and 'by the people'. The first item in the original triad—government 'of the people'—seems a rather empty idea at first: what would government *not* of the people be? Anarchy? But the thought is that a democratic state has power only over the people who make up the electorate. Ruling over a subservient class, or territory, is claimed to be antithetical to the true ideals of democracy.

All contemporary theorists at least implicitly agree that democracy should ideally satisfy the three-part description. But beyond this there is enormous dispute about what democracy amounts to. In contemporary politics a general assumption exists that democracy is a 'good thing'. Democratic status is often taken to be a litmus test for the legitimacy of regimes. If a government or state is thought to be undemocratic, it is subjected to intense international criticism. Even the word 'democratic' is fought over, and has been adopted by regimes that appear quite undemocratic. When, after the Second World War, Germany divided, the Soviets who had forced the split immediately claimed the name 'German Democratic Republic' for East Germany. The Allied forces had to be satisfied with the name 'German Federal Republic' for West Germany, even though, to western commentators at least, it was clear that it was far closer to their democratic ideals.

But does democracy really deserve its contemporary reputation? After all, for most of human history democracy has been almost universally detested. It has greatly flourished in recent times, and had a brief life in Ancient Greece—albeit in a very limited form—but for the 2,000 years or so in between a democratic state was hardly seen. If democracy really is as attractive as it is often claimed to be, why should so many thinkers throughout history have rejected it?

Moreover, not all contemporary theorists find democracy so attractive. It is not so much that they doubt its value as that they deny its coherence. 'Democracy', it is sometimes said, is not the name of a political system, but a term of praise. According to this view there is no single coherent theory of democracy. There is no political system that could be approved by all those who claim to be in favour of democracy.

This type of criticism may well be an exaggeration, but there is no doubt that it has some basis. Democratic theory contains serious tensions, and it will be helpful to explore some of the most fundamental problems in formulating democratic theory before looking at arguments for and against democracy itself.

One tension in democratic theory is between the idea of democracy as a system of 'majority rule', and the idea of democratic 'consideration for individuals'. When someone, in protest, says that 'I thought this country was meant to be a democracy', what she would normally mean is that she supposes that she has been treated unfairly in some way. Perhaps her home has been made subject to a compulsory purchase order, for example, to make way for a road. Maybe a new airport has been planned a short distance away, or her child has been refused a place in a local state school. Whatever the details, the basis of the complaint is that an individual's interests or rights have been treated with insufficient regard. And this, it is claimed, is undemocratic.

But is it? Suppose 51 per cent of the people want the road, or the airport, or to exclude the child. Then democracy, as a principle of majority rule, seems to imply that there is nothing undemocratic at all in this treatment of her interests. The majority has ruled against her.

Here we see a tension right at the heart of democratic theory. De Tocqueville brought out the point well, in his expression 'the tyranny of the majority'. Developing this idea, John Stuart Mill pointed out that before the large-scale establishment of democratic regimes, it was generally assumed that, if the people were ruling in their own interests, it would be impossible for political oppression to exist. For if the people governed themselves, why on earth would they pass repressive laws? But as Mill indicates, the fallacy here is to think of the people as a homogeneous mass with a single interest, each person affected in the same way by each policy. As we are not like this—we have different goals, interests, and plans; we live in different places and have different life-spans—it is quite easy to see how a majority could pass a law which has some very nasty effects for the minority. Is this undemocratic or not? Yes, if you think that a democratic state is one that must protect all individuals; no, if you think that democracy simply means majority rule.

Mill believed that steps must be taken to prevent the tyranny of the majority taking hold. We will examine his position in detail in Chapter 4. The point for the moment is simply that the theorist of democracy must decide whether democracy is essentially a rather crude principle of majority rule, or whether we should follow the 'Madisonian' view (after

James Madison, 1751–1804, often known as the 'father of the American Constitution') that democracy requires the protection of minorities.

A second debate concerns 'representative' and 'direct' models of democracy. In a direct democracy the electorate votes for or against laws or policies, rather than for candidates. Ideally, every major issue is put before the entire electorate, by way of referendum. A representative democracy, on the other hand, is the more familiar system in which the citizens vote to determine who will represent them at governmental level. It is these representatives who then go on to make laws. The former system, it seems, is truer to the pure spirit of democracy, yet it is virtually unknown in the modern world. Modern democracies adhere to the representative model, in which elections are used to determine who will form the government, rather than to decide the particular issues of the day. But if this representative system is thought undemocratic, then almost no democracies have ever existed on any large scale. This conclusion is drawn by many critics of contemporary 'liberal democracy'. Democracy would be a fine thing, they say, if only we had it.

These two debates—majority rule versus individual rights, and representative versus direct models—are fundamental to the formulation of a democratic theory. But they are far from exhausting the areas of controversy. For example, among the Greeks it was sometimes thought that voting for candidates was undemocratic: it gives the unpopular a less than equal chance! Therefore rulers should be elected by a lottery. Other theorists have suggested that we should find ways of measuring and taking account of the strength of different individuals' preferences. A minority with intense preferences, on this view, should take priority over an apathetic majority. Also, we should not ignore questions of deciding who is entitled to vote. In Ancient Greek democracies only a tiny proportion of the population was enfranchised: excluded were women, slaves, and foreigners, even those whose families had lived within the state's territory for generations. In the contemporary world, women were not treated on a fully equal basis in the United Kingdom until as late as 1928, and many countries still exclude 'guest workers' from the franchise.

On another level, we are familiar with somewhat less fundamental, if more intricate, wrangles about voting procedure. Many European countries have long debated the question of whether they should have a system of proportional representation, where the number of representatives is proportional to the total votes cast, as used in elections to the European Parliament, or a system of 'first-past-the-post' in each constituency, as in the United Kingdom. Such debates are, of course, of enormous importance, and the choice of system will have far-reaching consequences. For example, it is often said that Hitler was able to come to power only because Germany had a system of proportional representation. But from a more philosophical point of view, the pressing tasks are to be clear about what democracy is supposed to be, and why it might be thought valuable. As a first attempt to deal with these tasks we will look at one of the most powerful anti-democratic arguments: that of Plato, in the *Republic*, commonly thought to have been written between 380 and 360 BCE. By looking at this sceptical assault on the value of democracy we will begin to see whether it is worthy of the praise it so often receives.

Plato against democracy

Suppose the following to be the state of affairs on board a ship or ships. The captain is larger and stronger than any of the crew, but a bit deaf and short-sighted, and similarly limited in seamanship. The crew are all quarrelling with each other about how to navigate the ship, each thinking he ought to be at the helm; they have never learned the art of navigation and cannot say that anyone ever taught it them, or that they spent any time studying it; indeed they say it can't be taught and are ready to murder anyone who says it can. They spend all their time milling round the captain and doing all they can to get him to give them the helm. If one faction is more successful than another, their rivals may kill them and throw them overboard, lay out the honest captain with drugs or drink or in some other way, take control of the ship, help themselves to what's on board, and turn the voyage into the sort of drunken pleasure-cruise that you would expect. Finally, they reserve their admiration for the man who knows how to lend a hand in controlling the captain by force or fraud; they praise his seamanship and navigation and knowledge of the sea and condemn everyone else as useless. They have no idea that the true navigator must study the seasons of the year, the sky, the stars, the winds and all the other subjects appropriate to his profession if he is to be really fit to control a ship; and they think it's quite impossible to acquire the professional skill needed for such control (whether or not they want it exercised) and that there's no such thing as an art of navigation. With all this going on aboard aren't the sailors on any such ship bound to regard the true navigator as a word-spinner and a star-gazer, of no use to them at all?

> Plato, *The Republic*, ed. H. P. D. Lee ([380–360 BCE],
> Harmondsworth: Penguin, 1955), 282, 488a–d

Plato's opposition to democracy exploits another apparent tension within democratic theory. Just as 'monarchy' means 'rule by the monarch', 'democracy' means 'rule by the *demos*'. But what is the *demos*? In classical Greek it can be understood both as 'the people', and as 'the mob'. On the latter understanding, then, democracy is mob rule: the rule of the rabble, the vulgar, the unwashed, the unfit.

But this insult to democracy is a mere preliminary to Plato's main antidemocratic arguments. His basic weapon is the so-called 'craft analogy'. The point is very simple. If you were ill, and wanted advice on your health, you would go to an expert—the doctor. In other words, you would want to consult someone who had been specially trained to do the job. The last thing you would do is assemble a crowd, and ask them to vote on the correct remedy.

The health of the state is a matter of no less importance than the health of any given individual. Making political decisions—decisions in the interests of the state—requires judgement and skill. It should, Plato urges, be left to the experts. If the people are allowed to decide, they will be swayed by those who speak loudest and with most conviction—the Sophists—and so, like the deaf and short-sighted captain on the ship, will be swayed by the false reasoning of ambitious politicians. Meanwhile, those who are truly skilled in the art of navigation will be ignored. Just as a ship so navigated will lose its way and founder, so too, Plato argues, will the ship of state.

But where are expert rulers to be found? Here Plato's answer is simple, and, to many of his likely readers, initially rather flattering. The just society is impossible unless the kings become philosophers, or the philosophers become kings. Philosophical training, Plato argues, is a necessary qualification to rule. By the idea of becoming a philosopher, Plato does not mean merely spending a few years reading and thinking about philosophy. He has a plan for an entire life of education for the 'guardians', involving in its early years not only skills of literacy, but also musical, mathematical, military, and physical education. Philosophy is not studied at all until the age of 30. Five years of philosophy are then followed by fifteen years' military service, and those who have come through this with honour are then allowed to turn permanently to philosophy: a repose interrupted only by taking one's turn in the 'weary business of politics'.

It would take us too far out of our way to consider these and other aspects of Plato's *Republic* in much detail. In particular, we cannot go into the nature and content of the knowledge Plato intends his guardians to come to possess. But let us remember the craft analogy. Ruling, like medicine, navigation, or even farming, is a skill. A special training is necessary, and not everyone is naturally capable even of acquiring the skill. Just as medicine should be left to the experts, and a medical training only given to those most suited, so should ruling, and a training to rule. Any other arrangement will lead to worse results, and consulting the populace will lead to disaster.

On the face of it, Plato's argument against democracy seems devastating. If ruling is a skill, and a skill that can only be attained by the few, then democracy seems plainly absurd or irrational. The defender of democracy must find a response to the craft analogy. But does it have a weakness?

Problems with guardianship

The first thing to be said is that Plato's own system is a form of dictatorship, and just as there are general arguments that can be used to oppose any system of democracy, there are also general arguments which can be used against dictatorship. Even if we concede to Plato that in educating the guardians he is bringing into existence a class of expert rulers, it certainly does not follow that we should concede to them the power to run our lives.

The point is not that we should never defer to experts, but that giving unchecked powers to experts is to invite catastrophe. You may choose to take a doctor's advice, or consult an architect, but who would be happy if 'doctor's orders' had the force of law, or if architects allocated houses to people? However good these people are at their jobs, why should we trust them to make decisions on our behalf? They might be good at something else too: feathering their own nests.

This objection is an old one. What is to stop the guardian—the philosopher–king—from turning the situation to his or her own advantage? It is hardly a comfort to be told that the ruler is an expert. If we expect our rulers to be corrupt, we might prefer being ruled by incompetents. At least that way the corruption might be less damaging. In Plato's system, so the objection runs, who guards the guardians?

Plato did not overlook this difficulty. His response is to argue that the guardians must be placed in a position where the opportunities for corruption are minimized. So, for example, the philosopher–kings are not allowed to own private property. There would, therefore, seem to be no scope for the sort of corruption we have so often seen in the modern world: a ruling family or clique enriching themselves at the expense of their people. Clearly this would be ruled out on Plato's system—provided that the ruling against private ownership could be enforced.

But if we do assume that it could be enforced, we seem to have backed into the opposite difficulty. If the life of the guardian is not one of great wealth, why would anyone agree to rule? As Plato depicts the guardians, they are philosophers who would much rather spend their time reading, talking, and thinking about philosophy. Why should they give up their time? Plato's answer is, in a way, a negative one. The guardians agree to rule, not for the intrinsic or external rewards of the role, but to avoid being ruled by others. Rather than allow other people—worse still, *all* other people—to rule, they grudgingly accept this necessary duty.

Nevertheless, if the guardians decide to break the laws concerning private property, or even change the laws by proper procedures, who will have the authority and power to stop them? We cannot be fully reassured by Plato's laws designed to prevent corruption. If Plato wishes to persuade us that a proper philosophical education makes a person resistant to temptation, we might reply that full and proper public scrutiny, in the face of an empowered electorate, is a far more reliable remedy.

A further worry is the question of how guardians come to be appointed. Plato believes that potential guardians can be picked out at an early age, and then undergo various rigours which will allow for the selection of the very best. This seems perfectly possible: think how generals rise from the ranks of an army. But, in the case of the guardians, we can still wonder whether their claims to rule would ever be acceptable to the population as a whole. After all, most people will not have had the benefit of a philosophical education, and may not be able to judge who the best rulers would be.

If we add up these objections, what do they come to? Really not much more than the thought that we are very uncomfortable with the idea of Plato's system. Plato's society contains no guarantees that the guardians will always be able to resist temptation. And it may well be that the people do not accept their rule. But these problems with Plato's proposals hardly amount to a rousing defence of democracy. Perhaps another non-democratic system is the answer. Once more, if ruling is a skill, which can be possessed only by the few, then surely it is absurd to leave political decision-making to the rabble.

Knowledge and interests

Another kind of argument might help us to make progress. Plato claims that rulers need expert knowledge. But is such knowledge really attainable? If there really is no such thing as an expert ruler, then Plato's opposition to democracy would seem to dissolve into thin air.

Some critics have argued that we should be very sceptical about the claim that there could be expert rulers who possess a special level of knowledge. After all, it is often said, no one can be absolutely certain of anything at all. Virtually all claims to knowledge—whether in politics, science, or philosophy—are fallible. And so if we leave decisions on any subject to the so-called experts, we are deceiving ourselves about their abilities.

Although it is often rather satisfying to belittle the claims to wisdom of anyone who occupies some sort of position of authority, this reply does not take us very far. For the fact—if it is a fact—that no one can know anything for certain, does not tell against the more mundane point that some people are better judges than others. Like many, for example, I am often very sceptical about the claims to knowledge made by doctors. But if I believed my leg to be broken I would turn to a doctor for help, even though I firmly believe that doctors often make mistakes, including some very serious ones. But those untrained in medicine (for example, those people sometimes exposed in the popular press as masquerading as doctors) can rationally be expected to do even worse. So even if no infallible knowledge exists it does not follow that everyone is equally skilled, or rather unskilled, in all branches of enquiry. This way of trying to defeat the craft analogy is to assert that, in effect, there are no crafts. This is too implausible to believe.

But might it not be true that there is no expert knowledge applicable to ruling, even though expert knowledge exists on other topics? This, too, is hard to believe. Rulers today need quite subtle knowledge of economics, and of psychology and human motivation. They need (even if they do not always have) high intelligence, an enormous capacity for work, a keen memory, an excellent ability to deal with detail, and skill at handling other people. It is absurd to think that no one is potentially a better ruler than anyone else. A very good case can be made that ruling is, in large part at least, a craft.

Nevertheless, there is something about this objection that may push us in a more fruitful direction. Perhaps more could be made of the point that there is something special about political decision-making, which is not like asking for a show of hands to decide whether we should amputate a diseased limb. To bring out this line of thought we should take a closer look at the nature of voting in a democratic system. Plato implies that the point of voting is to register an opinion about what is best for the state as a whole. Obviously this is often one function of voting. But Plato seems to assume that this is all voting is, and his argument comes down to the claim that it is better to leave such decisions to the experts. However, if we can argue that there is more to voting than expressing an opinion about the public good, then perhaps a more robust defence of democracy becomes possible.

Remember one of the points made at the very beginning of this chapter: democratic governments rule *for* the people, that is, in the interests of the governed. Although Plato is opposed to democracy, he shares the assumption that the rulers should have the interests of the people at heart. What he denies is that the way to achieve this is through a system of rule *by* the people. One attempt to defend democracy is to try to argue that Plato's position cannot be sustained. Rule for the people must be rule by the people.

Why might this be? Plato advocates essentially a system of benevolent dictatorship. But even if the dictator wants to advance the interests of the people, how are those interests to be known? In a democracy people show their interests, it seems, by voting: they vote for what they want. Hence voting is more than a decision-making procedure. It is a way of revealing or expressing the very information that the decision needs to take into account: what the people want. Without some sort of voting procedure, how can this be discovered?

Plato might reply that the guardians are not only benevolent, but they are also experts too. They have wisdom and knowledge. Plato's kings are not the bombastic, ignorant tyrants seen from time to time in the modern world. They are philosophers. But, in response to Plato, does philosophical expertise really give them a way of knowing the interests of the people? Logic and metaphysics do not tell you what the people want. Neither does ethics, or even political philosophy. Philosophical knowledge and factual information seem to be two quite different things.

But is it true that political decision-making should be responsive to what the people want? Perhaps it should be responsive to the *interests* of the people—what is best for them. And could it be said that knowing the interests of the people is, indeed, the type of knowledge provided by a philosophical education? Perhaps everyone has the same interests. In that case, the philosophers' subtle powers of analysis put them in the best possible position to know the people's interests. However, whatever Plato thought about this, and whatever is true in the deepest metaphysical sense, in practical terms it must surely be false that we all have the same interests. Imagine that the building of a major road is under consideration. Some people will have an interest in that road being built. Others will have the opposite interest: for example, the owner of a business situated on the existing main route. Some people will have an interest in the road taking a certain route; others will benefit more from a different one. The building of the road will affect people in very many different ways. So there are multiple, and competing, interests to be considered here. Reading works of philosophy will not provide the solution to this problem.

On the other hand, an example like this might make us very doubtful about the value of democracy. How should the decision be made among the competing preferences or interests? It may well be that, because there are more than two options (the road can be built along several different routes) no one option will gain majority support. But even if one does, is it obvious that we should accept the majority preference? Perhaps this would be greatly unfair to the minority (remember the Madisonian element of democratic protection of minorities). Surely what we need is a ruling by someone who knows all the relevant interests, yet, with the wisdom of Solomon, makes the fairest and most judicious decision. This is even more necessary if we accept Hume's point mentioned in Chapter 2 that people are often very poor judges of their interests when their long-term and short-term interests divide. So, at most, we have an argument for detailed opinion-polling of the population, but not necessarily yet an argument for democracy.

In fact, the position is rather worse for democracy than it looks so far. Plato claims that we need expert rulers. The defender of democracy replies that experts need to know the people's interests, and only a vote will show what these are. The response to this is that it is not only false that only a vote will reveal people's interests, but that opinion-polling may well do a more effective job. A further, and more troubling, problem is that we can never be sure that a democratic vote tells us anything at all about the preferences or interests of the people.

To see this, let us consider a rather prosaic example. Suppose a group of people are in dispute about whether smoking should be permitted in a public place that they share and control—perhaps a student house. Suppose also that they agree to be bound by a majority decision. Does this mean that the group will vote to permit smoking if, and only if, a majority prefer there to be public smoking? At first sight this might seem obviously so, but a moment's reflection reveals that it need not be. It will be true that some people will vote as if they are expecting to answer the question 'Would you prefer there to be smoking or not?' These people will indeed vote according to their preferences. But others will vote as if the question they are answering is 'Do you think that smoking *ought* to be permitted?' Accordingly, some smokers will vote to deny their own pleasure, arguing that it is wrong for smokers to submit others to the adverse effects of their behaviour. Some non-smokers, too, will vote against their own preferences, arguing that smoking is a matter for individual decision. In other words, these people are voting in a disinterested fashion, and so do not reveal their interests by their vote.

In view of this, it is unsafe to assume that democracy is a way of making individual interests or preferences known. Some people will vote for what they most want. Others put their own preferences or interests to one side, and vote the way they do on moral grounds. We can never be sure what is motivating the members of any given electorate: in fact, they may not be sure themselves.

What is the consequence of this? If people do not always vote according to their preferences, we cannot represent the voting process as one that automatically reveals the preferences of the majority. So what does the vote reveal? If people are voting from mixed motivations—some out of preference, some out of concern for the common good—then it tells us nothing more than that a majority of people voted for one option over another. We cannot say with confidence that a majority of people believe the winning option to be in their interests; neither can we say that a majority of people believe that the decision is for the common good. Mixed-motivation voting, in short, is a mess. And what is worse, in present-day conditions it seems to be the normal case.

Voting and the common good

The problem of mixed-motivation voting seems to force us to decide which type of motivation voters should have. Whether we can ensure that voters will, in practice, have that type of motivation is a further, and perhaps more difficult, question. But let us first consider the theoretical question.

If we do not want to accept mixed-motivation voting then it seems we must choose between two models: one in which voters vote in accordance with their preferences, and the other in which voters vote in accordance with their estimates or opinions of the common good. The problem with the former, we saw, was that opinion-polling can be a far more sensitive way of gaining the necessary information. But perhaps the second idea—that all people should vote according to their ideas of the common good—can be used in a defence of democracy.

However, if we assume that the people are to vote according to their ideas of the common good, then we need a new argument for democracy. The last argument was that, without a vote, rulers would not be able to tell what the people want. But if people vote in accordance with their ideas of the common good, then voting will not tell us this either. It will only tell us what the majority think is in the common good, not where the majority preference actually lies.

But this suggests a different defence of democracy. If we allow people to vote according to their idea of the common good, and follow the majority decision, we surely have a very good chance of being right. The argument for democracy is that it now seems an excellent way of discovering the common good.

Unfortunately, this argument seems to play right back into Plato's hands. Why should we expect a vote among the rabble to do better than leaving the matter to the specially trained experts? We may as well ask the general population to navigate ships, make medical decisions, tend sheep, and so on. What possible reason is there to believe that the people will do better than the experts?

Surprisingly enough, there is a reason. The French philosopher and political theorist, Marie Jean Antoine Nicolas Caritat, the Marquis de Condorcet (1743–94), provided a very interesting mathematical argument that appears to show the advantages of allowing people to vote on the common good. Condorcet pointed out that if we assume that people, on average, have a better-than-even chance of getting the right answer, then allowing majority decision turns out to be an excellent way of getting to the right result. If a large number of people vote, then the chances of getting the right result tend towards certainty. In an electorate of 10,000, each with more chance of being right than wrong, then a majority decision is virtually certain to get the right result.

Condorcet's argument might seem a more than sufficient riposte to Plato. But it is vital to appreciate that it only works on two conditions. First, the average individual must have a better-than-even chance of being right (and Condorcet himself was very pessimistic about this when voting takes place on a large scale). Second, each individual must be motivated to vote according to his or her ideas of the common good, rather than out of particular interests. If the second assumption fails, then we are back to the confusion of what I called mixed-motivation voting. If the first assumption fails, things are even worse. If the people are, on average, more likely to be wrong than right, then it is almost certain that majority voting will lead to the wrong result.

So we have a reply to Plato only if the two conditions can be met. Is this possible? One philosopher who had a firm intuitive grasp of these points was Rousseau (even though he published his major writings on democracy twenty years before Condorcet produced his mathematical argument). Indeed, it is reasonable to see Rousseau's *The Social Contract* as an attempt—among other things—to show the conditions under which democracy will be superior to guardianship. But before we look at Rousseau's position in detail, there is another, complementary, response to Plato that we should consider.

The values of democracy

So far we have considered the question of whether democracy is better than Plato's system of guardians at achieving the common good. But there is something odd about this enquiry. Many people would argue that we should favour democracy even if it turned out that democratic systems were less good than others at achieving the common good. To put this another way, we have so far looked only at the question of whether there is an instrumental justification for democracy: is it a way of achieving something else we value? But perhaps we should consider another question. Is there something *intrinsically* good about democracy? That is, could it be that democracy is good (up to a point, at least), even if it is not able always to achieve desirable consequences?

Pursuing this thought may make us reflect again about the craft analogy. The craft analogy is premised on the idea that ruling is a skill; a skill aimed at achieving some external object. Democracy, according to Plato, is to be assessed purely on the basis of how well it is able to achieve desirable consequences. But as we are aware, we value skills not just for their results but, sometimes at least, for themselves too. It might seem rather homely to bring up such an analogy in this context, but think of exercising a skill as a hobby. Even if one's hobby is something very practical, like woodworking, the hobby is rarely valued on the basis that it is the most effective way of achieving a particular result. It may be a very nice table, but when you cost the time you spent making it, no doubt there are both better and cheaper ones in the department store. Hobbies allow people to enrich and test their physical and mental powers, and develop their sense of self-worth. And this type of value is independent of the value of the goods that may be produced.

This prompts the idea that democracy should not be judged simply in terms of how well it achieves the common good, even though that is important too. We should take another look at the craft analogy. Plato compares ruling to navigation: steering the ship of state. If we leave navigation to the mob, we can imagine what sort of chaos would ensue: a 'drunken pleasure-cruise', says Plato. We will never get where we want to go.

But need navigation always have such a clear purpose of efficient arrival at a pre-chosen destination? Consider, for example, a training voyage. In that case, we might give everyone a turn at the helm. Indeed, why shouldn't a journey in the ship of state be a drunken pleasure-cruise? What is wrong with that, at least if everyone has a good time and we all get home safely?

The serious and important point to make here is that there may be values involved in political decision-making that are different from the value of achieving given objectives. Defenders of democracy will say that democracy is valuable not only, or not necessarily, because democracies make better decisions than other types of political arrangements, but because there is something valuable about democratic processes in themselves. Democracy is most commonly thought to be expressive of two values we hold dear: freedom and equality. Freedom, as understood here, is a matter of giving people a say in political decision-making, particularly those decisions that affect them. Equality lies in this freedom being given to all. For Rousseau, the problem of political order is 'To find a form of association that will defend and protect the person and goods of each associate with the full common force, and by means of which each, uniting with all, nevertheless obey only himself, and remain as free as before' (*The Social Contract*, bk. I, ch. 6, 49–50). It is remarkable that Rousseau thinks he can solve this problem. How can any political system allow 'each associate [to] obey only himself'? It is time now to turn to Rousseau and to see how he sets out to defend democracy, both on instrumental grounds (as a way of achieving the common good) and in itself (as an expression of freedom and equality).

Rousseau and the general will

If children are raised in common in the midst of equality, if they are imbued with the laws of the state and the maxims of the general will, if they are taught to respect them above all things, if they are surrounded by examples and objects that constantly speak to them of the tender mother that nurtures them, of her love for them, of the invaluable goods she bestows on them, and of what they owe her in return, let us not doubt that this way they will learn to cherish one another as brothers, never to want anything but what the society wants, to substitute the deeds of men and citizens for the sterile and vain babble of sophists, and one day to become the defenders and fathers of the fatherland whose children they will have been for so long.

Rousseau, *Discourse on Political Economy* ([1755], Cambridge: Cambridge University Press, 1997), 21–2

Plato, we saw, argues that ruling requires a special training or education. Rousseau does not doubt this, but he denies that it is a training that ought to be given only to the few. Far better if everyone acquires the appropriate skills, and then takes an active—democratic—role as part of the 'Sovereign' (the term Rousseau uses for the body of citizens acting collectively, with authority over themselves). A democratic state should therefore place a high value on the education of the citizen.

Rousseau's citizens, then, are to be trained to 'will nothing contrary to the will of society'. This is essential to the health and preservation of the state. Citizenship, for Rousseau, also implies active public service: 'As soon as public service ceases to be the Citizens' principal business, and they prefer to serve with their purse rather than with their person, the State is already close to ruin' (*The Social Contract* [1762], bk. III, ch. 15, 113). Together with public service, Rousseau requires his citizens to play an active role in political decision-making. By means of a form of direct democracy, all citizens have a hand in the creation of legislation. However, this claim needs to be made out with some care, for there are passages in which Rousseau seems to argue against democracy.

In the strictest sense of the term, a genuine Democracy never has existed, and never will exist. It is against the natural order that the greater number govern and the smaller number be governed. It is unimaginable that the people remain constantly assembled to attend to public affairs, and it is readily evident that it could not establish commissions to do so without the form of administration changing. (*The Social Contract* [1762], bk. III, ch. 4, 91)

Thus, Rousseau concludes, 'If there were a people of Gods, they would govern themselves democratically. So perfect a government is not suited to men' (*The Social Contract*, bk. III, ch. 4, 92).

How should we understand Rousseau's position? We should start with the difficult concept of the general will. First, Rousseau distinguishes the will of all—the product of every individual's particular will—from the general will. Recall the earlier distinction between voting in one's interests, and voting on what one thinks is right. Exercising your vote in the first way—in your interests—is to pursue your particular will. Voting for what is in your view the morally correct outcome, or the common good, is, for Rousseau, a matter of voting in accordance with your idea of the general will.

So what is the general will? A helpful illustration is this: suppose a company has 1,000 employees, and a fixed sum of £1 million available for wage increases. It is in each individual's interests to get as much of this money as possible, so, at the limit, we could say the particular will of each individual is to try to gain an extra £1 million. Adding these particular wills together we get the will of all: a demand for £1,000 million, which, of course, was not on offer. But suppose the employees are represented by a trade union, which acts equally in the interests of all of its members. The union can do nothing except put in a claim for the £1 million, and then share it out equally between all of its members, giving them £1,000 each. This result represents the general will: the policy equally in the interests of all the members. This is not in anyone's special interests, although it is in the common interest. Hence we see an illustration of the difference between the particular wills of all the citizens, and the general will. The general will demands the policy that is equally in everyone's interests. Thus we can think of the general will as the general interest.

Rousseau also claims that the general will must be general 'in its object as well as its essence' (*The Social Contract*, bk. II, ch. 4, 62). That is, it must apply equally to all citizens. By this, Rousseau means that the general will must only make laws that, in principle at least, affect all the citizens, rather than executive orders targeted at particular individuals or groups. We should be ruled by laws, not by rulers. The point of this, for Rousseau, is to ensure that the general will expresses a common interest. Under these circumstances, Rousseau thinks, no one has any reason to vote for an oppressive or unnecessary law, for each person is equally affected by all laws. The people, as Sovereign, make laws expressive of the general will.

How, then, are the laws to be applied? After all, they will often require action that singles out groups, or even individuals. Legal punishment is the most obvious example. Rousseau's answer is that application of the laws is not the business of the Sovereign, but of the executive or government. The executive arranges day-to-day administration, and Rousseau's view is that it would be absurd to organize this task democratically, in the sense of involving universal active participation. An 'elected aristocracy'—a different sort of democracy, we might think— seems to be Rousseau's preferred arrangement, where the 'wisest should govern the multitude, so long as it is certain that they will govern it for its advantage and not for their own' (*The Social Contract*, bk. III, ch. 5, 93).

Note how Rousseau's system differs from Plato's. Even though Rousseau describes his scheme as one in which the wisest govern the many, it is important to remember how restricted a role the government or administration has. The government does not make laws, but only applies or administers them. This is not quite as trivial as it sounds: the government, for example, has the right to declare war. This is a particular act—it names a particular object—and so the people as Sovereign cannot legislate on the matter. All they can do is lay down the general conditions under which war may be declared. It is then for the government to decide whether the conditions are met, and to take the appropriate action. So the key contrast between Plato's philosopher–kings and Rousseau's elective aristocracy is that Rousseau's rulers do not have the power to make laws.

So how are the laws made? Rousseau argues that the 'Sovereign can act only when the people is assembled' (*The Social Contract*, bk. III, ch. 12, 110). This is how his system differs from those of contemporary democracies. For laws are made, not in parliament, but at popular assemblies. It is at such assemblies that the general will is discovered:

> When a law is proposed in the People's assembly, what they are being asked is not exactly whether they approve the proposal or reject it, but whether it does or does not conform to the general will, which is theirs; everyone states his opinion about this by casting his ballot; and the tally of the votes yields the declaration of the general will. Therefore when the opinion contrary to my own prevails, it proves nothing more than I made a mistake, and that what I took to be the general will was not. (*The Social Contract*, [1762], bk. IV, ch. 2, 124)

Of course, there are a number of objections to Rousseau's proposal. We might be particularly sceptical about the possibility of convening all the People to assemble together. But before considering these difficulties let us return to the reason why we began to look at Rousseau's position in the first place. The point was that Condorcet had demonstrated that there are conditions under which voting is an extremely good device for finding out the truth. If we assume that people have a better than even chance, on average, of being right, then a majority decision is very likely to get to the right answer, at least in a reasonably large electorate. But, to re-emphasize the necessary conditions for this account to apply, we have first to be sure that people are voting on their idea of the right solution—and not simply for the outcome that most favours them—and that the people do indeed, on average, have a better-than-even chance of being right. We introduced Rousseau as someone who had intuitively grasped the importance of these conditions, and had outlined a system that met them. Now we should examine whether this system really does so.

First, what justifies the assumption that, if the people are voting on the basis of their view of the general interest, they are likely to be right? Part of the answer must be our original observation that education was as important for Rousseau as it was for Plato. Individuals need to be educated into citizenship. But it is also vital that Rousseau wants to arrange political society in such a way that perceiving the general will should not be difficult, provided, at least, that one's vision is not clouded by particular interests. The common interest is the same for all individuals, and all are equally affected by all the laws passed.

But how can this be? Some are rich; some are poor. Some are employers; some are employees. How can it be that everyone is equally affected by the law? Class differences surely lead to distinct, even opposed, interests. The fact that laws single no one out is hardly enough to show that all will be treated in the same way by the law. This gives rise to two lines of scepticism. First, why should we think there is a general will at all—a policy that affects everyone equally? Second, even if there is one, it is unlikely to be easy to determine what it is.

Rousseau anticipated both these difficulties, and he has a radical solution to them. If his system is to be practicable, he asserts, then large inequalities must be absent. 'As for wealth, no citizen [should] be so very rich that he can buy another, and none so poor that he is compelled to sell himself' (*The Social Contract*, bk. II, ch. 11, 78). If class differences make the formation of a general will impossible, then classes must be eliminated. All should stand on an equal footing. At the very least, no one should be so rich as to be able to purchase other people's votes, nor so poor as to be tempted to sell their own. Rousseau does not dwell on the details of how such equality is to be achieved and maintained, but it is clear that a classless society has great advantages from the point of view of democracy. It will be much more likely that everyone will be affected in the same way by the same law, and, further, the complexities of finding out what the best law is are much reduced. Rousseau, of course, accepts that even some people acting in good faith will make errors, but 'the pluses and minuses ... cancel each another out, and what is left as the sum of the differences is the general will' (*The Social Contract*, bk. II, ch. 3, 60).

Even though the people meet regularly, they will not be called upon very often to make decisions. A good state needs to pass few laws. Therefore the people can use all their powers to inform themselves of what is required in the cases where they are called upon to vote.

The greatest obstacle to the emergence of the general will that Rousseau sees is not individuals' failure to perceive it, but their failure to be sufficiently motivated to act upon it. The difficulty is felt most keenly 'when factions arise, and [form,] partial associations at the expense of the large association' (*The Social Contract*, bk. II, ch. 3, 60).

To see this, let us return to the example used above to illustrate the distinction between the general will and the will of all. We imagined a sum of £1 million, to be divided between 1,000 employees. If these employees were represented by a single trade union then, assuming that there are no reasons for favouring one employee above another, the union would simply put in a request that the money should be split equally, and each should get £1,000. But suppose now that instead of one trade union there are ten, each representing 100 workers. Each of these unions would, no doubt, put in a claim for more than their 'fair share'. Membership of such a union would, in Rousseau's terms, distort one's vision. An individual would be liable to be swayed by spurious arguments 'demonstrating' why members of one's own union should get more. As Rousseau would put it, each of these unions would have a general will in respect to its members, but a particular will with respect to the whole. When 'interest groups' form, and people vote for the interest of their particular group, then there is no reason to believe that the general will would emerge from the process of voting.

Rousseau's main response to this is to recommend that either there should be no political parties, or factions, or, if there are any, there should be very many; a situation very different to the type of party-based democracy we are used to today. In this way the interests of particular groups should have little influence on the decisions of the whole.

Nevertheless, this still does not do enough to explain why citizens will vote for the general will, rather than for their own particular interest. Rousseau's main solution to this problem is that individuals must be made to identify very strongly with the group as a whole. He has a number of devices to ensure this. The most obvious of these devices we have already encountered: education for civic virtue. People need to be brought up the right way so that they learn to 'cherish one another as brothers'. This cements the social bond and widens each person's view so they take an interest in the state as a whole, and hence will naturally seek to advance the general will.

We might think that this is a somewhat sinister idea: it smacks of indoctrination. Despite Rousseau's obsession with the protection of the freedom of the individual, some critics claim to have noticed fascistic or totalitarian overtones in his thinking. People are to be moulded by education to forget themselves in favour of the state. There are two things to be said in reply to this criticism. First, Rousseau assumes that there should already be bonds of custom and tradition uniting a people before it is fit to receive laws. So education is a way of formalizing and consolidating links that are already present in a community, rather than of imposing an artificial order on a diverse group of people. Second, Rousseau would not be unduly concerned to hear that some of the measures he advocates are not to the taste of modern liberals. This is even more clear in the other two devices he proposes to ensure social unity: 'censorship' and 'civil religion'.

Rousseau supposes that the state needs an 'official censor' whose role is to encourage people to act in accordance with popular morality. Rousseau does not discuss censorship in its modern sense of the suppression of speech or images, although no doubt this would be included within the censor's role. Rousseau's main concern is with enforcing and discouraging types of behaviour. In essence, the job of the censor is to ridicule, and so discourage, certain forms of anti-social behaviour. As an example, Rousseau tells us, 'Some drunkards from Samos defiled the Tribunal of the Ephors: the next day the Samians were permitted by public Edict to be filthy. A true punishment would have been less severe than such impunity' (*The Social Contract*, bk. IV, ch. 8, 142). By such means the censor is charged with the duty of upholding, and clarifying where necessary, public morality.

As a final device to ensure social unity, Rousseau proposes that each state should be regulated by what he calls a 'civil religion'. In brief, there are three parts to Rousseau's account of religion. First, he requires that every citizen should subscribe to some religion or other, for this will 'make him love his duty'. Second, a diversity of religions should be tolerated, but only those which themselves include a principle of toleration. Otherwise some citizens will be compelled to become enemies, which is contrary to the idea of social peace. Finally, and most distinctively, in addition to private morality, each person should subscribe to the civil religion. This should have articles which are 'not precisely ... dogmas of Religion but ... sentiments of sociability without which it is impossible to be a good Citizen or a loyal subject' (*The Social Contract*, bk. IV, ch. 8, 150).

In sum then, if Rousseau's system were in existence it would seem to have a good chance of meeting the two conditions we have set down for Condorcet's argument to apply. The conditions were that people had to vote on moral grounds, rather than in their own self-interest, and to have, on average, a better than even chance of getting the morally right answer. In Rousseau's ideal state it is plausible that these conditions will be met. Of course, it does not follow that observing Rousseau's proposals is the only way in which the conditions can be satisfied: perhaps we could devise an alternative system. But let us concentrate on Rousseau. Even if we concede that his system meets Condorcet's conditions, is it a system we should adopt?

Freedom and equality

To recall the earlier discussion, we noted, in essence, two types of response to Plato. One was to argue that democracy, in principle, is a way of achieving the 'right result' that is at least as good as, or better than, rule by experts. This instrumental form of justification, as we called it, corresponds to the argument of Rousseau we have just considered. The second type of response was to consider the intrinsic value of democracy. In essence, we can see this as the question of how well democracy expresses or advances the values of freedom and equality. Discussion of this question will have the further advantage of helping us to decide whether Rousseau's system is one that we should wish to put into practice.

First, then, how expressive of the idea of equality is Rousseau's polity? One way in which equality entered the argument was through the idea that, without rough equality of wealth, factions would form. This would not only cloud the judgement of the voters but perhaps create an obstacle to the existence of a general will: a policy equally in the interests of all voters. For the rich would seek a set of laws which particularly benefited them, and would have the money and influence to arrange things in their own favour. So, as we noted, Rousseau assumes that genuine democracy presupposes a classless society.

The idea of the general will itself, however, is even more strongly egalitarian. The correct policy is one that benefits all citizens equally. On the face of it, then, it would be hard to devise a system which gives a greater weight to equality, particularly when combined with the democratic principle that all citizens have an equal say in the attempt to determine the nature of the general will on any given case.

Unfortunately, the appearance of equality within Rousseau's system is somewhat misleading. Rousseau always uses the masculine form to refer to the citizens. This is no accident of language. Rousseau believed that women were subordinate beings, and he simply seems to have assumed that the privilege of citizenship should be extended only to men. The doctrine of the equality of citizens is rather soured by Rousseau's assumption that there would naturally be inequalities between male citizens and female non-citizens.

This inconsistency in Rousseau's system was addressed by the major advocate of women's rights, Mary Wollstonecraft, in her *Vindication of the Rights of Women*, published in 1792. Wollstonecraft argued that there was no basis for the exclusion of women from the citizenry, a shocking and radical view in her time. But even she had a blind spot. The emancipated female citizen is assumed to have female domestic servants, and the idea that such servants should also have the vote is something that Wollstonecraft seems simply to have ignored. It was generally assumed, until relatively recently, that the only people entitled to vote were those with some property stake in the country. Those without property could not be trusted to use their votes 'responsibly'.

However, a motivation also moving Wollstonecraft, Rousseau, and, indeed, the Ancient Greeks, is the more mundane thought that those people who are active as citizens do not have the time to wash their own clothes or cook their own food. To perform your duty as an active citizen is enormously time-consuming, if you are both to keep yourself well informed and attend the public forum or assembly. Anyone engaged in public life needs domestic support staff. The Greeks took for granted that democracy was consistent with slavery, Rousseau that it was consistent with sexual inequality, and Wollstonecraft that it was consistent with the disfranchisement of the poor. Two things have brought about the changes that have made universal suffrage possible. One is the (rather depressing) view that a right to vote does not bring with it an onerous responsibility to keep yourself well informed about political and economic matters; the other that, in the developed world at least, household machinery has greatly eased the burdens of domestic work. It might be an exaggeration to say that the washing machine has made democracy possible, but it has certainly helped.

However, despite Rousseau's exclusion of women from the franchise, the real logic of his political thought implies that there is no good reason for this exclusion. We can, then, construct a model of genuine equality on the basis of Rousseau's proposals.

So much for equality; how about freedom? It is not difficult to detect significant limitations of freedom in Rousseau's chosen polity. The central restriction is simply the other side of the coin to the creation of the social bond. Freedom of thought is severely restricted, particularly in the area of religion. First, atheism is barred. Second, intolerant religions are not to be tolerated. Third, all must affirm the civil religion. And woe betide the hypocrite: 'If anyone, after having publicly acknowledged these same dogmas [of civil religion], behaves as if he did not believe them, let him be punished with death; he has committed the greatest of crimes, he has lied before the laws' (*The Social Contract*, bk. IV, ch. 8, 150). When we add to this the existence of the office of the censor, whose role it is to enforce public or customary morality, then individuals appear to lose any freedom to be unconventional. No doubt this would also include restrictions on people conducting 'experiments of living', to use a term we will encounter again in the examination of Mill on liberty in Chapter 4.

With this restrictive illiberal background in mind, we may ask how Rousseau can maintain that he has solved the problem of finding a form of association in which 'while each uniting with all, [each associate] neverthless obey[s] only himself, and remain[s] as free as before' (*The Social Contract*, bk. I, ch. 6, 49–50).

The answer is that Rousseau holds what was later to be called by Isaiah Berlin a 'positive' notion of freedom. We will look at this idea in more detail in Chapter 4, but the thought is that freedom is not simply a matter of being able to follow your desires, unconstrained by others (a 'negative' notion), but instead something that requires certain types of action. Typically, theorists of positive freedom define freedom in terms of 'living the life that the rational person would choose to live'. In Rousseau's case such a life—the rational life—is available only in civil society. 'The impulsion of mere appetite is slavery, and obedience to the law one has prescribed to oneself is freedom' (*The Social Contract*, bk. IV, ch. 8, 54). The way, of course, in which we prescribe laws to ourselves is through voting as a member of the Sovereign. It is only by acting in accordance with the laws created by the Sovereign—acting on the general will—that we can be said, according to Rousseau, to be truly free.

It has been pointed out by critics that, on this view, one can be 'forced to be free'; in fact, this is a phrase that Rousseau himself uses. Consider the case of someone who believes that the general will requires one policy (policy A), while the majority adopt another (policy B). Policy B, let us suppose, represents the general will. In that case our person will be forced to act according to policy B, and as freedom is identified with acting on the general will, then it follows that the person has been forced to be free. Rousseau would say that anything else—doing what one prefers, for example—is slavery to one's impulses, and not true freedom. Opponents of Rousseau have pointed out that on this basis even highly repressive regimes can be defended on grounds of their support of freedom. So even though we can rescue Rousseau's system from inequality, it is very unclear whether we can say—as Rousseau so wants us to say—that it advances the value of freedom.

Radical criticism of Rousseau

This criticism has been taken up and extended by contemporary writers, who, while being strongly influenced by Rousseau's writing, feel that his ideal of the state needs to be improved and repaired in a number of ways. There are three closely related criticisms to be made.

The first focuses on the idea of the general will. Even if it is true that in a closely unified, highly equal society a general will can be formed and relatively easily perceived, it is not true that contemporary societies conform to this ideal; nor is it desirable that they should. Economic class is not the only obstacle to the formation of a general will; we also belong to different religions, have different moral and philosophical ideas, and come from differing cultural, ethnic, and racial backgrounds. Now this does not mean that there can never be a policy equally in the interests of all: despite our differences, we all have similar basic needs. But beyond this, the fact that we value different things—economic progress or the protection of the natural environment, for example—can lead to conflict. On many issues it is very unlikely that there could be any policy that is equally in the interests of all. Or, if there were, that it would be easy to discover. Perhaps then, we must simply drop Rousseau's key assumption that citizens can form their wills into a general will.

Second, Rousseau's treatment of those who hold a minority view is hard to admire. Dissenters are to be 'forced to be free'. Those who first affirm the principles of the civil religion and then disobey them are to be put to death. Against the background of the tight unity of the state, dissent is a crime, and crime is treason. This might be marginally defensible if the majority were always right about the general will, and dissenters therefore either mistaken or anti-social. But if there is no general will, then this argument is appalling in more than one sense.

Finally, Rousseau's critics do not accept that freedom should be equated with obedience, even obedience to a law you make for yourself. Or, to put this another way, within Rousseau's system making the law for yourself is simply a matter of having some say in the decision-making procedure. But suppose, again, you are in the minority, and your views do not become law. Then, while it may be justified to coerce you to obey the law, it seems outrageous to say that such coercion makes you 'free', that you are being brought to obey a law that you have created for yourself. Even though the minority has taken part in the decision-making procedure, the law has been created despite them, not because of them.

The force of these criticisms can now be seen. In order for Rousseau to be able to argue that democracy is instrumentally justified—that it is a highly reliable way of achieving morally correct outcomes—he has to draw the bonds of social unity very tight. So tight, in fact, that the system becomes unacceptably repressive. So the same measures which, in Rousseau's model, make democracy defensible in instrumental terms also make it intrinsically undesirable. In an amended form it may achieve equality, but not freedom as we recognize it, nor pluralism, nor diversity. The price we have to pay for the general will is too high.

Rousseau's system needs repair. And, indeed, in the light of these criticisms we can point to another oddity in Rousseau's ideal polity—an oddity that has gone unremarked so far in this discussion. This is the extent to which Rousseau allows genuine political participation. Although Rousseau's citizens are regularly called upon to vote, somewhat paradoxically he seems to discourage them from taking too active a role in politics. First, as we saw, he does not advocate a democratic assembly, and second, the assumption that only clouded perception stands in the way of unanimity leads Rousseau to conclude that 'long debates, dissensions, disturbances, signal the ascendancy of particular interests and the decline of the State' (*The Social Contract*, bk. IV, ch. 2, 123).

However, once we drop the assumption that we can regularly and easily perceive a general will—in fact, if we drop the assumption that there is a general will altogether—then politics takes on a new cast. There now seems an urgent need to hear all voices, all arguments, and all positions. Voters can still be represented as aiming at 'the best' for the community. But perhaps what 'the best' is in any case can be a highly contested matter. Furthermore, it will probably be very controversial which policies would be most likely to achieve it.

Rousseau's critics have argued that extensive political debate is not a sign of decay, but vital to the functioning of democratic politics. Furthermore, outvoted minorities have no duty to change their mind about what is correct. In general we would expect them to obey the law, but they can continue to speak up, and, if they feel strongly enough, to agitate for change. Perhaps civil disobedience can also be justified on democratic grounds. If you sincerely believe that a wrong decision has been made by the majority, then you may have not only a right but a duty to draw attention to this, by whatever means necessary. Treating conscientious disobedience as treason, in order to preserve social unity, is surely a mistake. The dissenting citizen has a place. He or she should not be silenced for the sake of peace: perhaps the majority is wrong. But even if the majority is right, attention should still be paid to dissenters.

Participatory democracy

These objections have, in effect, led us to new models of democracy, much influenced by Rousseau, but with much more respect for the individual, for debate, and for minority views. These models go under the name of 'participatory democracy' and 'deliberative democracy'. There are many variants of these theories, but the most radical extend Rousseau's model in three ways.

First, they claim that we must find a great deal more room for individual involvement in political discussion and decision-making than Rousseau allows, and much more respect for dissenting voices. For example, theorists of deliberative democracy insist that democracy requires extensive public debates and sampling of the views of citizens to enrich and deepen the political process.

Second, they suppose that Rousseau's distinction between the Sovereign and the executive needs to be rethought. It may be that we cannot all join in every political decision for practical reasons. But, once we abandon the assumption that there is a general will, there is no reason why we should restrict individual decision-making to legislation. Perhaps all citizens should be involved in deciding the most important 'particular acts' of administration, especially when we remember that declaring war is considered by Rousseau to be an action of the executive, not the Sovereign.

Many of the practical difficulties recognized by Rousseau as standing in the way of more participatory politics could easily be overcome by modern technology. There is no need to gather all the people together, whether under an oak tree or in the public square. Rapid developments in information technology have created many alternatives to the town meeting. Any citizen can post political speeches digitally in numerous forms. Voting can be executed at the click of a mouse. You can do your democratic duty from the comfort of a favourite armchair, or even on the bus through a mobile device.

Finally, advocates of the idea of participatory democracy have argued that political decision-making should, in effect, go 'all the way down'. People should be consulted not only on matters of legislation, but in all decisions that affect them. It is proposed that we should follow democratic principles of decision-making not only in the public forum, but in the workplace, the family, and the other institutions of civil society. What use is a vote on issues of industrial policy when matters of most immediate concern—the nature of your working environment, whether you even have a job tomorrow—depend on the absolute decisions of another person, one's boss? As Marx observed, and as women have learnt to their cost, equal political rights are worth fighting for, but they are of little value if you are still treated unequally in day-to-day life. The removal of legal impediments or restrictions does not necessarily lead to an improvement in anyone's position.

Theorists of participatory politics claim that only active, democratic involvement in all matters of concern can achieve real freedom and equality for all. Only when we are involved in making the decisions that structure our lives in all spheres are we really free, they argue. And, to put this in the context of the discussion of political obligation from Chapter 2, only in a participatory democracy are the voluntaristic assumptions of social contract theory satisfied. In such a society we can genuinely be thought of as voluntarily contributing members of society. And so, on this view, it is only under these conditions that we even acquire an obligation to obey the state.

The idea of a participatory politics is, on the face of it, very attractive. We are the subjects of national and local decision-making—we have to obey the rules—so surely we should play our part as authors of those decisions. Only when we truly make the laws to which we are subject can we genuinely reconcile freedom and authority. But it is not difficult to find fault with the scheme as proposed, and it becomes more understandable why Rousseau proposed the limits to his system that he did.

The first difficulty is that fully participatory politics is barely conceivable, and, to the extent that it is conceivable, it is likely to be extraordinarily inefficient. John Stuart Mill pointed out that, while groups of people are much better than a single individual at deliberation, individuals are much better than groups at action. If a group wishes to have its decisions implemented, it must always ultimately delegate this to an individual.

In response, it will be said that no one has really proposed that somehow 'the whole people' is to carry out its own instructions. Of course, administrators must be appointed. But the whole people, or at least all those affected, will be involved in making the decisions. But again, although deliberation is better done in groups than by individuals, it does not follow that the bigger the group, the better the deliberation. Indeed, it is likely that a small, well-selected group will deliberate better than a large one. Large groups create noise, digressions, and confusion. The best arguments might never be heard. So surely there is room for expert deliberators within a democracy, and a fully participatory politics might find it hard to give such people a proper role. This is a modest version of Plato's worry.

The second problem is somewhat more subtle, but still obvious enough. In the computerized political fantasy we come home to find a list of questions for the day. But why should we find ourselves voting on one set of issues and not another? Who, in other words, sets the agenda? This is not a trivial question. Often the most powerful person is not the one who decides yes or no, but the person who puts the question in the first place. Participatory politics becomes far less appealing if the agenda is to be set by appointed officials.

In reply, it will be said that 'the people' can set the agenda. They will vote on which issues are to be voted on. But how will the agenda for this preliminary meeting be set? By vote? And so on. The idea that we could have participatory politics at every level is beginning to look naïve and even incoherent.

No doubt there are ways around this. Perhaps we could appoint, by lot, a 'president for the day', who gets to set the day's agenda. On reflection, though, the lack of continuity in such a system looks like a recipe for disaster. Rousseau's view that society will function better when fewer decisions need to be made by the people as a whole begins to look much more attractive. But even Rousseau had little to say about the problem of agenda-setting. The best he could do was propose that those who draft the laws upon which a vote is to be taken should themselves be excluded from the franchise. This seems like a way of arguing for a powerful, independent, apolitical civil service: an idea far removed from the goal of participation.

Finally, the most obvious problem was already pointed out by Rousseau. Oscar Wilde said that 'the trouble with Socialism is that it would take up too many evenings'. Many critics of participatory democracy have quoted these words as being even more appropriate in that context. The point is that, while we care about actively involving ourselves in decisions that concern us, we also care about many other things too. It is very unclear whether we should give up the other things we value— listening to music, talking to our friends and families, even watching television—for the sake of a say in every decision that affects us. And once we extend political participation to the workplace, participation takes up not only our evenings but much of our days too. In clamouring for all to play an active, equal role in politics, we risk, if not starving to death, then at least having far less productive working days.

In sum, while the idea of participatory democracy is a very attractive one, it is very hard to see that it can be made to work in a way that is worth the effort. Even if a participatory society is best from the point of view of preserving freedom and equality, it seems to do less well from the point of view of advancing prosperity and allowing the fulfilment of life plans. Can we do better?

Representative democracy

> Participation should be as great as the general degree of improvement of the community will allow; and that nothing less can be ultimately desirable than the admission of all to a share in the sovereign power of the state. But since all cannot, in a community exceeding a single small town, participate personally in any but some very minor portions of the public business, it follows that the ideal type of a perfect government must be representative.
>
> John Stuart Mill, '*Considerations on Representative Government*',
> in H. B. Acton, ed., *Utilitarianism* ([1861], London: Dent,
> 1972), 217–18

Any system of government—even the most radical participatory or deliberative democracy—needs administrators to execute policy. Carrying out the decisions of the people cannot be done by the people as a whole. A further question is what powers these administrators should be given.

One presumption is that administrators should be given very little power, with as much as possible being reserved for the people. In Plato's system, at the other extreme, the people have no role at all and the administrators—the guardians—have complete power. Rousseau decided the matter a third way: the people make the laws, and the administrators carry them out. But another, more familiar, model is available too. The people elect representatives who then both make laws and put them into practice. This is the idea of representative democracy, as defended by Mill.

For Mill, representative democracy is the only means by which democracy can survive in the modern world. To understand why Mill says this we should enquire, first, what he took the proper function of governments to be. What are the purposes of governments? For Mill, they are twofold: to 'improve' the citizens, and to manage their public affairs. Governments are to be judged by their effects on individuals, whether they improve them morally and intellectually, and by their efficiency in dealing with matters of public concern. In this latter respect Mill recognizes that there are many branches of government—jurisprudence, civil and penal legislation, financial and commercial policy—each with its own standards of success and failure. Although for Mill the ultimate standard for each of them is the same—how well it advances general happiness—this further claim is not essential to the main argument so far.

It is no surprise to be told that governments are required to manage society's affairs effectively. But Mill's conception of the other proper function of governments is more controversial. Do governments have any duty, or even any right, to concern themselves with the moral well-being of their citizens? One major theme of modern liberalism is that the moral welfare of the citizens is none of the government's business. And so it is odd to find Mill—one of the founders of modern liberal theory—making the claim he does. But we will leave this to one side for now, as we shall return to it in far more depth in Chapter 4.

Mill thinks it is easy to show the advantages of his system over what he calls good despotism, or absolute monarchy, which would also include Plato's guardianship. The management function of government, he concedes, could be carried out by a despot, though, so he claims, less well than by a democracy. But his main argument against despotism is the type of human beings it is likely to create.

Mill's claim is that despotism leads to passivity and inaction, for it produces a people who have no need to inform or educate themselves in the
business of the state. This affects not only the individuals themselves, but
also the likely prosperity of the state. 'Let a person have nothing to do for
his country and he will not care for it' (*Representative Government*, 204).
Or, if the subjects do inform and educate themselves, and take an active
interest in the affairs of the state, then they will not for long be content
with their subjection.

If further proof of the advantages of democracy were needed, Mill asks
us to:

> Contrast the free states of the world, while their freedom lasted, with the con-
> temporary subjects of monarchical or oligarchical despotism: the Greek cities
> with the Persian satrapies; the Italian republics and the free towns of Flanders
> and Germany, with the feudal monarchies of Europe; Switzerland, Holland
> and England, with Austria and ante-revolutionary France. Their superior
> prosperity was too obvious ever to have been gainsaid: while their super-
> iority in good government and social relations is proved by the prosperity, and
> is manifest besides in every page in history. (*Representative Government*, 210)

Mill's key assumption is that human beings flourish only under
conditions of independence. They need to be self-protecting and self-
dependent if they are to avoid oppression and make their lives worthwhile. Mill therefore feels confident that all citizens must play their role
in the exercise of sovereignty.

But what should the exercise of sovereignty come to? Not, Mill
argues, direct democracy. He might, if pushed, concede that direct democracy would be the best way of improving the citizens, both morally
and intellectually, but in terms of its efficiency as a form of government it is a disaster. One argument is that modern societies are simply
too large to make direct democracy possible. But, more importantly, in
words not far from Plato's, he argues that things will go badly wrong
if we let the people exert great influence over their appointed expert
administrators.

> At its best, it is inexperience sitting in judgment on experience, ignorance
> on knowledge: ignorance which never suspecting the existence of what it
> does not know, is equally careless and supercilious, making light of, if not
> resenting, all pretensions to have a judgment better worth attending to than
> its own. (*Representative Government*, 232)

However, critics of representative democracy argue that it is not so much a welcome move from direct democracy in the direction of realism as an unhealthy move away from democracy altogether. This is clearly Rousseau's view (remember his comments about the 'the English people' being mistaken about their freedom). Is representative democracy any more than a sham, behind which lurks elective dictatorship? If so, it can hardly be recommended as a system of equal power, or as a system that presupposes and extends the moral and intellectual development of the citizens.

Mill would accept that representative democracy can fail to achieve its purposes. But he is keen to propose a system that will do better. In particular, he emphasizes the importance of educating the citizens for citizenship. The most significant means of doing this is by participation in public business. Although, of course, this cannot mean participation in national government for everyone, there are other possibilities. So, for example, Mill emphasizes the importance of jury service and participation in local government, as this requires citizens to acquire a range of skills not likely to be available to those 'who have done nothing in their lives but drive a quill, or sell goods over a counter' (*Representative Government*, 217).

Nevertheless, Mill identifies a number of threats to democracy. One is the possibility that the system will encourage unworthy or unfit people to stand for election. Mill agrees with Plato that the people best equipped to rule us are those least likely to want to. Or, to make the point the other way round, the qualities most likely to lead to success in politics—flattery, duplicity, manipulation—are the ones we would least wish to have in our rulers.

At bottom, representative democracy must face the problem we saw with Plato's guardianship: how to protect ourselves from unsavoury leaders who may attempt to obtain power. This problem was considered in detail in *The Federalist Papers*, written by James Madison, Alexander Hamilton (1757–1804), and John Jay (1745–1829), and published under the pseudonym 'Publius' over a series of ten months in 1787 and 1788 in a number of New York City newspapers. The papers were written with a view to convincing the New York state voters to ratify the new Constitution of the United States. The Federalists supported what they called a 'republic', by which they broadly meant what we have been calling a representative democracy. Certain anti-Federalists, on the other hand, instead favoured participatory styles of democracy, and presented the Federalists with the problem of showing how to safeguard representative democracy from falling into an elected tyranny. The Federalists' main proposal on this score was to take over the idea of the 'separation of powers', found in John Locke and Charles-Louis de Secondat, Baron de Montesquieu (1689–1755), who had proposed that the legislative, executive, and judicial functions of government should be placed in independent hands. In theory this meant that the activities of any branch of government would be checked by the other two, and this would safeguard the people against the corruption of its rulers.

Mill accepts that power should be dispersed throughout the agencies of the state, to effect a system of 'checks and balances', so that the over-ambitious have little chance to exploit their power. But he also suggests further measures to prevent abuse of the democratic process. First, he proposes that there should be a limit on the money people are permitted to spend on their election campaign. How can we trust anyone prepared to pay a large sum of money to gain election? Surely they would seek a return on their investment. Second, Mill argues, somewhat surprisingly, that members of the government should not be paid. For otherwise a seat in the chamber 'would become an object of desire to adventurers of a low class' (*Representative Government*, 311). Those not of independent means, but obviously suitable and able, can be supported by private donations from their constituents.

The greatest obstacle to representative government, however, is the possible behaviour of the voters. For Mill it is vital that voters should vote in accordance with their ideas of the general interest; that is, they should vote for whichever candidates they feel most likely to improve the citizens and efficiently manage the affairs of the country in the interests of all. Here he uses an analogy with jury service:

> [The citizen's] vote is not a thing in which he has an option; it has no more to do with his personal wishes than the verdict of a juryman. It is strictly a matter of duty; he is bound to give it according to his best and most conscientious opinion of the public good. (*Representative Government*, 299)

Here we see the extra importance of real jury service as a form of participation. It educates voters by giving them a highly distilled and concentrated training for democracy.

Mill's worry is that a voter may give a 'base and mischievous vote ... from the voter's personal interest, or class interest, or some mean feeling in his own mind' (*Representative Government*, 302). Or it may also be that the voters are too ignorant to perceive the public good correctly.

One remedy Mill sees to the first of these problems is to have an open vote, rather than a secret ballot. As people have a duty to vote for the public good, it is reasonable that they should be held accountable for their vote. Therefore it should be a matter of public record. Public disapproval would be a force to keep people from exercising their vote out of self-interested reasons. The danger in this, Mill recognizes, is coercion. Secret ballots were introduced because powerful local individuals would press others—particularly their employees—to vote a particular way, with the threat of a loss of job, or of other favours, for failing to carry out the instruction. A secret ballot makes this threat empty: no one can know who has voted for which candidate. Mill, perhaps naïvely, believes that this is a lesser danger than the possibility of 'base' or self-interested voting, which would distort the poll. Mill's position, surely, is highly questionable.

Mill's other remedy—to prevent the distorting effects of class and personal interests—will, he hopes, also have the effect of neutralizing the influence of stupidity and ignorance. He argues that certain people are to be excluded from the franchise, at least temporarily. This includes those unable to 'read, write, and, I will add, perform the common operations of arithmetic'. And he goes on:

> I regard it as required by first principles that the receipt of parish relief should be a peremptory disqualification for the franchise. He who cannot by his labour suffice for his own support has no claim to the privilege of helping himself to the money of others. By becoming dependent on the remaining members of the community for actual subsistence, he abdicates his claim to equal rights with them in other respects. (*Representative Government*, 282)

Today, of course, it would seem scandalous to propose that those in receipt of welfare benefits should be excluded from voting, although for Mill it is a 'first principle'.

Mill's further proposal to avoid domination of the ballot by the unqualified is that although everyone who meets his conditions is entitled to a voice, 'that every one should have an equal voice, is a totally different proposition' (*Representative Government*, 283). Mill argues that people who are especially well qualified to exercise their judgement should be given more than one vote. He feels that the particularly intelligent or well educated should be favoured with two or more votes (he doesn't give final details).

Mill's most pressing concern is that the uneducated poor—the numerical majority—will, out of a combination of ignorance and class interest, make a terrible mistake. They will elect a government that will attempt to improve the position of labourers by raising the taxes on the wealthy, protecting home industries from competition, reducing uncertainty of employment, and other populist measures. Mill's objection is that such policies will make everyone—including the workers—worse off in the longer term by relaxing industry and economic activity, and discouraging saving and investment. Mill argues that the workers are likely to be mistaken about where their interests lie, and yet, being in the majority, would then tilt the country towards disaster.

We will return to the issue of the just distribution of property in Chapter 5. The details of the case do not really matter for the present argument. The point is simply that Mill wants to ensure that representative democracy contains safeguards to prevent it from being dictated to by stupidity and class interest. Hence we can see that Mill's main approach to democracy is to defend it on instrumental grounds, and to identify the steps to be taken if there is a danger that it might lead to undesirable consequences.

Would plural voting and partial disfranchisement achieve the goal Mill wanted? Perhaps, but there is something of a tension in his thought here. To protect industry we could bias the ballot in favour either of the rich or (so Mill thinks) the educated. He prefers the latter option, for it is vital that those with only one vote should be able to accept the reasoning that favours others with more than one. Each of the uneducated will accept that the educated 'understand the subject better than himself, that the other's opinion should be counted for more than his own accords with his expectations, and with the course of things which in all other areas of life he is accustomed to acquiesce in' (*Representative Government*, 284). But contrast this argument with another:

> I may remark, that if the voter acquiesces in this estimate of his capabilities, and really wishes to have the choice made for him by a person in whom he places reliance, there is no need of any constitutional provision for the

purpose; he has only to ask the confidential person privately what candidate he had better vote for. (*Representative Government*, 294)

This remark, made just ten pages after the first, occurs in the context of the discussion of a proposal that we should have two stages of election. We vote for a group of electors, who then go on to elect members of parliament. Mill has little time for this suggestion. He thinks that the only possible justification for it would be that perhaps we ought to leave such important decisions as electing our rulers to those whom we recognize as wise. Mill's response is that, if we think such people are wise, we need only ask them how to vote, and follow their instructions. Exactly the same reply has been made by Mill's critics to his proposal about plural voting. If the uneducated revere the educated, then we need not give the latter extra votes, for the uneducated can simply seek out their opinions. But if they do not respect such opinions, then they would not accept plural voting. Plural voting is either unnecessary or unjustified.

Protecting the minority

Although the case just discussed is one where, Mill claims, the ignorant majority will end up doing themselves harm by pursuing what they wrongly see as their own class interest, this type of example raises perhaps the main problem that troubled Mill about democracy: the place of the outvoted minority. Mill, we have seen, was particularly concerned to prevent the 'tyranny of the majority'. Most of us, of course, can accept being on the losing side from time to time. But sometimes an entrenched majority will win vote after vote, leaving the minority group permanently outvoted and ignored. So, in *Representative Government*, Mill takes great pains to ensure the representation of minorities in parliament. He declares his approval of a very complicated and elaborate system of proportional representation, involving the possibility of transferring your vote to a candidate in another constituency, should your favoured candidate fail. By such, or similar, means we ought to be able to ensure the representation of many minorities in parliament.

Nevertheless, representation is one thing, protection another. A represented minority could still be outvoted in parliament. Oppression on the basis of class, race, religion, or other factors remains possible under the system of majority rule, even when the minority are represented.

The best way, perhaps, of preventing oppression within a voting system is by giving the morally highly enlightened very many votes. But this returns us close to Plato.

In fact, Mill's solution—as we shall see in Chapter 4—is to restrict the legitimate sphere of government activity. Some things are just not the business of the government or of the majority. The government cannot legitimately interfere in particular areas of people's lives, and everyone has rights and liberties with which the government may not interfere.

However, to pass final judgement on Mill's model of democracy, we can see that it contains a form of the same tension that afflicted Rousseau's. The problem with Rousseau's view was that democracy could only be relied upon to produce decisions that were in accordance with the general will if it severely restricted the freedom of the citizens. In other words, if democracy is to be instrumentally justified, it cannot achieve the twin virtues of freedom and equality to which it aspires. For Mill, it is not freedom that is sacrificed, but equality. Some citizens are to be excluded from the franchise on educational or economic grounds, while others are given more than one vote. Mill's system leans more closely towards Plato than he is prepared to admit. Perhaps Mill should have had more faith in the abilities and virtue of the uneducated poor. Or perhaps any democratic system is bound to be compromised.

Conclusion

One upshot of the discussion so far is that we are very unlikely to be able to find an instrumental defence of democracy that also builds the values of equality and freedom into a feasible system. And however we restrict freedom and equality, there is no reason to think that democracies necessarily make better decisions than other types of systems. Indeed, we can conceive of systems combining extensive market research and wise administrators that are almost bound to do better. Nevertheless, few people are prepared to abandon democracy on this basis. Why not?

Clearly the answer has to be that democracy, for us, is not valued purely as a decision-making procedure, but for at least one other reason. What reason could that be? As a case study, consider the South African election of 1994, which was taking place while I was drafting the first edition of this book. This election—the fact of it, as much as the result—was celebrated the world over. Black South Africans were able to vote in national elections for the first time, but why was this seen as so signifi-cant? Surely the cause for celebration was not simply that black South Africans were more likely to be treated with justice than they had been in the past, although this was no doubt part of the reason for rejoicing. Rather, it seems, the main idea was that the mere fact that they now had the vote was a way of recording that black South Africans were at last treated as worthy of respect. That people are included in the franchise has symbolic or expressive value. In this case it symbolizes that, in some way at least, black and white South Africans stand together as political equals. Having a vote, then, seems to be important irrespective of what people do with the vote when they have it.

To think of this in another context, consider an argument commonly used in the early part of the twentieth century to deny women the vote. It was often said that women did not need to vote, because the interests of married women would be the same as those of their husbands, and of unmarried women the same as those of their fathers. There are so many things wrong with this argument it is hard to know where to start. To make the obvious objections, first, even if the claim about common interests is true, why should it not be the case that the interest is reg-istered for every person who holds it? Second, again, even if it is true, why is this a reason for giving men the vote and denying it to women, rather than the other way round? Third, it may well not be true. Why assume that women have the same interests as their husbands or their fathers? But the fourth objection is the most decisive. Whether or not women's interests are the same as men's, it is insulting and demeaning to give men a vote while denying it to women. Universal suffrage is a way of expressing the idea that we believe women, just as much as men, are owed respect as citizens.

Still, it is one thing to say that all the holders of the franchise are to be respected as citizens. But need we also say that everyone is owed equal respect, or is to be respected as equals? We have just seen one proposal that, while all should, in principle, have a say, sometimes this should be denied for some people, while others should have more than one vote: John Stuart Mill's plural voting scheme. It is interesting that no major thinker seems to have agreed with Mill on this issue. Few have even felt it necessary to give arguments to support their opposition. Why not? Simply because Mill's proposal violates the idea that democracy is a way of expressing *equal* respect for all. This, perhaps, is why many countries withdraw the vote from criminals: by their behaviour they forfeit the right to equal respect.

Is there anything else we can say in defence of the type of democratic system we now have? Perhaps the best we can add is this. In the contemporary world, we have to accept that we cannot survive without coercive authority structures. But if we have such structures, we need to have people to occupy the roles within them: rulers, in other words. In past centuries human beings may have been prepared to accept that some people had a natural right to rule. Perhaps they were thought to have been appointed by God. But this is not a line of reasoning we are now prepared to accept. We will accept that individuals have a right to rule only if they have been appointed by the people, and, perhaps even more importantly, can be removed by the people without bloodshed. That is, only democracy allows us an answer we can accept to the question 'Why should these people rule?', or 'What makes their rule legitimate?' By democratic means we can, of course, also exercise some measure of control over the rulers' behaviour. Perhaps this is the best we can hope for, both in terms of political structure and as a last-ditch defence of modern democracy.

4

THE PLACE OF LIBERTY

Mill on liberty

> The only purpose for which power can be rightfully exercised over any member of a civilized community, against his will, is to prevent harm to others. His own good, either physical or moral, is not a sufficient warrant.
>
> (Mill, *On Liberty,* in *Utilitarianism and Other Writings,* ed. Mary Warnock ([1859], 2nd edn, Glasgow: Collins, 2003), 94–5)

One simple principle

Once democracy is in place, what work is there left for the political philosopher? An optimistic view is that, as soon as we have a democratic decision-making procedure, the fundamental work of political philosophy is over. All decisions can now be left to the fair process of the electoral machine. Sadly, as we observed in Chapter 3, even if democracy is the best system we can think of, it is not a cure-all. And Mill suggests it has its own dangers: the threat of the tyranny of the majority. It is naïve to think that the existence of democracy rules out injustice. The fact that 'the people' make the laws does not rule out the possibility that the majority will pass laws that oppress, or are otherwise unfair to, the minority. Somehow the minority must be protected.

Mill's way out of this problem may seem surprising. After arguing for the virtues of representative democracy, the next thing he proposes is that we should severely limit its powers. His work *On Liberty* (in fact, published earlier than *On Representative Government*) is concerned with the question of 'the nature and limits of the power which can be legitimately exercised by society over the individual' (*On Liberty*, 88). Mill argues that we should reserve considerable powers for the individual. There are limits to state intervention, and also limits to the proper use of public opinion as a way of moulding beliefs and behaviour.

How much power should the state have? We have seen that a range of views is possible. At one extreme, the anarchist claims that the state has no justified power at all. This seems equivalent to the view that there is no acceptable limit to the liberty of the individual, or, at least, not a limit that the state may impose. At the other extreme, defenders of absolute government, such as Hobbes, argue that the state has no obligation to pay any regard at all to the liberties of its subjects. It may enforce whatever rules and restrictions it wishes.

Between these two poles, a spectrum of possibilities exists. Finding neither anarchy nor absolutism acceptable, Mill took it to be his task to define his position on this spectrum. Why, as a champion of liberty, did Mill reject anarchy, which many feel is the highest realization of individual liberty? As we saw in Chapter 2, Mill takes the view that if people are given complete freedom then some will surely abuse it, using the absence of government to exploit others. Hence he writes: 'All that makes existence valuable to any one depends on the enforcement of restraints upon the actions of other people' (*On Liberty*, 91). Anarchy means living without the law, and, according to Mill, our lives would then hardly be worth living. Mill takes it for granted that tyranny is no longer to be considered a serious option, and so sets out to determine the correct mix of freedom and authority.

On what grounds may the state interfere to prohibit people from acting as they wish, or force them to act against their wishes? Different societies, Mill observes, have 'solved' this problem in different ways. Some, for example, have prevented the practice of particular religions, or even suppressed religion completely. Others have imposed censorship on the press and other media. Many have outlawed certain sexual practices. Homosexual acts between men were illegal until as recently as the 1960s in many parts of the world and remain so in some, and while in many countries prostitution is not against the law, it is commonly illegal for a prostitute to solicit for customers. All these are limitations of people's liberty, carried out through the exercise of state power. But does the state have the right to interfere in people's lives and liberties in any of these ways?

Mill seeks a principle, or set of principles, that will allow us to decide each case on its real merits, rather than abandoning the matter to arbitrary custom and popular morality—Mill's greatest enemy. His answer is both radical and refreshingly simple. Mill's Liberty Principle (cited at the start of this chapter) announces that you may justifiably limit a person's freedom of action only if they threaten harm to another. To many modern readers this principle (also known as the 'Harm Principle') may seem blindingly obvious. But it has not been obvious through most of history. For centuries people have been persecuted for worshipping the wrong god, or for not worshipping at all. But what harm did they do to anyone, or anything, except perhaps to their own immortal souls? Mill's view should not even be obvious to us now. Suppose a friend is falling into drug addiction. May you forcibly interfere only to prevent harm to others? This example opens up serious issues regarding both the interpretation and plausibility of Mill's principle. Probably no society, past or present, has ever lived by the principle understood strictly. Indeed, as we shall also see, Mill himself shied away from some of its most unconventional consequences.

Before going any further, however, it is worth returning to one element in the statement of Mill's Liberty Principle. He says that it is to apply to 'any member of a civilized community'. So does he intend to accept restrictions on the liberty of the uncivilized? As a matter of fact, he does. He explicitly states that the principle is meant to apply only to people in 'the maturity of their faculties' (*On Liberty*, 95). Children and 'barbarians' are excluded, for 'Liberty, as a principle, has no application to any state of things anterior to the time when mankind have become capable of being improved through free and equal discussion' (*On Liberty*, 95).

Mill's point here is that liberty is only valuable under certain conditions. If those conditions do not apply, then liberty can do a great deal of harm. Children should not be free to decide whether or not to learn to read, and Mill shared the Victorian view that certain peoples were 'backward' and thus should also be treated as children. What is important at this stage in the argument is not whether Mill was right or wrong about barbarians (and we will return in Chapter 6 to look at some questions of justice and race), but the condition he laid down for the application of the Liberty Principle. Liberty is valuable as a means to improvement—moral progress. Under some circumstances liberty will, just as likely, have the opposite effect, and so progress will have to be effected by some other means. But Mill is in no doubt that when society is in its maturity—when we have progressed to an appropriately educated and civilized level—state interference in individual action should be regulated by the Liberty Principle.

An illustration: freedom of thought

One of Mill's most cherished beliefs was that there should be complete freedom of thought and discussion. He devotes almost a third of *On Liberty* to these vital freedoms, while accepting that there should sometimes be limits to what you are permitted to say in public.

The first thing to note, for Mill, is that the fact that a view is unpopular is no reason at all to silence it: 'If all mankind minus one were of one opinion, and only one person were of the contrary opinion, mankind would be no more justified in silencing that one person, than he, if he had the power, would be justified in silencing mankind' (*On Liberty*, 100). In fact, Mill argues, we have very good reason to welcome the advocacy even of unpopular views. To suppress them would be to 'rob the human race, posterity as well as the existing generation'. How so? Well, Mill argues that, whether the controversial view is true, false, or a mix of the two, we will never gain by refusing it a voice. If we suppress a true view (or one that is partially true), then we lose the chance to exchange error, whole or partial, for truth. But if we suppress a false view we lose in a different way: to challenge, reconsider, and perhaps reaffirm, our true views. So there is nothing to gain by suppression, whatever the truth of the view in question.

Is there really harm in suppressing a false view? We must first ask how we can be so sure that it is false. Even if the would-be censor claims to be certain of the truth of the customary opinion, there is quite a gulf, as Mill points out, between *our being certain of* a view, and *the view being certain*. Not to recognize this is to assume infallibility, but history provides enough evidence of how mistaken this assumption is. Many beliefs that were once held as certainties have been considered by later generations not only to be false, but also to be absurd. Think, for example, of those people who now claim to hold the once widespread belief that the earth is flat.

More dramatically, Mill reminds us of the cases of Socrates and Jesus, the first executed for impiety and immorality, the second for blasphemy. Both were tried by honest judges, acting in good faith. But both perished in societies where the assumption of infallibility led to laws prohibiting the advocacy of views contrary to established traditions. Of course, in western democracies we are unlikely to execute people for their views now. The point, however, is that the moral systems of both Socratic philosophy and Christianity were suppressed because they conflicted with established views 'known for certain' to be true. This illustrates the thought that the human race is capable of monumental error. Never, thinks Mill, have we the right to claim infallibility.

One further example may illustrate and extend Mill's point. The ancient Alexandrian library, one of the treasures of the ancient world, was reputed, at its height, to contain over 700,000 volumes. But in the year AD 640 Alexandria was captured by the Arabs, under the leadership of 'Amr, and this, according to the tale of the much later writer Abulfaragius (apparently a highly unreliable source) is what happened to the library:

> John the Grammarian, a famous Peripatetic philosopher, being in Alexandria at the time of its capture, and in high favour with 'Amr begged that he would give him the royal library. 'Amr told him that it was not in his power to grant such a request, but promised to write to the caliph for his consent. Omar, on hearing the request of his general, is said to have replied that if these books contained the same doctrine as the Koran, they could be of no use, since the Koran contained all necessary truths; but if they contained anything contrary to that book, they ought to be destroyed; and therefore, whatever their contents were, he ordered them to be burnt. Pursuant to this order, they were distributed among the public baths, of which there was a large number of the city, where, for six months, they served to supply the fires. (Quoted in *Encyclopedia Britannica*, IIth edn, 1910–11, i–ii, 570)

It is a pity that 'Amr did not have *On Liberty* available, for he would have done well to take pause and heed Mill's point that: 'There is the greatest difference between presuming an opinion to be true, because, with every opportunity for contesting it, it has not been refuted, and assuming its truth for the purpose of not permitting its refutation' (*On Liberty*, 102).

But before we feel too smug, we should note Rousseau's comments on the story of the library:

Our learned men have cited this reasoning as the height of absurdity. Yet suppose Gregory the Great in the place of ['Amr] and the Gospel in the place of the Koran, the library would still have been burned, and it might perhaps be the finest action in that Illustrious Pontiff's life. (*Discourse on the Arts and Sciences* [1750], Cambridge: Cambridge University Press, 1997, 26 n.)

The *Discourse on the Arts and Sciences* was written by Rousseau in 1750, for a competition set by the Academy of Dijon on the question 'whether the restoration of the Sciences and the Arts has had a purifying effect on morals'. Why would book-burning have been the finest act of Gregory the Great's life? Rousseau reports that the truth on such matters came to him on the road between Paris and Vincennes, on the way to visit the philosopher Diderot, who had been imprisoned for sedition. He realized, so he says, that developments in the arts and sciences, so far from aiding human progress, had caused more unhappiness than happiness, and, furthermore, had corrupted public morals. Unable to complete his journey, he sat down and scribbled out a draft of this highly controversial thesis, with which he won the prize.

It is hard to imagine a view further from Mill's. Rousseau suggests that we offer up a prayer: 'Almighty God! You who hold all Minds in your hands, deliver us from our Fathers' Enlightenment and fatal arts and restore us to ignorance, innocence, and poverty, the only goods that can make for our happiness and are precious in your sight' (*Discourse on the Arts and Sciences*, 26). Beneath Rousseau's rhetoric is a very serious objection to Mill's project. Can it be right to assume that it is always better to know the truth than to remain in ignorance? Mill's argument appears implicitly to assume that knowledge will lead to happiness, but why should we believe that? Just as an individual may sometimes lead a happier life in blissful ignorance of what his or her acquaintances really think of them, presumably there are times when society profits too by ignorance or false belief. Perhaps the truth is too hard to bear, or will dissolve the bonds of society. This is often said about belief in God and the afterlife. That is, so the argument goes, the reason why people should believe is not because there is a God and an afterlife—there may or may not be—but because unless these beliefs are widely held society will fall into selfishness and immorality. Therefore we should not allow the propagation of atheism, for, if it catches on, society will disintegrate. Whether or not we accept that argument, it does not take much imagination to come to the conclusion that human beings may well have been better off if we had never discovered some scientific truths: those, for example, which led to the development of the atomic bombs that destroyed Hiroshima and Nagasaki.

Should we then sometimes accept limitations on freedom of thought? The argument that we should rests not on truth, but on utility; the importance of a view to society. On this view, we can have good reason to suppress an opinion even if it is true. This argument against freedom of thought seems very strong, but so is Mill's reply. Everything depends on the theory that a view is necessary for social peace, and that its contrary will be destructive of that peace. But what makes us so sure that, say, disbelief in God will lead society into dissolution? Or that knowing about the structure of the atom will lead to more harm than good? We are just as fallible on that issue as we are on any. As Mill puts the point:

> The usefulness of an opinion is itself matter of opinion: as disputable, as open to discussion, and requiring discussion as much as the opinion itself. There is the same need of an infallible judge of opinions to decide an opinion to be noxious as to decide it to be false. (*On Liberty*, 104)

Indeed, Mill reminds us, Christianity itself was suppressed by the Romans on the grounds of the harm it would do to the preservation of society.

Still, the position is not quite as clear as Mill makes out. If we cannot know for certain whether believing the truth is more likely to lead to happiness or to harm, then we have no more reason, on this argument, to permit freedom of thought than to ban it. Mill must be making the assumption that, in general at least, believing the truth is a way of achieving happiness.

If that is so, what harm can be done by suppressing a false view? In fact, there are very strong reasons against doing so, Mill argues, even if we could know it to be false. If we do not consider challenges to our opinion, then 'however true it may be, if it is not fully, frequently, and fearlessly discussed, it will be held as a dead dogma, not a living truth' (*On Liberty*, 114). As Mill says, we 'go to sleep at [the] post as soon as there is no enemy in the field' (*On Liberty*, 120). One danger here is that the real meaning of the view might be lost or enfeebled if it is not constantly challenged and defended, and so becomes 'deprived of its vital effect on the character and conduct, the dogma becoming a mere formal profession, inefficacious for good' (*On Liberty*, 114). But perhaps the greater danger is that when challenged by a sparkling presentation of the opposite, false, view, the champions of the received truth will be unable to defend themselves. Not only will they look foolish, but also the false view may gain a popularity it does not merit, sometimes with disastrous consequences.

This, according to some accounts, is what happened to evolutionary theory in the United States. Believers in Darwinism, while realizing that the theory has some apparent flaws, nevertheless did not take seriously the thought that any intelligent, scientifically trained person could fail to accept the broad truth of evolutionary theory in some form or other. Consequently, when well-organized and skilful religious fundamentalists started packaging and deliberately mixing up sophisticated and plausible objections to Darwinism with their own advocacy of 'creation science'—the literal belief in the Old Testament—the Darwinian establishment was not ready to meet the challenge. And so the creationists developed a following way out of proportion to the scientific merits (nil) of their theory. Many Americans—in certain southern states a majority—have believed that evolutionary theory should not be taught in schools.

Two types of case have been considered so far: where the new view is true and where it is false. In each case, allowing the expression of the view will do good, not harm. There is a third case where this is even more obvious: where there is partial truth on both sides of the issue. This is the most common case of all. The only way in which truth might finally emerge is by allowing full and free discussion of all sides of the issue. So, Mill concludes, in all cases mankind will benefit from the expression of views opposed to the current orthodoxy, and so there is never a case for censorship.

Harm to others

While there is never a case for censorship, Mill accepts that there are occasions on which it is right to limit freedom of expression. An example he suggests is this:

> An opinion that corn-dealers are starvers of the poor, or that private property is robbery, ought to be unmolested when simply circulated through the press, but may justly incur punishment when delivered orally to an excited mob

> assembled before the house of a corn-dealer, or when handed about among the same mob in the form of a placard. (*On Liberty*, 131)

The fact that, in this case, freedom of expression is almost certain to lead to harm to others brings it, so Mill argues, within the scope of activities that can properly be regulated by governments.

Earlier we noted that, according to Mill, we may interfere with the liberty of an adult only to prevent harm, or threat of harm, to others. In severe cases, we can, with justification, use the force of law, while in other cases social pressure is the more appropriate restraint. But what does Mill mean by 'harm'? Suppose that a group of people want to set up a new religion, and worship in private. Mill's view is that as long as they do not attempt to coerce anyone into membership, then the rest of society has no business interfering. Why not? Because this behaviour does no harm to anyone else. But immediately the zealot of another, established, religion will object: of course they are causing me harm. First, their heathen behaviour causes me great offence and anguish. Second, they are thwarting my plans to convert the whole world to my religion. It is simply not true that they do no harm.

This objection can be put another way. We can divide actions into two classes: purely self-regarding actions and other-regarding actions. Other-regarding actions affect or involve at least one other person. Purely self-regarding actions concern only the agent, or if they do involve others it is with their free consent. Mill's Liberty Principle, then, comes down to the claim that, while we may regulate and supervise other-regarding actions, we have no business interfering in self-regarding actions. So far so good. But now Mill's critic asks for an example of a purely self-regarding action to fall into this protected realm. And, pretty much whatever we offer, the critic will be able to find some third party affected by the action. For example, whether I decide to wear black shoes or brown shoes today looks like a self-regarding action, if any action is. But then the makers of brown shoe-polish would clearly prefer me to wear brown shoes. Furthermore, my friends of highly refined sensibilities might suffer distress and embarrassment on my behalf if it turns out I am wearing the wrong shoes for the occasion. So even a trivial example like this seems to turn out to be other-regarding. If we try very hard we might find some examples of purely self-regarding action. For example, if I live alone it is perhaps hard to see how my decision whether to sleep on my front or my back could affect anyone else (although the pillow-making industry may have an opinion, as may the health service if I am more likely to avoid back pain one way or another). But if we have to resort to such examples then Mill is lost. If we interpret the Liberty Principle as giving the individual freedom, but only over self-regarding actions understood this way, then it is left without a serious range of application.

Mill could not have intended to be understood in this manner. He was determined that the sphere of liberty was not to be left to the 'likings and dislikings' of society. So it is obvious that he must distinguish between those actions that society, or its members, dislike, or find annoying or offensive, and those actions that cause *harm*. Mere offence, or dislike, for Mill, is no harm. So what did Mill mean by harm?

Mill often uses the terminology of 'interests' in his statements of the Liberty Principle. So, for example, he says that his view authorizes 'the subjection of individual spontaneity to external control, only in respect to those actions of each, which concern the interest of other people' (*On Liberty*, 95–6). Harm, then, is sometimes read as 'damage to interests'. Understood in this way, the Liberty Principle essentially reads 'act as you like, so long as you do not harm the interests of another person'.

This gives us some help, but unfortunately no one seems to have been able to give an adequate definition of 'interests' in this sense. The term is most commonly used in connection with financial interests. If someone has a financial interest in a scheme, then they stand to gain or lose money depending on the success of that venture. However, Mill was not exclusively concerned with people's financial well-being, and so we must add that individuals have, at least, an interest in their personal safety and security. Therefore murder, assault, rape, theft, and fraud would all count as actions that harm the interests of the person attacked or defrauded. The Liberty Principle then would, quite rightly, allow us to restrict individuals' freedom of action to prevent such acts.

But we must be careful here. Mill does not say that society may rightly interfere with someone's freedom of action whenever he or she threatens to harm your interests. We have already seen an example that illustrates this. My decision to wear black shoes may, in some small way, harm the interests of the brown shoe-polish manufacturers, but Mill gives them no right to intervene. In fact, Mill himself points out many much more serious examples of this: 'Whoever succeeds in an overcrowded profession, or in a competitive examination; whoever is preferred to another in any contest for an object which both desire, reaps benefit from the loss of others, from their wasted exertion and their dis-appointment' (*On Liberty*, 163). Mill intends that none of these forms of competition will be ruled out by the Liberty Principle, despite the fact that they are capable of doing severe harm to the interests of the losers. Clearly, then, we have not yet got to the bottom of the Liberty Principle. In Mill's view, harming another's interests is not enough (not a suffi-cient condition) to justify constraint. Indeed, we will later see reason to question whether Mill even thinks it is a necessary condition. To make further progress we must broaden our view.

Justifying the Liberty Principle

> [Each person] should be bound to observe a certain line of conduct towards the rest. This conduct consists ... in not injuring the in-terests of one another; or rather certain interests which, either by express legal provision or by tacit understanding, ought to be con-sidered as rights.
>
> (*On Liberty*, 147)

Liberty, rights, and utility

In the passage just quoted Mill appeals to a new idea: interests that ought to be considered as rights, or 'rights-based interests'. Perhaps this can help us understand the Liberty Principle. For example, while there are laws to enforce my right to keep my property against your attempts to take it by force, I have no similar right to be protected against economic competition. Indeed there are many interests that do not normally seem to give rise to claims of right. When my rich aunt strikes me out of her will, my interests may suffer, but she does not infringe my rights.

This may seem a promising approach, but there are two serious mat-ters to consider. First, how do we know what rights we have? Suppose I claim a right for my business to be protected against competitors. What can Mill say to show me that I have no such right? Second, it is very odd to see Mill using the concept of rights at such a crucial point in the argu-ment. For early in the essay he writes (or should we say boasts?): 'It is proper to state that I forego any advantage which could be derived to my argument from the idea of abstract right, as a thing independent of utility' (*On Liberty*, 95). But how is this consistent with the appeal to the idea of 'rights-based interest'? This statement of intent apparently contradicts the explicit appeal to rights in the passage just noted.

Perhaps it will be thought that the most charitable thing to do would be simply to ignore Mill's statement that he will refrain from appeal to the notion of an 'abstract right'. But this would not really do. Mill has very good reasons for making this statement, as we can see if we look, for a moment, at the idea of a right.

Within liberal circles it is often taken as a fundamental axiom that people have some basic rights. Normally included are the right to life, free speech and thought, free assembly, and freedom of movement, together with rights to vote and stand for office. Some theorists, although not all, add rights to a decent standard of living (shelter, food, and health care). Most often these rights would now be collected together under the name of 'human rights' or 'universal human rights'. In the past they would have been called 'the rights of man' or 'natural rights'. Anything—particularly any action by a government—that violates a human or natural right is morally wrong, and should be remedied. It is a familiar and comforting notion that we all have rights, and that these must be respected. Countries that ignore the rights of their citizens are often subject to intense international criticism.

Nevertheless, the idea of a natural right is highly problematic. In fact, one of the features which makes a theory of natural rights initially so attractive turns out to be one of its main weaknesses; that is, the theory claims that natural rights are basic, fundamental, or axiomatic, and are the ultimate ground of all further decisions. This is attractive because it makes the theory seem so rigorous and principled. But the disadvantage is that we are left with nothing more fundamental to say in defence of these rights. Suppose an opponent doubts that there are any natural rights. How can we reply? Short of saying that the opponent must be insincere or confused, there seems nowhere left to turn. Using the terminology of natural rights may be a successful tactic in disputes between those who agree that there are such things, but otherwise it seems to leave us dangling and exposed.

A further, related, difficulty is that, if natural rights have a fundamental status, and so are not arrived at on the basis of some other argument, how do we know what rights we have? This difficulty was exploited by Bentham, who pointed out that if it is 'self-evident' that people have natural rights, why do different theorists have different ideas about what those rights should be? There are major inconsistencies between the accounts given by different political philosophers. This raises not only the question of how to adjudicate between different accounts, but also leads to the troubling thought that a statement of what natural rights we have often seems little more than one person's opinion.

Bentham's best-known attack on the idea of natural rights starts with the observation that a right seems to be a legal idea. We think of rights and duties as being distributed by laws. The laws give you rights to vote, to receive welfare benefits, to protection by the police, and so on. In Bentham's view this is all there is to a right: 'Right is with me the child of law ... A natural right is a son that never had a father' (*Supply Without Burthen* [1795], 73). If this is correct, then it makes the idea of a natural right—a right independent of the law of the land—'nonsense on stilts' (*Anarchical Fallacies*, written 1796, first published 1814, 53). There just cannot be such a thing.

Of course, not everyone will accept Bentham's argument. Theorists like Locke simply deny Bentham's major assumption: that rights can only be created by legal decree. But Mill favoured Bentham's view, and was very suspicious of the idea of natural rights. This is what he means by saying that he intends to make no use of the idea of abstract right. But how, then, can he use the notion of rights-based interests? Does he mean 'those interests *already respected* by the law as rights'? A moment's thought is enough to dismiss this idea. After all, Mill saw himself as putting forward a doctrine with radical, reforming consequences, critical of the current state of affairs. To accept the present system of rights would put him back into the hands of custom and prejudice, and this is precisely what Mill wanted to avoid.

If Mill can neither accept natural rights nor rely on conventional rights, then what is left for him? The answer lies in how he completes the passage where he declares his opposition to abstract rights, partially cited above. After saying that he will make no use of the idea of abstract right, as a 'thing independent of utility', he adds: 'I regard utility as the ultimate appeal on all ethical questions; but it must be utility in the largest sense, grounded on the permanent interests of a man as a progressive being' (*On Liberty*, 95).

Mill intends to defend a view of rights that makes them not natural or fundamental, nor a simple echo of whatever happen to be the laws of the land, but derived from the theory of utilitarianism. We took a preliminary look at utilitarian theory in Chapter 2, and we also saw the 'indirect utilitarian' argument used to justify rights. It is worth, briefly, going over the main lines again, before showing how this theory can illuminate Mill's doctrine of liberty.

Mill explains and defends the utilitarian system in his work *Utilitarianism* (1861). As he defines it, utilitarianism is the theory which: 'holds that actions are right in proportion as they tend to promote happiness, wrong as they tend to produce the reverse of happiness. By happiness is intended pleasure and the absence of pain; by unhappiness pain and the privation of pleasure' (*Utilitarianism*, 186). Broadly we might summarize the view as saying that utilitarianism requires us to maximize the sum total of happiness or pleasure in the world. (This will not quite do as a summary of Mill's view, as he claims that some pleasures—of the intellect, for example—are qualitatively more valuable than other more bodily pleasures. But we can ignore this complication.)

How can we connect the idea of a right with utility? Mill claims: 'To have a right, then, is, I conceive, to have something which society ought to defend me in the possession of. If the objector goes on to ask, why it ought? I can give him no other reason than general utility' (*Utilitarianism*, 226).

In brief, the basic idea is to lay out a system of rights that will maximize the general happiness. That is, we grant people particular rights so that more happiness can be achieved within the structure of those rights than would be possible under any alternative system. Perhaps the best way of thinking about this is to put yourself in the position of a utilitarian legislator. Suppose you are responsible for setting out the legal system, and you want to set it up in such a way that laws maximize happiness. Naïvely, it might be thought that under such circumstances you should make just one law: 'Act to maximize happiness.' But this is not so obvious.

We must remember a distinction made in Chapter 2 between direct and indirect utilitarianism. A direct utilitarian believes that an individual should perform an action whenever that action will lead to more happiness than any available alternative. On this view, we saw, it is sometimes said that it is acceptable to punish someone who is innocent if that will placate an angry mob and defuse a potentially disastrous situation. The direct utilitarian must weigh up the distress to the innocent victim, the likelihood that the deception will become public, the likely effects of allowing the mob to try to find the guilty party, and any other factors that might affect the balance of pain and pleasure that will flow from the situation. If the sums reveal that we will maximize happiness by punishing the innocent, then this is what we should do.

The indirect utilitarian follows a more subtle strategy. On this view, it is accepted that the goal of law and morality is that happiness should be maximized, but it is claimed that this goal will not always be achieved by allowing individuals to seek to maximize happiness themselves. Consider the last example. Suppose it is true that utility is sometimes advanced by making some people scapegoats. Suppose, too, that everyone knows this. Everyone, then, realizes that there is a possibility that they will be picked on and victimized. Knowing this is likely to cause an atmosphere of anxiety and gloom. The possibility of scapegoating would be detrimental to the general happiness. Therefore the indirect utilitarian might calculate that the general happiness will best be served by ensuring that no one is ever punished unless they are proven guilty. Although there might be a few, very special, occasions when we might profit from scapegoating, in the long term we do much better in utilitarian terms by giving everyone immunity—a right—against victimization. This, then, is a sketch of how to derive a utilitarian theory of rights. While it is true that, in the short term, we might do better to violate a right, when we take long-term effects into account utilitarianism suggests that rights are to be obeyed.

Indeed indirect utilitarianism can be taken one step further, although Mill did not do this himself. Henry Sidgwick (1838–1900), the most thoughtful and sophisticated of the early utilitarians, suggested that, while utilitarianism is the correct moral theory, it might sometimes be better if this were kept secret. Perhaps most people should be given some very straightforward, simple maxims to follow: do not lie, do not murder, do not cheat, and so on. His reason for this is that, should ordinary people know the truth of utilitarianism, they would be likely to attempt to calculate in direct utilitarian terms. Not only would this be a bad thing for the reasons already given; most people would also make poor calculations through lack of care, or ability, or through the magnification of their own interests. (Compare Hume on our powers of reasoning in

Chapter 2.) It is much better, thought Sidgwick, to keep utilitarianism as an 'esoteric' doctrine, revealed only to the enlightened elite. (This view has been called 'government house utilitarianism' by its opponents. It treats citizens in the patronizing fashion that European powers treated their colonial subjects in the days of empire.)

As I said, Mill did not go this far, and, it is true, his own indirect utilitarianism is implicit in his view rather than explicitly stated. But once we have appreciated the idea of indirect utilitarianism, we can see how a utilitarian theory of rights is possible. This, then, will inform the utilitarian legislator. The insight of indirect utilitarianism is to note that, instead of setting out a single law—maximize happiness—the utilitarian legislator might do much better, in terms of the general happiness, to set out a larger body of law, which guarantees and respects secure rights of individuals. Indeed, it may well be that Bentham and Mill thought of themselves as primarily addressing law-makers, rather than the public. After all, Bentham's major book on the topic is called *An Introduction to the Principles of Morals and Legislation* (1789).

And now we can begin to see how the pieces fit together. According to Mill, the greatest happiness will be achieved by giving people a private sphere of rights-based interests where no intervention is permitted, while allowing a public sphere where intervention is possible, but only on utilitarian grounds.

How does this solve the question of where to draw the line between the private and public spheres? Mill himself is not explicit, but there is a ready answer. First, we acknowledge that the private sphere is identified with the sphere of 'rights-based interests'. Then we raise the difficult question of what makes the difference between rights-based interests (my interest in personal safety) and other interests (my interest in not being struck out of my aunt's will)? The answer to this question is given by the theory of utilitarianism. It will serve the general happiness if we pass a law that protects people's interests in walking down the street free from attack, but it will diminish general happiness if we set out restrictions about whether aunts can or cannot strike their nephews out of their wills.

Other examples might help to make this clearer. As we saw in detail, Mill wants to protect freedom of thought. Why? Because this is most likely to achieve the truth, and (Mill implies) knowledge of the truth increases happiness. So we are assumed to have a rights-based interest in freedom of thought. But Mill does not want to protect an individual's business against fair competition. Why not? Because according to Mill the utilitarian advantages of free trade mean that no other system can advance happiness to the same extent. (The feudal system, for example, in which individuals purchased licences to be the monopoly supplier of a particular good, led to enormous inefficiencies.) Therefore people are to be given rights to compete in business, not rights which protect their financial interests against competition. The position is somewhat complex, because, of course, Mill accepts that we have to have rights in our property to protect it from theft and fraud. But indirect utilitarianism, in Mill's view, does not extend to protection against economic competition.

This utilitarian defence of the Liberty Principle seems very plausible. The utilitarian theory of rights supplies exactly what is missing: a doctrine of rights that does not rest on what Mill regards as the false foundation of natural rights theory, nor on the shifting sands of convention. It appears to allow us to make perfect sense of Mill's proposal. Yet the idea that a utilitarian defence can be given of Mill's Liberty Principle has met with strong criticism. And it is not difficult to find examples where utility and liberty seem to conflict. As one critic has said: 'A drug addict who has successfully kicked the habit is thoroughly justified on utilitarian grounds in stopping some incautious young experimenter from taking the first steps down a road which may prove to have no turning' (R. P. Wolff, *The Poverty of Liberalism*, 1968, 29). In other words, utilitarianism would seem to encourage exactly the type of paternalistic intervention that the Liberty Principle expressly rules out: remember that the Liberty Principle does not permit anyone to interfere with another, even for their own good. So, it is thought, liberal rights cannot be justified in utilitarian terms.

This objection brings out that even if it is possible to construct a utilitarian theory of rights, it does not yet follow that the utilitarian theory would be a liberal theory. Why should we think that, in the long term, there would be more happiness in Mill's society than in the society, governed by customary morality, which he sought to replace? Or in some other society in which enlightened, experienced elders are given the right to direct the lives of its younger members?

To appreciate Mill's response to this problem we need to take yet another look at the wording of the passage in *On Liberty*, where Mill declares his allegiance to utility: 'I regard utility as the ultimate appeal on all ethical questions; but it must be utility in the largest sense, grounded on the permanent interests of a man as a progressive being' (*On Liberty*, 95). 'Utility in the largest sense' presumably means that we should include all sorts of pleasures and forms of happiness—intellectual and emotional, as well as bodily—in the calculation. But why does he add 'grounded on the permanent interests of a man as a progressive being'? There are some further aspects of Mill's view that we will have to understand before everything falls into place.

Individuality and progress

The key to solving this problem lies in Chapter 3 of *On Liberty*, entitled 'On Individuality, as one of the Elements of Well-being'. It is here that Mill tries to show that the general happiness will be best advanced by assigning people a large private sphere of rights to non-interference. In this chapter, Mill argues that freedom is essential to originality and individuality of character. And, Mill claims, 'the free development of individuality is one of the leading essentials of well-being' (*On Liberty*, 132). Here Mill wants to make several points, and it may be helpful to set them in the context of a criticism made by one of Mill's earliest and more impressive critics, James Fitzjames Stephen (1829–94), in his book *Liberty, Equality, Fraternity*, first published in 1873.

Stephen argued that it is absurd to think that liberty is always good in itself. Rather, he claims, it is like fire. It would be irrational to ask whether fire is good in itself; it all depends on the purpose to which it is put. And Stephen has chosen his analogy well. Controlled fire has given us many of our most important technological achievements—the internal combustion engine, for example—but uncontrolled fire is a great fear and, often, a great disaster. This, supposes Stephen, is the case for liberty too.

Mill is prepared to accept that liberty does not always lead to 'improvement'. But he stresses, 'the only unfailing and permanent source of improvement is liberty' (*On Liberty*, 143). Advancing liberty contributes much more to human happiness than any other possible competing policy might. Mill has several reasons for saying this.

First, he argues that, even though people do make mistakes, individuals are still *more likely* to be right about what would make them happy than anyone else. After all, they pay more attention to the issue, and give it more thought than anyone else is likely to. Nevertheless, Mill recognizes that people could exercise liberty far more than they do at present, for he notes that people commonly abuse this power, and before acting ask: 'what is suitable to my position? what is usually done by persons of my station and pecuniary circumstances? or (worse still) what is usually done by persons of a station and circumstances superior to mine?' (*On Liberty*, 136). Independence of judgement, Mill claims, will surely lead to superior consequences. But he does not mean that no one should ever try to influence other people's behaviour. On the contrary, he is keen to emphasize that each of us has a duty to try to convince others of their mistakes, if we feel that they are embarking on foolish or damaging courses of action. We may reason and plead with people. But this is all we may do. Force is out of the question:

> Considerations to aid [another's] judgment, exhortations to strengthen his will, may be offered to him, even obtruded on him, by others: but he himself is the final judge. All errors which he is likely to commit against advice and warning are far outweighed by the evil of allowing others to constrain him to what they deem his good. (*On Liberty*, 148)

Such measures must, in Mill's view, nevertheless fall short of concerted social pressure, although how in practice we can draw this distinction he does not make clear. But overall Mill's position is that leaving people to themselves will tend to make them happier than if we insist that they follow society's recommendations.

A second reason for liberty is that it will not only lead to better decisions in the long run, but also that the exercise of freedom of choice is itself vital to the full development of human nature. Those who are slaves to custom, Mill suggests, will never develop into rounded, flourishing individuals; not necessarily because they will be unhappy, but because they will fail to develop one of their most distinctively human capacities, the capacity for choice.

Mill's third—and most important—reason for championing liberty and individuality is this:

> As it is useful that while mankind are imperfect there should be different opinions, so it is that there should be different experiments of living; that free scope should be given to varieties of character, short of injury to others; and

that the worth of different modes of life should be proved practically. . . . [This is] quite the chief ingredient of individual and social progress. (*On Liberty*, 132)

Mill claims that 'In proportion to the development of his individuality, each person becomes more valuable to himself, and is therefore capable of being more valuable to others' (*On Liberty*, 137). Mill's idea is that human progress is best served by giving individuals the licence to engage in 'experiments of living'. Those who take up this opportunity may well conduct 'successful' experiments, and so arrive at styles of life which others can choose to follow. In other words, role models can show others how to live (or not to live) their own lives, and from these role models the less creative can take up various new possibilities for themselves.

It is at this point that we see Mill at perhaps his most optimistic, and we see the point of his appeal to 'utility in the largest sense, grounded on the permanent interests of a man as a progressive being'. Mill's view is that mankind is progressive, in the sense that human beings are capable of learning from experience, to the long-term benefit of all. Through the experiments of some individuals we may learn things of great value, for the permanent benefit of mankind. Those of us too timid to conduct experiments of our own may nevertheless learn from the more adventurous. It is by observing, and trying out, the various possibilities that we are presented with that mankind will be able to learn what sorts of lives will lead to genuine human flourishing. Liberty is vital as a condition of experimentation. This, it seems, is the primary reason why Mill is convinced that liberty will—in the long run—secure the greatest possible happiness for humankind.

Is Mill too optimistic? That was certainly the opinion of James Fitzjames Stephen. His immediate criticism is that Mill was wrong to think that giving people liberty is likely to lead to vigorous experimentation. Freedom from the interference of others is just as likely to lead to idleness, and lack of interest in life. But a deeper point can also be made, one far more threatening to Mill's project.

In the interpretation of Mill I have presented, the great weight of his position comes down on his assumption that human beings are progressive, capable of learning from experience. Does the experience of recent centuries give the lie to this view? If so, then the heart drops out of Mill's position. Humankind keeps on repeating its mistakes. If people will not learn from others' experience, then we lose Mill's reason

for encouraging experiments of living. What is the point of other people demonstrating new lifestyles to us, if we are not prepared to learn?
Without some such defence of experiments of living, there is far less
justification for individuality and liberty, on the arguments Mill gives.
Indeed some have said that human beings, generally, are in the state
Mill reserved for 'children and barbarians': incapable of being improved
by free and equal discussion. And, as Mill himself argues, such people
are not fit recipients of liberty, at least, not according to the utilitarian calculus. Perhaps this pessimism about the possibility of human improvement is a great exaggeration. But if the truth lies somewhere in the
middle, if humans are less capable of improvement than Mill imagines,
the utilitarian case for liberty is correspondingly weakened. Progress is
the cornerstone of Mill's doctrine.

Liberty as an intrinsic good

Could it be that Mill was wrong to attempt to defend the Liberty Principle in utilitarian terms? In effect Mill has presented liberty as *instrumentally* valuable: it is valuable as a way of achieving the greatest possible
happiness for society. But perhaps he should have argued that liberty is
intrinsically good, good in itself. If we take such a view, as many contemporary liberals claim to, then we avoid the problem that maximizing happiness perhaps requires a non-liberal society. Liberty is valuable,
whatever its consequences.

Some will object that there are no intrinsic goods: everything is valued
for something else, rather than for itself. But Mill himself accepted that
there is at least one intrinsic good: happiness. Utilitarians claim that happiness is the only intrinsic good. Everything must be justified in terms of
its contribution to the total sum of happiness. But then, why shouldn't
we say that there are *two* (or more) intrinsic goods, happiness and liberty? In fact, some commentators have been tempted to say that this is
Mill's real view, even though he denied it.

Mill would reject this interpretation of his views. He is clear that
liberty is good primarily as a means to improvement, and where it fails
to have that effect—in the case of children and barbarians—there is
no case for liberty. Liberty is good only when it adds to our happiness,
but then it is 'part of happiness' rather than an independent value.

Furthermore, unconstrained liberty would lead to anarchy. Utilitarianism provides an account of what liberties we should have, and which we should not have. For example, Mill argues that we should be free to compete in trade, but not free to use another's property without their consent. His position allows us to set out limits to liberty, while paying it great respect.

This is not a conclusive argument for Mill's approach. It is not true that only utilitarianism can set out restrictions to liberty: perhaps liberty can be restricted for the sake of other liberties, or fairness. And there are other ways of defending liberty without relying on utilitarianism (we will see John Rawls's non-utilitarian approach in Chapter 5). Mill's argument is only one way of trying to defend liberalism. Yet the Liberty Principle gives us a reasonable, if problematic, statement of a liberal political philosophy. Is it one we should accept? Not everyone thinks so.

Problems with liberalism

> Euthanasia or the killing of another at his own request, suicide, attempted suicide and suicide pacts, duelling, abortion, incest between brother and sister, are all acts which can be done in private and without offence to others and need not involve the corruption or exploitation of others.
>
> (Lord Devlin, 'Morals and the Criminal Law' [1958], in his *The Enforcement of Morals*, Oxford: Oxford University Press, 1965, 7)

Poison, drunkenness, and indecency

What would life be like if we tried to regulate society according to the Liberty Principle? As I mentioned early on in this chapter, Mill himself falls short of endorsing some of the most shocking implications of his view. In his final chapter, Mill sets out some of the 'obvious limitations' of the Liberty Principle. One limitation concerns restrictions on liberty that are justifiable to prevent crime. So, for example, Mill argues that if the only reason why people bought poison was to commit murder, then society would be entirely justified in banning its production and sale. The fact is, however, that most poisons have other functions too, and so Mill recommends that the law should require chemists to keep a register, recording full details of sales, including the name of the purchaser, and their declared purpose. Accordingly if someone is later found poisoned, the police will already have a list of prime suspects. Strictly, a purchaser, with innocent intent, might complain that this arrangement is intrusive, and in violation of personal liberty. But Mill's view is that the violation is trivial in the light of the benefits of the system, and so this is an obvious exception to the generality of the Liberty Principle.

Another exception is that, while drunkenness, ordinarily, is no crime, anyone who has been convicted of violence to others when drunk should, according to Mill, be prohibited from drinking. Here, for Mill, the danger of harm outweighs an individual's right to drink alcohol.

Although some liberals might worry that these cases—particularly the latter one—are overly restrictive of human liberty, Mill's point is that restrictions are justified to ward off serious harm, even if that harm is a fairly remote possibility. A further example, however, raises much more serious issues of principle:

> there are many acts which, being directly injurious only to the agents them-selves, ought not to be legally interdicted, but which, if done publicly, are a violation of good manners, and coming thus within the category of offences against others, may rightly be prohibited. Of this kind are offences against decency; on which it is unnecessary to dwell, the rather as they are only con-nected indirectly with our subject, the objection to publicity being equally strong in the case of many actions not in themselves condemnable, nor sup-posed to be. (*On Liberty*, 166)

Mill's prose on this delicate subject does not have its usual clarity, but the intention of the passage is clear. Certain actions—sexual intercourse between husband and wife, for example—would be condemned by no moral code if performed in private, but would be acceptable to very few people (and certainly not to Mill) if performed publicly.

But how can Mill make this view consistent with the Liberty Princi-ple? What harm does 'public indecency' do? After all, Mill insists that mere offence is no harm. Here Mill, without being explicit, seems to allow customary morality to override his adherence to the Liberty Prin-ciple. Few, perhaps, would criticize his choice of policy. But it is hard to see how he can render this consistent with his other views: indeed, he appears to make no serious attempt to do so.

Once we begin to consider examples of this kind we begin to under-stand that following Mill's 'one simple principle' would lead to a society of a kind never seen before, and, perhaps, one that we would never wish to see. Some of the apparent inconsistencies in the liberal position were brought out very well by Lord Justice Devlin, in his essay 'Morals and the Criminal Law', published partly as a response to the Wolfenden Re-port of 1957, which recommended the decriminalization of homosexual acts between consenting adults. The Wolfenden Report also argued that prostitution should not be made illegal. These recommendations seem fully in accord with the Liberty Principle. Yet, as Devlin observes, many of the laws of contemporary societies are very hard to defend in terms of the Liberty Principle. Some examples are laws against duelling, incest between siblings, and euthanasia.

To make his point, Devlin focuses on the question of prostitution. Why is the liberal prepared to permit it to exist? The standard answer might be that it is simply none of the law's business: prostitution is a matter of concern only for the prostitute and the customer. But then, asks Devlin:

> If prostitution is … not the law's business, what concern has the law with the ponce or the brothel-keeper …? The Report recommends that the laws which make these activities criminal offences should be maintained … and brings them … under the head of exploitation.… But in general a ponce ex-ploits a prostitute no more than an impresario exploits an actress. ('Morals and the Criminal Law', 12)

Devlin's own view is that we can understand these matters only by as-suming that society holds shared moral principles, which it enforces through the criminal law. If anyone breaks these principles they are thought of as offending society as a whole.

While Mill would certainly deny Devlin's claim that the law ought always to uphold customary morality, there is no doubt that he would have felt uncomfortable if faced with Devlin's examples. This is not to say that liberals like Mill could never find grounds for objecting to eu-thanasia or brothel-keeping. The real question is that, if the Liberty Prin-ciple is intended as seriously as Mill suggests, why should the liberal be concerned if it comes into conflict with customary morality? Mill's pretended adherence to 'one simple principle' does not reflect how com-plicated his beliefs really are.

Marxist objections to liberalism

Criticism of a quite different sort comes from the Marxist tradition. Marx's own writings on this topic appear most famously in his early essay 'On the Jewish Question', published in 1844, when Marx was 26. In 1816, laws were passed in Prussia that restricted Jews to rights that were far inferior to those of Christians. Marx's own father, Heinrich, for example, converted to Christianity the year after the anti-Jewish laws made it impossible for him to remain both a lawyer and a Jew. The Rhenish parliament had voted for Jewish emancipation in 1843, but the king vetoed the proposed legislation. Hence the Jewish Question was a matter of intense debate among liberals and intellectuals in Prussia.

'On the Jewish Question' was written in response to Marx's friend and colleague Bruno Bauer, who had surprisingly written against Jewish emancipation, albeit from an atheist rather than conservative perspective. Bauer's position was that religion stood in the way of both Christians and Jews. If the people of Germany were to gain emancipation, then both the state and its citizens had to be emancipated from religion. Religion had to be abolished.

Marx claims to disagree with Bauer, although what he really does is to set Bauer's remarks in a deeper, more theoretical context. According to Marx, Bauer overlooks a crucial distinction: between political emancipation and human emancipation. This goes hand in hand with a failure to recognize the distinction between what Marx calls 'the state' and 'civil society'.

The demand for political emancipation is the demand for equal rights. In the context of religious emancipation, the emancipated state is one whose laws contain no religious barriers or privileges. For Marx, the United States was an example in which political emancipation was nearly complete. Marx was wrong: he apparently overlooks the fact that at the time the United States was still a slave society, and it would be another eighty years before women would be given the vote on equal terms to men. But Marx's point is that the laws of most of the American states, even in 1843, took people to be equals irrespective of their religion. Yet discrimination can exist at another level. Even if the laws of the state are 'religion-blind', individuals can remain full of religious bigotry and hatred. In consequence, members of some religions suffer discrimination in employment, education, and other areas. In the private world of day-to-day activity, of economic life—civil society—discrimination exists even in a politically emancipated state. Thus, Marx asserts, 'a state can liberate itself from a limitation without man himself being truly free of it' ('On the Jewish Question', 51). Political emancipation is not human emancipation.

This sets the scene for Marx's critique of liberalism. Liberalism seeks a regime of rights to equality, liberty, security, and property: political emancipation. Yet not only does the possession of such rights fall short of human emancipation; liberal rights are actually an obstacle to it. For liberal rights are egoistic rights of separation: rights that, according to Marx, encourage each individual to view others as limitations to his or her freedom. Marx's idea is that the genuinely emancipated society is one in which individuals see themselves, and act, as fully co-operating members of a community of equals. Liberalism parodies this by setting out, at the level of the state, a sham community of 'equal' citizens, which cloaks the egoistic day-to-day activity of competition between unequals in civil society, where man 'treats other men as means, degrades himself to a means, and becomes the plaything of alien powers' ('On the Jewish Question', 53). The rights granted to the citizen reinforce the egoism and antagonism of civil society.

For Marx, political emancipation—liberalism—is a great advance over the hierarchical, discriminatory state that preceded it. But it is a long way from his ideal, a communist society in which emancipation extends all the way down to civil society. This change, of course, Marx believes can only be accomplished by revolutionary action. Liberalism, by contrast, appears to Marx to be a shallow, superficial doctrine.

Communitarianism and liberalism

Is Marx right? Few interpreters now have any confidence that Marx has given us much understanding of what he really means by human emancipation, or how it is to be achieved. However, the underlying point of his critique has been taken up in quite a different way by some contemporary critics of liberalism who call themselves not communists but communitarians. Communitarians share Marx's opposition to what they see as the atomism or individualism of liberalism. But, unlike

Marx, they see the remedy for this not in some imagined community of the future, but in the culture and traditions of existing society.

Liberalism, it is said by communitarians, conceives of people as isolated individuals who, in their own little protected sphere, pursue their own good in what they take to be their own way. Liberal individuals see themselves as having no special attachment to the customs, culture, traditions, and conventions of their own societies. Communitarians argue, in response, that we are thoroughly social beings, and that our identities and self-understandings are bound up with the communities in which we are placed. If we did not find ourselves in our particular, local, social settings, with our commitments and allegiances, we would, quite literally, be different people. Mill, himself, in *Utilitarianism* pays lip-service to this view, suggesting that:

> The social state is at once so natural, so necessary, and so habitual to man, that, except in some unusual circumstances or by an effort of voluntary abstraction, he never conceives himself otherwise than as a member of a body; and this association is riveted more and more, as mankind are further removed from the state of savage independence. Any condition, therefore, which is essential to a state of society, becomes more and more an inseparable part of every person's conception of the state of things which he is born into, and which is the destiny of a human being. (*Utilitarianism*, 207)

Yet communitarians would charge that Mill has not understood the significance of his own words. Only on the contrary, isolated individualist, view, does liberty as Mill understands it seem so valuable. For Mill, liberty allows us to throw off the crushing weight of the bonds of custom and conformity. But, the communitarian argues, not only does this presuppose a false view of human nature (that it is *possible* for us to throw off these 'bonds'); it also has most dangerous consequences. By denying the importance of our community we set out on a path that will lead to individual alienation, and, ultimately, the dislocation of society. The communitarian alleges that liberalism offers a false picture of human nature and social relations, and with it a misleading and damaging vision of what it is possible for human beings to achieve politically. Instead, we must acknowledge the importance of customary morality—the bond that holds society together. We must also acknowledge that no one can expect to be given the right to do anything that will seriously undermine social morality. Of course, we need not see customary morality as static and unchanging—there can surely be disputes about what it is and what it should become. But the room for moral reform is constrained by the customs and traditions we already have.

A likely reply to the communitarians is that they are proposing a highly repressive form of society that gives little place to individual freedom or liberty. But communitarians also argue that liberals are mistaken about the nature of real liberty. Many liberals assume what we saw in Chapter 3 that Isaiah Berlin called a 'negative' definition of liberty: you are free to the extent that you are able to make your own choices about how to live. But, communitarians argue, this is a crude, and indeed false, view. You do not make people free by leaving them alone. On the contrary, it is necessary to bring people to a position where they can make the *right* choices about how to live: the choices that the rational person would make.

The distinction between negative and positive liberty is sometimes put in terms of the difference between 'freedom from' and 'freedom to'. On that account negative liberty is freedom from constraint, and positive liberty is freedom to act. However this is not a very helpful way of explaining the difference, for, as is commonly noted, freedom is always a 'three place relation', which means that freedom connects a person (place one), a constraint or set of constraints (place two) and an action or goal (place three). To say, for example, that I am free to go out this evening, is to say that I am free from constraints (such as other commitments or plans) to perform the action of going out this evening. On the other hand, if I had made a promise to stay in, that would act as a constraint rendering me unfree to perform the action of going out.

A better way to understand the distinction between positive and negative liberty takes us back to Rousseau. Negative liberty, we have seen, is essentially the liberty to act on my desires. But Rousseau, we saw in Chapter 3, believes that following your desires doesn't always make you free. It may sound odd, but it is not absurd to call someone a 'slave' to his or her desires. We might say that about a drug addict, or someone with a dominant obsession about a film star, for example. In order to become free the drug addict or obsessive needs to be able to form and act from more reasonable desires. They have to achieve self-control or self-mastery. To do so would be to enjoy freedom or liberty in the positive sense.

It is this alternative view of 'positive liberty' that the communitarian is likely to endorse. And on one version of this view, thorough socialization is a preliminary to the recognition of your real interests and the possibility for you of achieving positive freedom. But no one has an interest in anything that undermines their society, and with it their identity. And so, it is said, it follows that your (positive) freedom is in no way limited if you are not permitted to engage in actions which compromise important parts of customary morality.

Mill and the communitarian will view each other's doctrine of liberty with mutual suspicion. If Mill's negative definition leads to isolation and alienation, then the communitarian's positive definition leads to repression in the name of freedom. But the dispute between Mill and the communitarian really seems to come to this: which would be a happier society—one that follows a (modified) form of the Liberty Principle, or one that follows a (modified) form of the customs and traditions of society? In fact, we can see that the views might even meet in the middle: perhaps a compromise between the two will be best of all.

Conclusion

It is, I think, fair to say that Mill was right to value (negative) liberty, and to believe that a liberal society is likely to be happier than many illiberal ones. But, as we have seen, his own defence of liberty rests very heavily on the idea that human beings are capable of making moral progress. That, for Mill, was an article of faith. But if he was wrong it may well be that a communitarian society would be preferable to a liberal one on utilitarian grounds: perhaps experiments in living will do more harm than good if no one will learn from them. Defenders of liberty, then, must either show that people are capable of making moral progress or find an alternative foundation for their view.

I cannot resist ending this chapter with an anecdote. In the mid-1980s I met a Spanish lawyer who had studied law and philosophy during the highly autocratic Franco era. I asked him whether it had been possible to study political philosophy, and he said that he had indeed taken such a course. For most of the year they studied the Ancient Greeks, but in the last few weeks they had also covered the moderns. After studying Hobbes, Locke, and Rousseau, they spent some time on Hegel, and then had a two-hour seminar on Marx. But they were given only a few minutes on John Stuart Mill. It was Mill, not Marx, that Franco's regime chose to censor. This makes perfect sense. The doctrines of Karl Marx were unlikely to turn the heads of affluent provincial law students. But John Stuart Mill on free speech and liberty was quite another thing.

5

THE DISTRIBUTION OF PROPERTY

The problem of distributive justice

> We shall suppose that a creature, possessed of reason, but unac-
> quainted with human nature, deliberates with himself what rules
> of justice or property would best promote public interest, and
> establish peace and security among mankind: His most obvious
> thought would be, to assign the largest possessions to the most ex-
> tensive virtue, and give every one the power of doing good, pro-
> portioned to his inclination ... But were mankind to execute such
> a law ... the total dissolution of society must be the immediate
> consequence.
>
> (Hume, *An Enquiry Concerning the Principle of Morals* in
> *Enquiries*, ed. L. A. Selby-Bigge ([1751], 3rd edn,
> Oxford: Oxford University Press, 1975), 192–3)

Liberty and property

How should property be distributed? As Hume indicates, this is a topic
fraught with difficulties. Obvious answers to the question might be disastrously naïve.

The liberty of the citizen, in Mill's view, requires the protection of each
person from harm. For Mill, one form of harm is harm to property: theft,
fraud, or damage. But, he argues, we have no right to protection from
the effects of a normal functioning market, no rights to protection from
economic competition. Mill favours *laissez-faire* capitalism—at least for as
long as individuals are in their present state of moral imperfection. (In a
late work, *Chapters on Socialism* (1879), he suggests that socialism would
be a more appropriate form of economic organization for the morally

perfected beings of the future.) Mill also supposes that the individual has a duty to pay his or her share of the expenses of running the government, and should also be taxed to support those unable to support themselves.

To what extent is a commitment to these policies a consequence of accepting the value of liberty? And what other values are relevant in assessing the justice of a system of property? In fact, in defending his views of distributive justice Mill makes a fairly direct appeal to utilitarianism. Others, such as Locke, have thought that in deriving a just system of property we should appeal to natural property rights. And others again have given a more fundamental role to the idea of equality.

Let us consider, for a moment, whether accepting the value of liberty has any consequences for the question of distributive justice. How should a liberal society distribute property? Opinions differ widely. One tradition, following Locke, supposes that valuing liberty requires the recognition of very strong natural rights to property. In the libertarian development of this view—the most eloquent presentation of which is *Anarchy, State, and Utopia*, published in 1974 by the Harvard philosopher Robert Nozick (1938–2002)—these rights are so powerful that the government has no business interfering with them. The government in Nozick's 'minimal state' has the duty to enforce individual property rights, but may not tax individuals beyond the level required for the defence of the citizens against each other and foreign aggressors. In particular, on this view, the state violates individual rights to property if it attempts to transfer property from some (the rich) to others (the poor). Distribution is to be left to the unimpeded free market, gifts, and voluntary charitable donations.

The libertarian, then, tries to argue from the value of the liberty of the individual to a very pure form of capitalism. In effect, this places an individual's property within his or her 'protected sphere' of rights, where no one else, government or individual, may interfere without consent.

An opposing view points out that libertarianism is bound to lead to vast inequalities of property, which in turn will have a detrimental effect on the liberties—or at least the opportunities—of the poor. This view, welfare liberalism, argues that property must be redistributed from the wealthy to the less fortunate to ensure equal liberty for all. Property remains outside an individual's protected sphere, and the government has the duty to supervise and intervene where necessary (subject to the laws of the land) to protect liberty and justice. The most important variant of welfare liberalism is contained in *A Theory of Justice*, published in 1971 (three years before Nozick's book) by Nozick's Harvard colleague, John Rawls (1921–2002). In fact, much of contemporary political philosophy has been inspired by Rawls's work, whether in defence of it, or, like Nozick, in opposition.

Nozick and Rawls, then, give different answers to the question of distributive justice. A fully worked-out view requires responses to a number of questions. Are there natural property rights? What place is there for the free market? Should we tolerate large inequalities of wealth? What should the government's role be? There is no shortage of answers to these questions. But which answers are right?

The income parade

It is hard to jump right into these questions without some aids to reflection. The problem of distributive justice is the problem of how goods should be distributed. And, it seems, one excellent way of prompting thought about 'how things should be' is to consider how they are. So perhaps we should start with some facts.

Raw income statistics, while no doubt useful, often fail to sink in. It is all very well to be told that the top few per cent of the population hold so much of the wealth, but it is often hard to appreciate the significance of such dryly presented figures. For this reason a Dutch economist, Jan Pen, in his 1971 book *Income Distribution*, decided to present the facts about the income distribution in the United Kingdom in a rather different way. Of course, much has changed since 1971, but Pen's way of presenting the data is so powerful that it remains an excellent place to begin.

Pen invites us to imagine a Grand Parade of everyone in the United Kingdom economy who earns a wage of any sort, including those who receive social security. The Grand Parade is in single file, with people ordered by income, the lowest earners in the front, and the highest at the back. We are to suppose that the entire parade passes us by in one hour. The peculiar feature of the parade is that everyone's height is determined by their pre-tax income. That is, the more you earn, the taller you are. Those who earn the average wage will be of average height, those who earn double will be twice the size, and so on. Suppose that, as spectators, we are of average height, and watch the parade go by. What would it look like?

First, for a few seconds we see extraordinary people of negative height. These are individuals who own loss-making businesses. But they are soon replaced by people the size of a matchstick or a cigarette. In 1971, these were typically married women who had worked only for a week or so, and so do not have an annual income, schoolchildren doing paper rounds or odd jobs, and so on.

These folk take five minutes to pass, and after ten minutes people about 3 feet tall—the height of a 2-year-old child—begin to come through. These include many unemployed people, old-age pensioners, divorced women, some young people, and owners of shops doing badly. Next follow ordinary workers in the lowest-paid sectors. Dustmen, transport workers, some miners, unskilled clerks, and unskilled manual workers. There are many black and Asian workers within this group. After fifteen minutes the marchers finally reach 4 feet tall. And for the next fifteen minutes there is very little change in height, as skilled industrial workers with considerable training and office workers pass by.

Pen comments at this point: 'We know that the parade will last an hour and perhaps we expected that after half-an-hour we would be able to look the marchers straight in the eye, but that is not so. We are still looking down on the top of their heads' (*Income Distribution*, 51). It is forty-five minutes before we see people of average height. These people include teachers, executive civil servants, shopkeepers, foremen, and a few farmers.

In the final six minutes the parade becomes sensational, with the arrival of the top 10 per cent. At around 6' 6" we see headmasters, young-ish university graduates in various jobs, more farmers, and departmental heads, most of whom had no idea that they were in the top 10 per cent. Then, in the last few minutes, 'giants suddenly loom up'. A lawyer, not exceptionally successful, 18 feet tall. The first doctors, 7, 8, 9 yards. The first accountants. In the very last minute university professors appear, 9 yards tall; managing directors, 10 yards; a permanent secretary, 13 yards; high court judges, accountants, eye surgeons—20 yards or more.

For the last few seconds we see people the size of tower blocks; businessmen, managing directors of major companies, film stars, members of the royal family. Prince Philip is 60 yards tall, the singer Tom Jones nearly a mile high. At the back comes John Paul Getty: between 10 and 20 miles tall.

As we observed, these figures are, of course, rather old. An up-to-date version would see new technology entrepreneurs and hedge fund managers in the final seconds, with the last few minutes dominated by lawyers, accountants, bankers, stockbrokers, and company directors, with public sector employees (especially university professors!) rather further back than they were some decades ago. But though they are dated, presented this way the statistics are quite startling. It is hard to read through the account without thinking that there *must* be something wrong with any society so unequal. But is such a reaction justified? Other types of response are just as possible. One is to say that the parade simply does not give us enough information to allow a properly considered judgement. Another, complementary, reaction is to say that the parade is seriously misleading. Developing this last point, the claim could be advanced that this pretended 'scientific' presentation of bare data is 'value-laden', in the sense that the selection of data would only be made by someone who wishes to persuade us that current society is unjust.

It is true that a defender of the current system would hardly choose to present it in this way. So if the parade is misleading, how? What does it exaggerate, distort, or leave out? Pen himself questions the nature of the 'reference unit', that is, the parade includes everyone in the economy who earns any sort of income. Accordingly some spectacular effects of the parade are the result of admitting children with spare-time jobs, women who worked for just a few weeks or a few hours each week, and others who do not attempt to live solely off their own wages. These people, generally, are members of families where the family's combined income will be more substantial. So it is obvious that if we take families, or households, as the basic unit of comparison, then many of the lowest incomes will be eliminated.

A more philosophical objection is that presenting the data this way simply ignores many pertinent facts. For example, we do not know who obtained their money by honest trade or by theft or fraud; by working hard or by exploiting others. How can we assess the justice of a society without knowing these things?

Property and markets

> The first man who, having enclosed a piece of ground, to whom
> it occurred to say *this is mine*, and found people sufficiently simple
> enough to believe him, was the true founder of civil society. How
> many crimes, wars, and murders, how many miseries and horrors
> Mankind would have been spared by him who, pulling up the
> stakes or filling in the ditch, had cried out to his kind: Beware of lis-
> tening to this impostor; You are lost if you forget that the fruits are
> eveyone's, and the Earth no-ones.
>
> (Rousseau, *'Discourse on the Origin of Inequality'*, in *The Discourse and*
> *other Early Political Writings*, ed. S. Gourevitch ([1755], Cambridge:
> Cambridge University Press, 1997),161

Locke on property

One way of arguing that a society is just, despite its inequalities, would
be to show that the individuals in that society who hold property have
moral rights to that property. Can such a theory of property rights be
constructed?

According to Nozick, a theory of property rights needs three different
principles: 'justice in initial acquisition'; 'justice in transfer'; and 'justice
in rectification'. John Locke, whose ideas we looked at in Chapters 1
and 2, addressed himself primarily to the first question in his writings on
property: how can an individual form a right to property appropriated
from its natural state?

This is a very puzzling issue. Every object now owned by someone was
either once owned by no one, or is ultimately made from something that
was owned by no one. This book is made from paper. Most paper is made
from wood. The trees from which that wood came might have been
deliberately planted as a crop, but those saplings came from seeds, and
those seeds were descended from trees which once belonged to no one.
At some point an object, be it tree or seed, which belonged to no one,
became someone's individual property. How could that be? How could
someone gain the right to exclude others from the use of that object?
This question is even more pressing in the case of land. Anyone may
use unowned land. As soon as it becomes private property no one may
use it without the permission of the owner. How can someone come to

have the right to exclude others in this way? To answer these questions requires an account of justice in initial acquisition.

Locke's *Second Treatise* contains a chapter on property, and in it are several arguments designed to show that justified initial acquisition is possible. Locke takes for granted that if you are the rightful owner of property you have various rights over that property. Not only can you use it, but you can also transfer it to others by sale or gift. And this includes bequeathing the property to your heirs. Locke's aim is to justify property rights broadly as they were understood in his time (the seventeenth century), which in its essentials is not so far away from how we understand property rights in contemporary society.

There is still great scholarly disagreement about how we ought to read Locke's arguments. Not even Locke could have thought that they are clearly expressed. But there is no doubt that for Locke labour is all-important in the appropriation of property. On one reading of the text we can discern at least four strands of argument in Locke's defence of initial appropriation of property. How many arguments Locke thought he was making is another matter.

The first idea is the argument from survival. Locke assumes that initially the world was owned in common by all human beings. How, then, could anyone come to own anything as individual private property? Locke first relies on the 'fundamental law of nature' discussed in Chapter 1 of this book: mankind is to be preserved as much as possible. If no one could take anything, we would all die. So we must be permitted to take what we need in order to survive. Locke gives this a further theological defence. Not to permit human beings, put on earth by God, to survive would be to offend against God's rationality. Nevertheless, our appropriation from nature must be constrained by two conditions—the 'Lockean provisos'—if it is to be justified: we must not take more than we can make use of (the non-wastage proviso); and we must leave 'enough and as good' for others. These two provisos apply not just to the survival argument for property, but to all of Locke's arguments.

While eminently reasonable, the survival argument has some obvious limitations. First, it justifies the appropriation only of objects we need to consume in order to survive—fruits and nuts, for example—rather than land itself. Second, it does not specify how exactly objects are to be taken into private ownership. Both these flaws are remedied by Locke's next argument, contained in the famous chapter on property in the *Second Treatise*:

> Though the Earth, and all inferior Creatures be common to all Men, yet every Man has a *Property* in his own *Person*. This no Body has any Right to but himself. The *Labour* of his Body, and the *Work* of his Hands, we may say, are properly his. Whatsoever then he removes out of the state that Nature hath provided and left it in, he hath mixed his *Labour* with, and joyned to it something that is his own, and thereby makes it his *Property*. It being by him removed from the common state Nature placed it in, it hath by the *labour something annexed to it*, that excludes the common right of other Men. For this Labour being the unquestionable Property of the Labourer, no Man but he can have a right to what is once joyned to, at least where there is enough, and as good left in common for others. (*'Second Treatise'*, in John Locke, *Two Treatises of Government*, ed. Peter Laslett ([1689], student edn, Cambridge: Cambridge University Press, 1988) s. 27, 287–8)

Locke here starts from two premises: you own your own labour; and in labouring on an object you 'mix your labour' with that object. Thereby, so long as that object is not already justly claimed by another, you come to own the object on which you have laboured (provided you leave enough and as good for others). Not surprisingly this is commonly known as Locke's 'labour-mixing' argument. The great advantage of this argument over the previous one is that it seems it can justify the appropriation of land, as well as nuts and berries.

The basic thought behind this argument is very attractive. Those who are the first to work on a plot of land should be entitled to keep it. We are reminded of wild-west pioneers, staking their claim on the frontier, and working the land to prove their title. One common adverse reaction is that this seems very hard on those unable to work. But Robert Nozick has pointed out a more fundamental flaw. The argument that mixing your labour with land entitles you to the land seems to rely on a missing premiss: if you own something and mix it with something else that is presently unowned (or owned in common by all), then you come to own that other thing. But this premiss is surely false, and Nozick provides a counter-example: 'If I own a can of tomato juice and spill it in the sea so that its molecules (made radioactive, so that I can check this) mingle evenly throughout the sea, do I thereby come to own the sea, or have I foolishly dissipated my tomato juice?' (*Anarchy, State, and Utopia*, 175).

How can we save the labour-mixing argument? Perhaps we should take Locke's key idea to be not *mixing*, but *labour*. That is to say, mixing labour is not analogous to mixing tomato juice, for there is something special about labour. But what is this? Here we encounter Locke's third argument: the 'value-added' argument. Consider the amount of food that could be gathered from a plot of uncultivated land. Now consider the amount that could be provided by a plot of the same size under cultivation. Locke suggests that the cultivated plot will be perhaps a hundred times as productive. From this Locke concludes that 'labour ... puts the difference of value on every thing' (*Second Treatise*, s. 40, 296). In other words, in labouring on land one massively increases its value. This is why labouring entitles the labourer to appropriate cultivated land.

But this argument too has an obvious difficulty. We might be persuaded that labouring entitles you to keep the *added* value. But the land is not part of the added value: it was there before you came, and, in normal circumstances, would still have been there had you never laboured. So this is an argument, at best, for keeping the fruits of production. It seems to give no right to keep the land worked on. Is there anything that could yield that consequence?

A fourth argument might help. Locke says that God gave the earth to the use of the:

> Industrious and Rational . . . not to the Fancy and Covetousness of the Quarrelsom and Contentious. He that had as good left for his Improvement, as was already taken up, needed not complain, ought not to meddle with what was already improved by another's Labour: If he did, 'tis plain he desired the benefit of another's Pains, which he had no right to, and not the Ground which God had given him in common with others to labour on. (*Second Treatise*, s. 34, 291)

In this passage, Locke wants us to consider someone who has appropriated and improved land (Industrious) and another person (Quarrelsom) who makes a claim for the land Industrious has worked on. Provided that there is plenty of land left, Quarrelsom's only reason for wanting Industrious's land is laziness: not being prepared to put in the work that Industrious has. But this is no good reason, and so no good reason to complain about Industrious's appropriation. Behind this, I suggest, is an implicit appeal to the notion of desert. If Industrious has worked hard, she deserves the fruits of her labour. At least no one else has a valid claim.

Unfortunately, this argument shares the defects of the earlier ones. The fruits of labour may be deserved, but the land would have been there anyway. Perhaps the argument justifies a temporary title to the land—it is yours to use for as long as you are making good use of it, but for no longer. Yet property rights are rarely thought of as conditional in this way: certainly, Locke did not think so. This argument gives you no right to sell your land, or to leave it to your children. Furthermore, those unable to fend for themselves will rightly feel aggrieved if labouring is made a necessary condition of acquiring property. However strongly we feel the attraction of the view that labouring on land should entitle one to it, it is very hard to explain why this should be so, at least within Locke's framework.

A further and related problem concerns the 'enough and as good' proviso. Perhaps Locke is right to suppose that there is no good reason to object to another's appropriation if there is plenty of equally good land left. But what should we say once land becomes scarce? The logic of Locke's position would seem to suggest that property rights dissolve at this point. But of course he says no such thing. Probably his view was that as long as people are better off working on other people's land than they would have been in the state of nature, then they have no justified complaint about another's property rights. And in 'proof' of the benefits brought by labour and property rights Locke claims that a king of a large and fruitful territory in America (where little of the land had been transformed by labour) 'feeds, lodges, and is clad worse than a day Labourer in England' (*Second Treatise*, s. 41, 297).

However, unless we read the 'enough and as good' proviso literally— that there really is enough and as good land left for others to take— Locke's defence of property rights is far less persuasive. For if land is scarce, then it will be taken by those first to stake their claim by labour. Those born to a later generation, unable to find land of their own, will complain that they have been unjustly treated in comparison with those who have inherited land: not because they are quarrelsome and contentious, but because they will feel that they have been denied something given to others. Why should you have land and I have none, if the only difference between us is that your ancestors were industrious and mine not? And what can be said in response?

Surely some sort of response, or new argument, is needed to defend property rights. After all, virtually the entire non-liquid surface of the earth is now claimed as the private property of individuals, firms, or states. And so it seems that either these holdings are illegitimate, or that there must be justified ways of coming to acquire property. In fact, however, virtually no progress has been made in improving upon Locke's argument, if we start from Locke's premises.

It is easy to see why not. We noted earlier that before an item of property comes to be appropriated by an individual or group, everyone is at liberty to use that item. Once it becomes an individual's property, this liberty of non-owners is cancelled. Others can use it only with the owner's permission. What could I possibly do to a piece of land, or other object, which could have such powerful effects? Why should anything *I* do to an object overturn *your* previous liberty to use it? It is very hard to find an answer, and so it is very hard to find a satisfactory principle of justice in acquisition. Perhaps it is impossible.

Does this mean that property is theft (in Proudhon's famous formulation)? That would be too simplistic a conclusion. A more modest response is to suppose that there may be something wrong with the schema we set up at the beginning. That, is, perhaps it is wrong to focus on the issue of justice in acquisition as a separable element in a theory of distributive justice. Possibly we could argue for a system of distributive justice that included ownership of private property as one element of the system. That way we might be able to justify private property as an intrinsic part of a theory of justice without worrying too much how property was originally appropriated from nature. And this is just what many defenders of the free market try to do.

The free market

One alternative to Locke would be to attempt a utilitarian justification of property rights. We can see how such an argument would go: allowing people to appropriate property and to trade it and leave it to their descendants will encourage them to make the most productive use of their resources. As a result, this would make a greater contribution to human happiness than any alternative arrangement. Such an argument is already implicit in Mill's view, outlined above.

This utilitarian argument concerns itself less with the process by which people come to acquire property than with the benefits of trade and inheritance. It is part of the argument that individuals should hold property, but it is less important *how* they come to hold that property. To put this another way, for the utilitarian the issue of justice in transfer takes priority over the issue of justice in initial acquisition. And many utilitarians stress the importance of the capitalist free market as a mechanism of transfer.

The 'pure model' of a capitalist free market includes a number of essential features. First, property in land, raw materials, and other goods (including labour) is held by individuals or firms, under a system of secure property rights. Second, goods are produced for profit, rather than to satisfy the consumption needs of the producer, or of other needy people. Third, all goods are distributed by voluntary exchange on a market regulated by laws of supply and demand. Finally, free competition exists: anyone may produce and offer for sale any good.

This is the pure model. No real economy perfectly incorporates all these features: generally all are modified in some way. For example, in many countries the state owns and runs some enterprises such as the post office. Second, most countries have a significant 'voluntary' sector, producing goods and services on a partly charitable basis. Third, some goods cannot legally be traded on the open market (plutonium, heroin). And fourth, various state-enforced limitations to trade exist which prevent newcomers from entering a particular industry. For example, in most countries that permit gambling there is a limit to how many casino licences can be granted by the government. However, it is also clear that most countries now increasingly aim to approximate to the pure free market model to a greater or lesser extent. Are they right to do so?

What is the alternative to the capitalist free market model? First, as we have just seen, it can be modified by restricting the type of exchanges people can make. But the most radical alternative is the planned economy. It contrasts with the free market in all essential features. Here the state, in the name of the people as a whole, controls all property used for production. Second, production is not for profit, but to satisfy the needs of the citizens. Third, distribution is by central allocation, rather than by trade. Finally, the state has ultimate control over who may produce how much of each good. Enterprise is carried out in accordance with a central plan, allocating resources to various industries.

The free market looks less autocratic than the planned economy, but, superficially at least, less rational. The free market leaves all decisions to individuals acting alone. How, then, do they co-ordinate? How can we make sure that there will be enough of each good provided? How can we avoid wasteful overproduction where too many companies compete to satisfy the same demand? Planning from the centre will, it seems, ensure that enough of each good is produced to satisfy the demands of all. Marx's collaborator, Friedrich Engels (1820–95), wrote:

> Since we know how much, on the average, a person needs, it is easy to calculate how much is needed by a given number of individuals, and since production is no longer in the hands of private producers but in those of the community and its administrative bodies it is a trifling matter to regulate production according to needs. ('*Speeches in Elberfeld*', in K. Marx, F. Engels, and V. I. Lenin, *On Communist Society* ([1845], Moscow: Progress Press, 1974, 10)

According to many commentators, arguments like this led to one of the most costly mistakes of the twentieth century. Despite the rational appeal of planning, all attempts to put a planned economy in place have failed—and they would have failed much sooner if they had not been supplemented by extensive, illegal, black markets. The market has been able to achieve a far higher level of efficiency and well-being for its citizens than the planned economy, despite its 'anarchic', uncoordinated, nature. But why should that be so?

The best answer was provided by the Austrian economist and social theorist F. A. von Hayek (1899–1992). To understand his reasoning we must take a brief look at how the free market can be expected to function. Suppose that a particular good—garlic, say—costs 50 pence per bulb. Then a respected scientist publishes a report indicating that consuming a bulb of garlic a day wards off cancer and heart disease. Accordingly, demand for garlic soars. Garlic retailers sell out rapidly, and prices spiral as customers scramble and outbid each other for available supplies. Huge profits are made in the garlic industry.

The prospect of such profits will prompt new producers to enter the garlic market. Eventually supply begins to rise, and as it does the price falls again, until a new equilibrium is established. Eventually demand equals supply at a price where garlic producers achieve roughly the same profit levels as are available elsewhere in the economy. We may well end up back at 50 pence a bulb, although the new equilibrium price could be higher or lower.

This rather banal example of economic life shows the remarkable powers of markets. First, the price system is a way of signalling and transmitting information. The fact that the price of a good rises indicates that it is in short supply; if the price falls, then it is oversupplied. Second, the profit motive gives people a reason to respond to that information. If prices rise in a sector because of increasing demand, this normally means that larger-than-average profits are to be made, and so new producers rush in. If prices fall, because of falling demand, generally profits fall, and so some firms will leave the industry. In both cases, equilibrium will eventually be established, where the rate of profit for the industry broadly matches the average rate of profit for the economy as a whole.

These are the two key features of the market: it signals information, and it gives people an incentive to respond to that information by changing production patterns. Nor should we forget the importance of competition in driving down prices, and driving up quality. In combination these factors lead to the consequence that, in general, in markets people (with money) get what they want from other people. And the position of the consumer is almost always improving. But not because others are being altruistic. As Adam Smith (1723–90) pointed out:

> It is not from the benevolence of the butcher, the brewer, or the baker that we expect our dinner, but from their regard to their own interest. We address ourselves, not to their humanity but to their self-love, and never talk to them of our own necessities but of their advantages. (*The Wealth of Nations* ([1776], Harmondsworth: Penguin, 1970), 119)

Many theorists accept that the market can distribute goods to individuals in a way that no planned economy could match. If I want something and if I have the money I can go and buy it. I can express my preferences in my purchasing behaviour, and others try to make as much profit as they can by responding to them. In the planned economy there are two problems. How will the planner know what I want? It might be common knowledge that people like ice cream, and need socks, but how can the planner know that I prefer vanilla ice cream to chocolate, or plain socks to patterned ones? And why should the planner take the trouble to make sure I get what I want? Real planned economies have been plagued by chronic shortages of some goods, such as winter tights, overproduction of others such as low-grade vodka, and a depressing lack of quality and variety in those goods that are available. In order to run an economy as efficiently as the free market, the planner needs a level of omniscience, omnipotence, and benevolence rarely attributed to mere human beings.

This is essentially a utilitarian argument for the free market: it will advance human happiness to a level that could not be achieved by the planned economy. Arguments based on liberty have also been offered. The planned economy involves restrictions on individual behaviour. In his important study, *The Economics of Feasible Socialism*, first published in 1983 and now translated into a score or more of languages, Alec Nove quotes a passage from a novel by Vasili Grossman:

> I wanted since childhood to open a shop, so that any folk could come in and buy. Along with it would be a snack-bar, so that the customers could have a bit of roast meat, if they like, or a drink. I would serve them cheap, too. I'd let them have real village food. Baked potato! Bacon-fat with garlic! Sauerkraut! I'd give them bone-marrow as a starter, a measure of vodka, a marrow-bone, and black bread of course, and salt. Leather chairs, so that lice don't breed. The customer could sit and rest and be served. If I were to say all this out loud, I'd have been sent straight to Siberia. And yet, say I, what harm would I do to people? (*The Economics of Feasible Socialism* (London: George Allen & Unwin, 1983), 110)

Robert Nozick puts essentially the same point more succinctly: 'The socialist society would have to forbid capitalist acts between consenting adults' (*Anarchy, State, and Utopia*, 163).

It will be better to postpone discussion of the liberty argument for the free market until later: it comes out in sharpest focus as a criticism of Rawls's views, which will be discussed shortly. First, we should take stock. So far the main discussion has shown some substantial utilitarian advantages of the free market over the fully planned economy. But from this comparison it does not, of course, follow that the free market is the best possible system. It is easy to derive improvements under a utilitarian analysis. This can clearly be seen in cases of 'market failure' for goods with what are called 'externalities'.

Externalities come in two types: positive and negative. A negative externality is something you get for nothing, but would rather not have: polluted air, or noise, for example. A positive externality is again something you get for nothing, but in this case are pleased to have: for instance, a pleasant view over your neighbour's front lawn. One important category of goods with positive externalities is 'public goods'. This consists of goods that, if provided, benefit all, whether or not the recipient has contributed to their production. Consider street lights. The benefits of street lights cannot be restricted only to those who have helped pay for them. They are public goods in this sense.

The free market will tend to oversupply goods with negative externalities and undersupply goods with positive externalities. It is easy to see why. Creating a negative externality is often a way of dumping your costs on another: literally. If it is cheaper to use a noisy production process than a quiet one, other people are inadvertently 'subsidizing' my use of the noisy process by bearing the cost of being disturbed by the noise. Public goods, on the other hand, are subject to the free-rider problem. Why should I contribute to supply street lights if I will get the benefit whether or not I contribute? But if everyone thinks like this—and the market encourages this type of reasoning—no lighting will be provided. It is normally assumed that the solution to these problems is to make the state the supplier of public goods, taxing citizens to pay for them. Similarly the state can make pollution illegal, returning the costs to the polluter. More recently other approaches have been considered, and some enacted: giving those people who suffer from negative externalities the right to recover damages, and those individuals who supply goods with positive externalities the right to charge those who benefit.

We can see, then, that there are utilitarian arguments for modifying the market, whether by state intervention or the creation of new legal rights. But is modification enough? Are there deeper problems with the market? The most powerful objections come from the Marxist and socialist tradition: the market is wasteful; it alienates the worker; it is exploitative; and it leads to unjust inequalities. Let us consider these in turn.

Arguments against the market

In his *Speeches in Elberfeld*, quoted above, Engels complains that the free market is extraordinarily wasteful. This is essentially a utilitarian argument against the free market, and Engels has two main charges. The first is that the free market inevitably leads to crisis after crisis, in which individuals are thrown out of work and businesses are ruined as goods are wasted or sold at a loss. Engels was one of the first theorists to point out that the capitalist market is punctuated by a 'trade cycle' of boom and bust. Try as they might, economists and politicians have never been able to work out a method by which capitalism can avoid this destructive cycle of prosperity and recession. Engels's second argument is that capitalist society contains an enormous number of people who perform no productive role. A communist planned economy could incorporate these people into production, improving efficiency and reducing the working day. They include not only the unemployed, but also members of the police and armed forces, the clergy, domestic servants, and, most despised of all, 'speculating, swindling superfluous middlemen, who have forced themselves in between the producer and the consumer' (*Speeches in Elberfeld*, 11). It is interesting that defenders of the market see middlemen as heroes of enterprise, essential to the efficient running of an economy by moving goods from where they are oversupplied to areas where they are in high demand. For Marx and Engels, they are bloodsucking parasites.

Suppose Engels is right. How convincing is his case against the market? Well, what would be better? We can no longer share his confidence in the self-evident rationality of the planned economy. A modified market, as outlined above, despite its flaws, may well be more efficient than anything else that has been proposed.

But the market is wasteful in another sense: wasteful of the potential of the worker. This is the second criticism of the market: that it leads to alienation. The central thought here is that in the capitalist free market the nature of work is degraded and unfitting for human beings. The profit motive requires capitalists to adopt the most efficient methods of production available. This generally means incorporating a highly developed form of the division of labour, in which each worker performs a highly specialized, boring, and repetitive task. In essence, then, the nature of work under capitalism is alienating in that the worker becomes subordinate to a machine 'and from a man becomes an abstract activity and a stomach' (Karl Marx, *Early Writings* [1844], 285). The potential of the worker as an intelligent, creative human being is frustrated. It has been said that under capitalism for many workers the day's most skilled activity is driving to and from work.

The question for critics of the market, however, is whether alienation is a consequence specifically of the capitalist form of production, or
whether it is a consequence of modern technology more generally. Can
we really conceive of a form of production that will produce enough to
satisfy our needs, but will not depend on an alienating system of production? If there is one, it has not yet been discovered.

A third criticism is that capitalists exploit workers in the free market.
For Marx exploitation is essentially the extraction of surplus labour. The
worker is paid for a day's work. In that work the worker creates profits
for the capitalist that are in no way proportional to the work the capitalist puts in. Indeed, shareholders take a portion of profits but do no work
at all. At bottom, then, the thought is that those who receive rewards in
the market without putting in a proportional level of work are exploit-
ers. Those who receive less than they create are exploited.

The most natural defence of the free market is to claim that capitalists
in fact receive fair return for the use of their property, or for the risk of
their money. After all, labour alone produces nothing. Someone must
supply raw materials, machinery, factories, and so on. The debate about
exploitation, then, comes down to the question of whether capitalists
are entitled to earn a reward for using their property. But are they morally entitled to own this property? It seems that we cannot address the
question of whether the free market leads to exploitation without settling
first the more basic issue of the justification of private property rights.

Finally, the most common criticism of the market made by Marxists,
socialists, and many liberals is that it is bound to lead to very large, unjust, inequalities. Unconstrained, the free market can lead to devastating
poverty. Consider Engels's description of the area of St Giles, in central
London, in 1844:

> All this is nothing in comparison with the dwellings in the narrow courts and
> alleys between the streets, entered by covered passages between the houses,
> in which the filth and tottering ruin surpass description. Scarcely a whole
> windowpane can be found, the walls are crumbling, door-posts and window-
> frames loose and broken, doors of old boards nailed together, or altogether
> wanting in this thieves' quarter, where no doors are needed, there being
> nothing to steal. Heaps of garbage and ashes lie in all directions, and the
> foul liquids emptied before the doors gather in stinking pools. Here live the
> poorest of the poor, the worst paid workers with thieves and the victims of

prostitution indiscriminately huddled together ... and those who have not yet sunk in the whirlpool of moral ruin which surrounds them, sinking daily deeper, losing daily more and more of their power to resist the demoralising influence of want, filth and evil surroundings. (*'The Condition of the Working Class in England'*, in *Marx and Engels on Britain* ([1845], Moscow: Marx-Engels-Lenin-Stalin Institute, 1953), 60–1)

All countries that are wealthy enough to do so have accepted that society has a duty to protect people from such a fate, and so various welfare provisions are made—some more effective than others. Unemployment and disability benefits, income supplements, and other grants now allow the vast majority of individuals in wealthier societies to obtain a level of income to provide them with a minimal standard of living.

Is the level of inequality generated by the market, even as modified by the welfare state, acceptable? Such a society is depicted by the income parade discussed above. Is it just? Arguably, the considerations presented here demonstrate that societies so characterized can be given a utilitarian justification. This contention might seem surprising. It is often supposed that utilitarianism would recommend a roughly equal distribution of resources, rather than the inequalities of the income parade. The central assumption in the utilitarian argument for equality is that people have 'diminishing marginal returns' for goods. The utility or pleasure derived from eating a first chocolate biscuit is much more than that derived from the second. So if there are two of us, and two biscuits, then utilitarianism is likely to recommend one each. Similarly, a given sum of money provides much more utility for the poor than for the rich. To maximize utility we must share things out, and so redistribution from the rich to the poor maximizes utility.

The weakness in the argument just given is that it seems to assume that *how goods are distributed* does not affect the *quantity of goods available for distribution*. But it is often supposed that an egalitarian distribution will suppress initiative and enterprise: why work hard, or try to develop new products, if doing so will make a negligible impact on your income? Allowing at least some inequalities, on the other hand, will produce incentives for people to innovate and to work more productively. So it seems that an unequal society may well produce more wealth than an equal one, and so it is possible that it will do better in utilitarian terms, even if we accept that most goods have diminishing marginal returns.

Utilitarian defenders of the free market claim that the market makes a far stronger contribution to human happiness than the planned economy or equality could do. But the market can be improved by allowing governments to provide public goods and to introduce legislation to reduce the supply of 'public bads' (goods with negative externalities). The government should also introduce some form of welfare provision to eliminate the worst aspects of poverty. Such a system might be the best we can do in utilitarian terms. Is this enough to show that such an economy is just? Many are not convinced. Rawls's theory of justice is the most powerful recent attempt to try to do better.

Rawls's theory of justice

> Certain principles of justice are justified because they would be agreed to in an initial situation of equality.
>
> (Rawls, *A Theory of Justice* ([1971], Oxford: Oxford University Press, rev. edn, 1999), 21 [19]

A hypothetical contract

What is the just society? How could we know? To get started, let us think about a fairly simple example in which a question of justice seems to arise. Suppose two people—you and I—are playing poker. I deal, and you pick up and look at your cards. Before picking up my own hand I notice a card—the Ace of Spades—lying face up on the floor. Seeing this, I propose that we throw in the hand and that I should deal again. But you argue that we should play the hand out. So we disagree. What should we do?

Ultimately, of course, one of us might bow to superior pressure, even physical force. But before we come to blows we should realize that several strategies are open to us to try, if we wish, to resolve the issue by determining what the fair or just outcome should be. One, for example, might be that we have already made an agreement that covers the case. Before sitting down we might have drawn up a lengthy document outlining what to do in just this eventuality and many others like it. Presumably reference to such an agreement would decisively settle the dispute. More realistically, we might have made a verbal agreement to play by a certain well-known set of rules of the game. Again, reference to the rules settles the matter.

But perhaps, as is more likely, there is no actual agreement we can refer to. What else can we do? A second thought is to ask the advice of an 'impartial spectator'. There might be an onlooker we both respect, or, if we are playing in a club, a referee. Or if we are children—brother and sister, say—we might ask our mother for a decision. Again, by this method we ought to be able to come to a definitive ruling.

But what if there is no one like this around either? A third strategy would be to conjure someone up in the imagination—a hypothetical spectator. 'What would your father say if he were here?' Admittedly this does not guarantee a resolution; we might have the same dispute again over what he *would* say. But it is not unheard of for someone to realize that he or she is in the wrong by reflecting on how an impartial person would view the situation. So this tactic can, in some cases, yield a helpful answer.

Finally, we could appeal to a hypothetical agreement. We might, in our imaginations, consider the question of what agreement we would have made if one or other of us had raised the issue before the game started. Perhaps I can convince you that, if we had discussed the matter, we would have agreed to throw the hand in under these conditions. You only disagree because you are distracted by the actual hand you have been dealt. Maybe it is your first good hand of the evening. This blinds you to the justice of the situation. Imagining what you would have agreed to before you were dealt this hand is a way of trying to filter out the bias caused by your own special interests. And it is this idea that Rawls adopts in his attempt to argue for his principles of justice.

It is clear that, if we are to use the hypothetical agreement method to solve problems of justice, we must suppose that the hypothetical contract will take place under some sort of special conditions. For consider again the card game: we cannot use the method if we suppose the hypothetically contracting parties (you and I) are placed exactly as we are in real life. For in real life we have a dispute—I want a re-deal, you do not—and the hope is that we can find a method to resolve this dispute. If we are to reach a hypothetical agreement we must abstract from real life. In the card game this is easy enough. We imagine what agreement we would have made before the cards were dealt. So we assume some ignorance. Neither of us knows what hand we have. If we can success-fully imagine this, then we will be in a position where we cannot be biased by our particular interests; that is, by whether we have a good hand or a bad one. If we do not make this abstraction, then the chances that we can find a hypothetical agreement are very slim.

Rawls, then, uses a hypothetical contract argument to justify his prin-ciples of justice. Accordingly we can divide Rawls's project into three elements. The first is the definition of the conditions under which the hypothetical agreement is to take place; the second is the argument that his principles of justice would be chosen under such conditions; and the third is the claim that this shows that they are the correct principles of justice, at least for modern democratic regimes. Let us consider the first of these elements, the conditions of the contract, which Rawls calls the 'original position'. What ignorance or knowledge do we need to attribute to the contractors if an agreement about social justice is to be possible?

Were we to try to imagine a hypothetical contract between everyone in a modern society, we would fail. There are no terms to which literally everyone would agree (or if there are some, these would hardly amount to a complete conception of justice). We can expect some rich people, for example, to be strongly opposed to taxation, while some poor people will want the rich to be taxed more than they are at present, in order to increase welfare benefits. Hence we have a dispute, and the point of a theory of justice is to attempt to resolve such disputes.

Rawls supposes that people's views of justice are often biased, in part, by their own particular interests. Because they already know what social cards they have been dealt—intelligence, strength, and so on—people will often fail to take a properly impartial stance, as required by a con-cern for justice. Rawls's leading thought is that, while justice requires impartiality, impartiality can be modelled by assuming ignorance. This opens the way for a hypothetical contract argument. To make this clearer, consider the following example (not, by the way, one of Rawls's own).

Suppose, in the not-too-distant future, the supply of football referees dries up. (Imagine they are so disillusioned by the abuse they get from the players that they all take up archery.) For many games it becomes impossible to find a neutral referee. Suppose that this is true of the game between United and City, and suppose, too, that the only qualified referee at the match is the manager of United. Understandably, City objects to the proposal that he should referee the game. However, the Football Association is aware that this difficulty arises from time to time, and so it has invented a drug. If you take this drug you behave perfectly normally, except in one respect. You have a highly selective loss of memory. You are unable to remember which football team you manage (and cannot hear anyone who tries to remind you). Having taken this drug how should the manager of United referee the game?

The answer is that he may as well be impartial. He knows he manages one of the teams, but not which one. Accordingly, if he randomly picks one of the teams to favour he may find himself doing his own team harm. If we assume that he does not want to run the risk of unfairly damaging his own team's prospects, then all he can do is act as fairly as he is able, and let the game run according to the rules. Ignorance spawns impartiality.

With this in mind, we can consider Rawls's construction of the original position. People in the original position—the hypothetical contractors—are placed behind a 'veil of ignorance' that makes them unaware of their particular circumstances. Because of this ignorance they do not know how to be biased in their own favour, and they are apparently forced to act impartially.

The people in the original position, Rawls says, do not know their place in society or their class position. They are ignorant of their social status, their gender, and their race. Importantly, they are also ignorant of their possession of 'natural assets'—their abilities and strengths. In all these respects they do not know which cards they have been dealt.

Is this enough to allow them to come to an agreement? It would be, were it the case that the only thing that divides people on questions of justice is personal interest. But Rawls recognizes that this is a crude and insulting oversimplification. People also disagree because they value different things. They have different 'conceptions of the good', that is, different ideas about what makes life worthwhile. People have different moral, religious, and philosophical views, and different aims and ambitions. They also have different views about what the good society should be like. Rawls excludes all this information too. People in the original position do not know their own conception of the good, and neither, says Rawls, do they know their 'special psychological propensities'.

To illustrate the power of this method, the suppositions so far seem to be enough to explain why people in the original position would agree to what Rawls calls the Liberty Principle—that each person is to have an equal and extensive set of basic liberties. To choose a different principle to regulate liberty would, in effect, be to discriminate against a certain group, or to accept diminished liberty for all. But who would agree to do this if they did not know which group or groups they belonged to? Who would choose to discriminate against a particular race if they did not know their own race? And why would anyone choose to limit everyone's liberty? The Liberty Principle seems an obviously rational choice.

On the other hand, an objection is that individuals might choose lesser or unequal liberty if this would make everyone better off. Rawls denies this, and we will look at his reasons shortly. But a more subtle objection is that people as so far described would simply be unable to make any choices or decisions. They do not know what they are like, or what types of things they like. How, then, can they make any sort of decision about how society ought to be? Without a conception of the good, how can they even know that they value liberty?

Rawls's answer is to presuppose a certain type of motivation. The parties in the original position, he stipulates, are assumed to possess a 'thin theory of the good'. The first, and most important, element of the thin theory of the good is that agents in the original position know that they want what Rawls calls 'primary goods'. These are liberties, opportunities, wealth, income, and the rather mysterious 'social bases of self-respect'. What these have in common, Rawls supposes, is that they are what people should rationally want, whatever else they want. That is, whether your conception of the good is a life of unadulterated pleasure, monastic virtue, hunting, shooting, and fishing, consciousness-raising, or whatever, Rawls's primary goods are desirable. You always want liberty, opportunity, and money, supposes Rawls, as all-purpose means to your personal ends in life. So agents in the original position are presumed to know that they want primary goods.

Rawls adds that they prefer more of these primary goods to fewer, and that the agents are rational, in the sense that they will take the most efficient means to achieve their ends. Also they are not envious, and so will not be resentful of anyone else's good fortune. Finally, they are 'mutually disinterested'. They take no interest in the plight, whether positive or negative, of anyone else.

It is important to try to keep clear that Rawls is *not* saying that this is what people in the world are really like. People are often envious, or irrational, and we certainly often do care very much about how other people's lives go. Rather, he is creating a hypothetical—fictional—model of a person who will take part in the original position. In the card game, in order to come up with a fair, hypothetical agreement, we supposed that the players had not been dealt their hand, even though they had. Similarly, in the case of the original position we suppose a far more radical level of ignorance and knowledge to ensure impartiality between the contracting parties. We end up with a view of people in the original position who are very unlike real people. But this is not a criticism of the theory. The conditions of the original position, behind the veil of ignorance, are not meant to describe the nature of a person, but to act as a methodological device; a device to help us come to a view about the correct principles of justice.

There are just a few more pieces to add before the picture of the original position is complete. Rawls assumes that people are ignorant of particular facts about their society. They do not know its economic and political situation, its level of civilization or culture, or the generation to which they belong. However, they do know that people—real people, people in society—have a sense of justice and are capable of having a conception of the good.

They also know that their society is in what Hume called 'the circumstances of justice'. Hume pointed out that in some conditions the idea of justice seems not to apply. If we are in a condition of dire scarcity, so bad that we cannot even ensure everyone's survival, then the idea that we should criticize anyone's actions as unjust seems absurd. If simply to stay alive you must take what you can from others, then considerations of justice look completely irrelevant. At the other extreme, if we were in a situation of such abundance that we could all have as much as we desired, then conflicts of justice would not arise. If you have what I want, why should I dispute with you about it if I could get another just like it, without any difficulty? Accordingly, the circumstances of justice are 'between scarcity and abundance', and Rawls assumes that his parties know that they are deciding on principles to regulate a society placed in such conditions.

Choosing principles of justice

Having constructed the original position, what principles of justice would be the outcome? Rawls says that any of us can think our way into the original position at any time. If we do, we will see for ourselves whether or not we would, in fact, choose his principles of justice. The principles we would choose, says Rawls, are:

1. Each person is to have an equal right to the most extensive total system of equal basic liberties compatible with a similar system of liberty for all.
2. Social and economic inequalities are to be arranged so that they are both:
   (a) To the greatest benefit of the least advantaged ... and
   (b) Attached to offices and positions open to all under conditions of fair equality of opportunity. (*A Theory of Justice*, 302 [266])

Principle 1 is the Liberty Principle, 2(*a*) the Difference Principle, and 2(*b*) the Fair Opportunity Principle. According to Rawls, the Liberty Principle has 'lexical priority' over the other two, as does the Fair Opportunity Principle over the Difference Principle. What this means, for Rawls, is that once we have reached a reasonable level of wealth in society, considerations of liberty should have absolute priority over matters of economic well-being or equality of opportunity. On this account, for example, it is no defence of slavery that it makes the slaves better off than they would be with their freedom, even if that were true. The fact is that enforced slavery is inconsistent with recognizing equal liberty, and so must give way whether or not it has economic advantages for the slaves. Similar things can be said about the priority of the Fair Opportunity Principle over the Difference Principle.

The main object of our interest in this chapter is the Difference Principle. Note that it is a broadly egalitarian principle in the sense that, for Rawls, there is a general presumption in favour of an equal distribution of goods among all citizens. However, Rawls takes notice of an argument discussed earlier that often seems to generate a powerful criticism of egalitarianism: that it leaves no room for incentives. That is, some people will work much harder if they know that they will get extra rewards for doing so. But the hard work of the highly productive is capable of benefiting us all: either directly through new job and consumption opportunities, or indirectly through raised tax revenues. Now, if an inequality benefits everyone, then what can be the objection against it? After all, who does it harm? On these grounds egalitarianism is sometimes accused of being both inefficient and irrational, or even 'the politics of envy'.

Rawls accepts the conditional statement that *if* an inequality is necessary to make everyone better off, and, in particular, to make the worst off better off than they would otherwise be, then it should be permitted. This idea yields the Difference Principle. However, *whether* incentives are necessary in the manner outlined is a question not to be answered by philosophers, but for psychologists and economists.

In the previous section I suggested that a utilitarian political philosophy would probably yield a free market with a welfare state. Such a system would allow far greater inequalities than the Difference Principle could justify. But how can Rawls show that the Difference Principle is to be preferred on grounds of justice? His answer is to use the device of a hypothetical contract. From the original position, people would choose his principles of justice in preference to utilitarianism. But why would they do that? Why not choose utilitarian principles?

It may help to consider an adaptation of the original position. Suppose you have just woken up in a hospital bed. First, you realize that you are suffering from an extensive memory loss. Looking down you see that you are swaddled from head to toe in bandages. You don't remember your name, sex, or race, nor can you discover these by self-inspection (the tag on your bandaged wrist has only a number). Facts about your family, occupation, class, strengths, skills, and so on are all lost to you. You do recall some general theories you once learnt in economics and sociology classes, but you cannot remember anything from your history lessons. In fact, you could not even say what century it was. Then into the ward walks a man in a white coat. 'Good morning,' he says, 'I am Professor John Rawls. Tomorrow your memory will return, your bandages will be removed, and you will be free to leave. So we don't have much time. What we need you to do is to tell us how you would like society to be designed, bearing in mind that, from tomorrow, you will be living in the society you have chosen. We want you to design society purely in your own interests. Although you do not know what your actual interests are, I can tell you that you want as many primary goods as possible—liberties, opportunities, wealth, and income—and you should not consider the fortunes of anyone else. I will come back this evening to see what you have decided.' Under these circumstances what would it be rational to choose?

Note, in passing, that we have slipped into talk of 'choice' of principles rather than the idea of 'agreement' we started with. In practice this makes no difference. People in the original position are assumed to be the same. Therefore they will all reason in the same way, and so we may as well concentrate on the choice of just one person. This does no harm, and it makes the argument easier to handle.

So would you choose the Liberty Principle? We have already seen the main reason why you should. As you do not know which group or groups you belong to, it would be irrational to discriminate against one portion of society. For all you know you would be discriminating against yourself. This is a reason for choosing equal liberty. But why the *most extensive* equal liberty? This seems to follow from Rawls's assumption that people not only want Primary Goods, they also want as much of as many of them as possible. From behind the veil of ignorance, or from your hospital bed, the Liberty Principle seems an obvious and automatic choice. (No doubt similar things can also be said about the Fair Opportunity Principle.)

Remember, though, that Rawls argues that people will not only adopt the Liberty Principle, but also that they will give it 'lexical priority' to the other principles. According to this view we cannot sacrifice liberty for the sake of anything else. But it could be argued that giving such an absolute priority to liberty is hardly rational. There are times when liberty should be sacrificed for the sake of security—think of wartime blackouts and curfews. Or in times of great economic hardship and scarcity we might accept a restriction on political and civil liberties if this is the only way we will get fed. How, then, can we accept the priority of liberty?

Rawls deliberately ignores cases of emergency, like wars, wanting to understand the more 'central' cases of justice before looking at these less common problems. And he has also said that we can assume that we are choosing principles of justice for a society placed in 'the circumstances of justice'. That is, we already know that resources in our society are not in dire scarcity, and so we need not concern ourselves with such problem cases. Rawls's plausible view—although one that could be questioned—is that, given moderate prosperity, basic rights and liberties should always be preferred to further material advances.

So now we turn to the derivation of the Difference Principle. This, of course, is the principle that says that the distribution of wealth and income in society should be equal, unless an inequality will be to everyone's advantage. In particular it must be to the advantage of the worst off. Why should such a principle be chosen?

In effect we are now addressing an example of the problem of rational choice under uncertainty. To decide what principles of justice it would be rational to select, we first need to know what principles of rational choice it would be appropriate to use in this case. Seeing matters in this way means that we can help solve the problem by tapping into the resources of 'rational choice theory'.

To see the type of issue in play, let us start with a very simple case as an example. Suppose you are sitting down to a meal in a restaurant and are faced with having to choose a first course. It is a fixed-price menu, so you need not worry about the relative costs of the items. Also ignore any dietary or religious concerns you may have. The choice is a reasonably simple one. There are only two items on the menu, mussels and melon. Melon is a safe option. This is a good restaurant, so they would only serve ripe melons of high quality. You can be sure that you will find it enjoyable. Mussels, however, are more of a gamble. Normally they give you great pleasure—very much more than melon—but a bad mussel can spoil your whole week. From past experience you can assume, let us say, that one dish of mussels in ten will have a bad effect. Given these facts, what should you choose?

It will help to bring things out if we set this information in tabular form. The numbers are supposed to represent the relative amounts of utility—'pleasure' and 'displeasure'—you get from the options.

Melon 5 (whether good or bad)
Mussels 20 (If good—90% chance)   **−100** (If bad—10% chance)

One theory of rational choice says that we should 'maximize expected utility', or 'maximize average value'. What this means is that we derive an average figure for what each option is worth, and then choose the option with the highest average. This average figure is the expected utility. Of course, calculating the average utility of the melon is trivial; whatever happens you will get 5. Calculating the expected utility of the mussels is slightly harder work. What we do is take the utility of each possible outcome and multiply it by its probability. Then we add together each of these amounts and so arrive at our average figure. So we begin by multiplying 20 (the utility of good mussels) by 0.9 (the probability that they will be good) and obtain 18. We then multiply −100 (the utility of bad mussels) by its probability and obtain −10. Adding these together (18 and −10) gives us 8, which is the expected utility of the mussels.

Another way of seeing this is to imagine that you are in a long-run series of this 'game'. Suppose you eat at this restaurant 100 times, and each time order mussels. If the probabilities run true, then you would have had ninety 'good' experiences and ten 'bad' ones. Each good experience is worth 20, so totalling these gives 1,800. Each bad experience is worth −100, yielding a total of −1,000. Consequently, 100 dishes of mussels will yield a 'profit' of 800, and so the average profit—the expected utility—is 8. It is important to realize that calling this 'expected utility' does not mean that this is what you would actually expect to get. In fact you will never get 8; you will either get 20 or −100: expected utility is an average figure.

If you are to maximize expected utility, then you will choose the mussels. Is this the most rational thing to do? Some people, no doubt, would strongly disagree. Mussels, although in some sense a good bet, remain very risky. It is foolish to take such a risk, some will say, when there is a perfectly decent alternative. The melon is a good, safe option, and, for some people at least, this makes it the more rational choice. Nothing can go wrong. Those who reason this way can often be represented as adopting the 'maximin' principle of rational choice. This instructs us to make sure that the worst possible outcome is as good as possible: maximize the minimum. Used in real life, this is a principle for pessimists. It tells you that you should not rush across the road (you might get killed), but wait for the traffic signals to show that it is safe to cross. Maximiners will do this, even if the chance of death is very slight, and the inconvenience of not crossing very high. Maximiners, then, will choose the melon.

So far we have two candidate principles of rational choice: maximize expected utility and maximin. In fact there is no limit to possible principles of rational choice. To illustrate a third—maximax—consider an extension to the original example. Suppose the waiter, before taking your order, says 'and today's special is fish eggs'. On further enquiry he reveals that this is a novelty dish prepared by the chef, who, at the beginning of the meal lays out fifty plates, one of which contains caviar, while the other forty-nine contain lumpfish roe. Accordingly, there is a 2 per cent (1 in 50) chance of getting caviar, and a 98 per cent chance of lumpfish roe. You are also assured that if you do strike lucky and get the caviar it will be served up with great ceremony, and so you will certainly know that you have got it, whether or not you can actually taste the difference.

You calculate that if you do get the caviar it will be such a thrill that it will be worth 50 to you. On the other hand, if you get the lumpfish roe (pasteurized, of course) it will not do any harm, but you will get no pleasure out of it. Probably you will leave most of it. So you value it at zero. Now, if you were playing maximin you would stick with the melon. This still has the 'best worst' outcome: 5 is better than 0. Similarly, maximization of expectations still dictates the mussels. (Fish eggs have an expectation of 1, as can easily be calculated.) But some will argue that it is rational here to go for the fish eggs. After all, if the gamble comes off, the pay-off is very large indeed. Someone reasoning this way might well be implicitly relying on the 'maximax' principle, which tells us to choose the option which has the 'best best' outcome (however unlikely): maximize the maximum, a principle for risk-taking optimists. As fish eggs is the option with the best possible outcome (even if this outcome is very unlikely to occur), it is the one that should be chosen.

Maximax is really a joke principle; it is not a serious idea. Whoever would choose fish eggs in this example surely would not continue to do so if, should the gamble be lost, instead of receiving lumpfish roe, they were to be taken out to the back of the restaurant and shot. Probably those who think of themselves as maximaxers follow the more complex principle of 'maximax constrained by disaster avoidance'. But let us leave this to one side. The point so far is that, in the restaurant example, we have identified three different principles of choice, and each issues in a different decision. Having now identified and illustrated these principles we can return our attention to the social case, and rational choice from the original position or the poor unfortunate in the hospital bed.

It may not be easy to see immediately, but selecting a principle of rational choice for use in the original position turns out to be vitally important. For each of the three principles we have identified yields a different model of the just society. Those who choose to maximize expectations are looking for the outcome with the highest average score. Accordingly, from the hospital bed they should choose some version of the average utilitarian theory of justice: we should make the average position in society as good as possible. Maximaxers, by contrast, have their eyes only on the best outcomes. So they are likely to choose a highly unequal form of society with a privileged, wealthy, and powerful, ruling class. Finally, maximiners look only to the worst off, wanting to make the worst off in society as well off as possible. In other words, they would choose Rawls's Difference Principle.

We can now see that the burden of Rawls's argument comes down to the claim that the rational principle of choice in the original position is maximin. This is not to say that Rawls believes maximin to be a suitable principle of choice for every case of decision under uncertainty. Melon is not the uncontroversially rational choice on the menu. Sometimes it seems more rational to take some risk. However, Rawls suggests there are reasons to think that the very special circumstances of the original position make maximin the only rational choice in this case. We need now to examine his arguments.

Reasons for maximin

What, then, is the rational principle of choice to use in the original position, or hospital bed? Before attempting to answer, a few more remarks about the nature of the choice need to be made. First, we might ask, why not choose a principle like 'Everyone should live in a palace'? That way I would be sure to be well off. But, of course, Rawls would reply that you cannot know that your society would be able to sustain such a situation; almost certainly, it would not. Your society is in the 'circumstances of justice'—between scarcity and abundance—and you must choose a principle that will be suitable for all levels of productivity between the two extremes. So, we might say, there are *physical constraints* on your choice.

And, we need hardly add, there are *logical constraints* too. Whatever you choose must be logically possible. So you cannot choose the principle 'Everyone should have slaves', or 'Everyone should be richer than everyone else'.

More importantly, Rawls claims that there are also *formal constraints* that reflect the idea of a hypothetical *contract* model of justification. The thought is that formal conditions need to be met if people are correctly to be said to have entered a contract, and Rawls imports these conditions as further constraints on choice. One is that the terms must be known, or at least knowable, to all the parties. There is no contract if its terms are deliberately concealed from one or more of the contracting parties. This is the constraint of *publicity* and it is enough to rule out the sort of 'two-level' or 'government house' style of utilitarianism we saw advocated by Sidgwick in Chapter 4.

A second formal constraint is that of *finality*. If a contract is made in good faith, then the parties will not seek to have it revoked just because things turn out badly. Many contracts have terms to cover unlikely contingencies. For example, one party may contract to compensate the other in the event of non-delivery. If you enter such a contract, then you must be prepared to bear these 'strains of commitment'. So, in this example, if I know in advance that I will not, in fact, compensate you if I fail to deliver, then I have not entered the contract in good faith. The upshot of this idea for the Rawlsian contract is that I must not make a choice that I would want to go back on if things turned out badly. Suppose that, from my hospital bed, I choose a very unequal society, and then find that, in actual society I do badly by these arrangements, and find myself near the bottom of the heap. If I am then discontented and want the system changed, then I have not made my choice in good faith, as I am not prepared to bear the strains of commitment. This idea is clearly important if we think that the just society should also be stable in the long term. We will shortly see the work to which Rawls puts this idea.

We are, then, looking for a principle of rational choice that yields a decision that is physically and logically possible, and does not violate the constraints of publicity and finality. This is not yet enough to determine the choice of a single principle, for it seems that choosing either on the basis of the maximization of expectations (average utilitarianism) or of maximin (the Difference Principle) both remain possible. So what do we do now?

It might be helpful to proceed in the other direction. Under what circumstances would maximization of expectations be a rational principle of choice? Within economic theory maximization of expectations is virtually taken to be the definition of rationality. Why should this be? The answer is that in a long-run series of decisions, which are discrete in the sense that what happens in one does not depend on what has happened or will happen in another, you almost certainly do better by being a maximizer of expectations than by following any other policy. Suppose, for example, that at the end of each day's work you were given wages of £50, but also told that you could gamble those wages for a 50 per cent chance of £150. The expected value of this gamble is therefore £75. If you were offered this gamble every day, and were sure that the person offering it was honest, then it would simply be stupid to follow a regular policy of playing safe. Should you do so, you would ensure a wage of £250 for a five-day week, whereas gambling will bring you in, on average, £375. So in such a long-run series, maximization of expectations is surely the rational strategy—and economic theory assumes that individuals are indeed faced with many such choices and decisions (albeit of less regularity and predictability than in the case described).

Now it is important for Rawls that the choice from the original position is not the first in a long-run series of choices. It is a one-off, unrepeatable offer. If things go badly you do not have another chance. Therefore maximization of expectations is not so obviously the rational policy, for it involves taking risks (remember the dish of mussels). Might this mean that the choice is a matter of temperament, rather than rationality?

On the contrary, Rawls argues that the use of the maximin principle, and, therefore, the selection of the Difference Principle, is the more rational decision because of the special circumstances of the choice. He has a number of arguments, not all of them equally convincing, but the best one is that alternative principles of choice involve taking risks so grave that to do so would be foolish in the extreme. If you decide to gamble, and you lose, you are stuck. There is no second chance. The original position will not be replayed. If you choose to maximize expectations, and so select utilitarianism, there is always the possibility that you will have the misfortune to end up very badly off.

Admittedly, we have already assumed that the Liberty Principle would be chosen—people should not gamble with their liberty—so you will not end up as someone's slave. This guarantee already marks a very important distinction from utilitarianism. But you might be very poor, unemployed, and homeless. Perhaps the existence of disadvantaged people is an inevitable side-effect of a particularly efficient type of market economy. Why take the risk of this if something better can be guaranteed by use of the maximin principle? And, Rawls adds, perhaps unfairly, if the gamble failed how would you justify your taking such a risk to your descendants, whose life prospects would also be diminished by your choice?

As a follow-up, Rawls argues that, if you did decide to take the gamble, and ended up in poverty, then you would not consider such a society just, and may well press for change. But this would be, in a sense, to 'go back' on your initial agreement. In other words, if the gamble failed you would not be able to bear the 'strains of commitment'. Accordingly you have not made the contract in good faith, and so have violated the 'constraint of finality'.

This further argument seems to depend on taking the idea of a contract very literally; perhaps more seriously than we ought. But the argument doing the real work is simply that maximin is to be preferred because alternative principles of rational choice involve taking chances that are just too risky to be rational in the circumstances, given that this is a once-only choice, with no going back. And this certainly seems to be a good reason for rejecting the principle of maximization of expectations.

But is it a strong enough reason to use maximin? Perhaps Rawls has not played fair by making his main comparison one between maximin and maximization of expectations. A defeat for utility maximization is not automatically a victory for maximin. There may be other, intermediate principles, which share some of the advantages of both. Consider the choice situation in which you are told that if you open Box B you will receive 5 units, and if you open Box A you have a 50 per cent chance of 4 units, and a 50 per cent chance of 10 units. In this situation if you were to use the maximin principle then you would be required to choose B, for this has the higher minimum result: 5. Yet one has to think of a very special case in which option B would be the rational one, whether we are talking about pounds, millions of pounds, or just pennies. (Perhaps you need exactly £5,000 for a life-saving operation.) So, thinking again, can we come up with a new principle of choice which allows you to choose A over B, but avoids the grave risks associated with maximization of expectations (or indeed maximax)?

One answer is to select the principle of 'constrained maximization'. That is, one should use a principle that says, roughly, 'maximize expectations, but exclude any option that contains a very bad possibility'. This is a principle that allows you to gamble, but does not permit you to risk everything. And such a principle seems nicely to overcome the problem of avoiding grave risks, but without endorsing the 'boring' maximin principle. Anyone using such a principle of 'maximization constrained by a safety net', as we might call it, might well be prepared to choose a society of great inequality if it boosts the average position in society, provided that no one is left too badly off. In other words there would be a minimum income, provided, if necessary by the government, to make sure that no one is left in too desperate a plight. We might even think that contemporary western societies largely fit this model: the free market modified by the welfare state.

Rawls thinks that the argument for constrained maximization fails. The problem, he believes, is that from the standpoint of the original position it would be impossible to set the social minimum in a non-arbitrary way. As we do not know the actual circumstances of our society we cannot decide that, say, 'everyone should get at least £200 per week'. Given how society actually turns out, that might not be enough for someone to be kept fed, clothed, and housed. Or it might turn out not to be economically possible. A more general principle is needed: one that is applicable however society turns out. How about 'No one should get less than half the average income'? But why half? Why not a quarter? Why not three-quarters? And how can we be sure that any of these would be sufficient to guarantee an acceptable standard of life? Rawls suggests that the contracting parties, in trying to set a social minimum, would finally settle for this suggestion: 'Make the worst off as well off as possible.' But that is simply the Difference Principle, and so, it seems, this form of constrained maximization collapses back into maximin.

Some suspect that Rawls has not been imaginative enough in trying to set the social minimum in a non-arbitrary fashion. Why not set it, for example, so as to overcome the 'strains of commitment'? Rawls's case is far from made, although in fairness to Rawls he does use another important argument, based on the ideas of 'fraternity' and 'reciprocity', to try to defend the Difference Principle. These ideas appeal to the notion that in a just society no one will want to benefit unless all do so. Rawls's argument here is a subtle one, and it is a controversial question of how exactly it is to work. Still, there is some plausibility in the idea that the Difference Principle would be chosen from behind the veil of ignorance, in the original position. And we have already accepted that the Liberty Principle and the Fair Opportunity Principle would also be selected, although it is less clear that they should be afforded the priority Rawls gives them. So far, then, Rawls's project seems a (qualified) success.

But the argument is not over yet. For even if Rawls is correct that his principles would be chosen, what does that prove? Why is that supposed to be a justification of the principles? After all, we are not, now, in the original position, and so why should we care what people in such a position would do? What, in other words, justifies Rawls's method? This is our next topic.

Rawls and his critics

> A hypothetical contract is not simply a pale form of an actual con-
> tract; it is no contract at all.
>> Dworkin, 'The Original Position' ([1973], reprinted in Norman
>> Daniels (ed.), *Reading Rawls* (Oxford: Blackwell, 1975; reissued
>> Stanford, CA: Stanford University Press, 1989),18)

The hypothetical contract method

Why, then, should we take Rawls's argument seriously? Here is one bad reason. Rawls has presented a hypothetical contract argument. Whatever can be shown to be the result of a hypothetical contract is just. Therefore the outcome of Rawls's method is just.

The weakness in this attempted justification is the claim that whatever can be shown to be the outcome of a hypothetical contract is just. This is simply false. Imagine that, in exchange for a copy of this book you were to give me all your worldly possessions. This supposition is a hypothetical contract, as is any fictional contract that we could devise. But the result of it is hardly just, and in any case it obviously conflicts with the results of many other hypothetical contracts (for example, the one in which you will not accept a copy of the book unless I also give you all my worldly possessions). Something obviously needs to be said to show why Rawls's hypothetical contract should be taken more seriously than either of these joke hypothetical contracts.

Rawls claims that his hypothetical contract has a privileged status because every element of the contracting situation—the original position—can be shown to be fair. The original position is, he says, 'a device of representation'. Every element represents something we accept, or could be brought to accept, on moral grounds. For example, making the parties in the original position ignorant of their sex reflects our belief that sexual discrimination is wrong. As we saw before, Rawls ensures impartiality by imposing ignorance.

That said, we are now able to see two quite different constraints on the make-up of the original position. One is that all its elements, all the assumptions about knowledge and ignorance, must properly reflect relatively uncontroversial moral beliefs shared by all, or almost all. The other is that agreement from the original position must be achievable. People must be characterized in the original position in such a way that they can come to some agreement or other; otherwise, the method would have failed. It would be a very powerful argument against Rawls if it could be shown that, in order to reach agreement between the contracting parties, he has incorporated elements into the original position that are not fair.

One important criticism of this type questions Rawls's justification for requiring people to choose in terms of primary goods: liberties, opportunities, wealth, income, and the social bases of self-respect. We should recall that primary goods were introduced as a consequence of Rawls's decision to make people ignorant of their conception of the good. Consequently, Rawls had to posit a 'thin theory of the good' so that people in the original position could make some choice or other, for otherwise, without a conception of the good, they would not know what they preferred. Rawls assumes that people want primary goods and that they prefer more of them to less. The philosophical justification of this move is to say that this is what rational people want, whatever else they want. That is, whatever you want from life, these goods—liberty, opportunity, income, wealth, and the social bases of self-respect—will be a help. They are 'all-purpose means'. Hence they are neutral between conceptions of the good. But, in criticism, it has been said that these goods are not neutral. They are particularly suitable for life in modern capitalist economies, built on profit, wages, and exchange. Yet surely there could be non-commercial, more communal, forms of existence, and hence conceptions of the good in which wealth and income—even liberty and opportunity—have lesser roles to play. So, runs the criticism, Rawls's original position is biased in favour of a commercial, individualist, organization of society, ignoring the importance that non-commercial, communal goods could have in people's lives.

A different criticism focuses on the fact that Rawls wishes to make the contracting parties ignorant of their natural and social assets. Again, this may be necessary to achieve agreement between the parties, but how does it reflect a moral belief that we are all supposed to share? Rawls's answer is that one's possession of natural and social assets is 'arbitrary from a moral point of view'. No one deserves to be stronger, more intelligent, or better looking than another, or to be born to wealthy and especially cultivated parents, and so no one deserves to benefit from these accidents of birth. This belief, then, is modelled by making people in the original position ignorant of these factors. We make natural assets 'common assets': things from which all members of society gain a benefit.

But is this right? Many people would resist the idea that we never deserve to benefit from using our talents. In particular, if someone has worked harder than others to develop a talent or skill that they use to good effect, then we often feel they deserve some reward for doing so. But Rawls says that even the ability to make an effort, or strive conscientiously towards a given goal, is so influenced by social and natural factors beyond one's control that you cannot even claim that developed talents deserve reward.

Perhaps Rawls is right about this, but he will not have convinced everyone by this argument. In that case some people will not accept that his description of the original position is correct, and they will also reject the claim that Rawls has justified his two principles of justice. For that attempted justification depends on the two principles being chosen from the original position, and on the original position being drawn up in such a way that whatever comes out of it will be fair. We have seen reasons for doubting both claims. But let us now turn to a different type of challenge to Rawls's views.

Nozick and patterns

Some have suggested that the main difficulty with Rawls's theory is not so much the method he uses, but the results he achieves with it. In particular, some critics have argued that Rawls's two principles of justice are inconsistent. Specifically, they say it is not possible consistently to follow both the Liberty Principle and the Difference Principle. This type of argument comes in two, diametrically opposed, forms. One argument contends that if we are concerned to equalize liberty then we must also equalize property—for it seems obvious that the rich can do more than the poor, and hence have more liberty. It can be argued, then, that the Difference Principle allows inequalities of liberty, in conflict with the Liberty Principle. However, the opposite complaint is made more often, and, if correct, is quite devastating to Rawls's project: to give people liberty means that *we cannot impose any restrictions on individual property holdings*. Limiting how much property people can acquire, and what they can do with it, is a way of reducing individual liberty. A proper respect for liberty rules out the Difference Principle, or, in fact, any other distributional principle. Robert Nozick has produced the most important version of this argument. It forms a central part of his libertarian defence of the free market, touched on in the first part of this chapter.

Nozick's argument against Rawls begins with some classification. First, he distinguishes what he calls 'historical' and 'end-state' theories of justice. An end-state theory of justice supposes that you can tell whether or not a situation is just simply by looking at its structure. So, for example, if you felt sure that the distribution depicted in the income parade described earlier in this chapter was unjust (or if you felt it was just) simply on the basis of the description given, it might well be that you hold an end-state theory. But if you think that more information is needed about how people obtained their resources, or about the basis on which the resources were allocated, then you believe in a historical theory.

Nozick distinguishes two types of historical theory: patterned and unpatterned. Patterned theories say, obviously enough, that the distribution should be made according to some pattern: 'To each according to their ...'. To each according to their need, to each according to their ability, to each according to their desert, or to each according to their status, would all be examples of theories that appeal to a pattern. Unpatterned theories do not do this. Essentially they are 'procedural' theories. On an unpatterned theory the essence of just distribution is a matter of each person acquiring the goods they hold through legitimate procedures. Nozick's own theory is unpatterned. Almost all other theories, so he claims, are either patterned or end-state. And all can be defeated by a single example that shows the consequences of giving liberty proper respect.

Nozick begins by asking us to imagine society regulated by our favourite pattern, whatever that may be. Suppose your view is that justice requires distribution according to need. The more one needs, the more one should have. Suppose, then, that property is distributed in society so that people are given money in proportion to their needs. Call this distribution of property D1. Nozick then asks us to imagine that a basketball player—Wilt Chamberlain—has made an arrangement with his team so that he gets 25 cents for every spectator who attends a home game. In addition to the standard gate money that they pay at the turnstile, they must each drop a quarter into a special box as they pass through the gate. At the end of the season a million people have dropped their quarter into the box. Accordingly, Wilt Chamberlain is now $250,000 better off, and so a new distribution of property is the result. Call this new distribution D2. On the basis of this very simple example Nozick feels entitled to draw several important conclusions.

The first is that any pattern—whatever it is—is liable to disruption by people's free actions. In this case the pattern was 'each according to their needs', and it was disturbed, essentially, by people's consumption decisions. A million people decided to watch Wilt play, rather than, say, spending their money on chocolate. Whatever the pattern, it seems, some free actions (exchanges, gifts, gambles, or whatever) are capable of disrupting it.

But what if people decided to stick to the pattern? This might be difficult to achieve in practice, but it might not be too difficult to stay within a certain range of variation. On the other hand, is it reasonable to expect everyone, or almost everyone, to be motivated in this way? If society is divided about the correct pattern, then, it appears, any pattern will be vulnerable.

Nozick's second claim is even more significant. If D1 is just, and people voluntarily moved from D1 to D2, then, he argues, surely D2 is also just. But once we have conceded this, then we have admitted that there can be just distributions which do not obey the original pattern. So all patterned conceptions of justice are refuted. It is vital, then, for defenders of patterns to resist this move. One strategy is to deny that the move from D1 to D2 was voluntary. Although it would seem foolish to argue that Wilt's supporters did not give him the money voluntarily, it does not follow that they realized that, in doing so, they would be bringing about D2. This is a subtle point. Although D2 has come about as a result of voluntary action, it does not follow that people have brought about D2 voluntarily. How could they have if they did not even know that D2 would be the result of their actions?

Another way of resisting the argument is to say that even if D2 has come into existence in a purely voluntary way, it does not follow that it is just. Perhaps Wilt's riches will put him in a position to do other people harm, by exerting power through the market, hoarding goods, speculating, or whatever. After all, not everyone chose to pay to watch Wilt play, and these people—including the as-yet unborn—might have a legitimate complaint against Wilt's new wealth.

However, even if this reply can be sustained, Nozick's third argument is the most important of all. Patterns, he argues, can only be enforced at grave cost to liberty. Suppose we decided to maintain a pattern. Given that some people would wish to engage in Wilt-like exchanges, it seems likely that the pattern will soon be disrupted. So what should we do? Nozick argues that we have just two alternatives. Either we maintain the pattern by banning transactions that might disrupt it (remember Vasili Grossman's would-be cafe owner) or we constantly intervene in the market to redistribute property. Either way we need to make intrusions into people's lives: by stopping them from doing what they want to do, or by investigating their holdings of wealth and income, and removing some from time to time. But whichever we choose we will be severely impeding people's liberty. Proper respect for liberty, then, rules out enforcing a pattern.

Nozick argues that these conclusions hold even for those who want to abolish private property altogether. In 'non-money communism' people will still have to be allocated goods, and some will want to make trades. Skilful traders may turn a profit. Furthermore, little industries could start up. Perhaps some will manage to make machines out of their legitimately acquired furniture or saucepans, and produce extra goods for exchange. This way, even without money, inequalities of possession will emerge.

What are the implications of the Wilt Chamberlain argument for Rawls? As far as Nozick is concerned, the Difference Principle represents a patterned conception of justice. Property is to be distributed so that it makes the worst off as well off as possible. But once people are given income and wealth according to the Difference Principle, some will spend it, while others will acquire more, and so sooner or later the Difference Principle will no longer be satisfied. Property will have to be redistributed. And, so Nozick has argued, this will greatly interfere with people's liberty to live their lives free from interference. Now recall that for Rawls the Liberty Principle takes priority over the Difference Principle. So if it really is true that maintaining the Difference Principle restricts liberty then, it seems, Rawls's own arguments compel him to give up the Difference Principle. A proper regard for liberty, so Nozick has argued, is incompatible with enforcing any patterned distribution of property.

Rawls, however, has several potential replies to this argument. The first is to point out that the Liberty Principle does not distribute liberty as such. Rather it is concerned with giving individuals an extensive scheme of what Rawls calls 'basic liberties', such as freedom of speech, or the right to run for public office. It does not say that people should be absolutely free from interference. So there is no formal inconsistency between Rawls's two principles of justice.

Nevertheless, something more persuasive than this is needed to blunt the force of Nozick's attack. Even if there is no formal inconsistency in Rawls's views, should he not be troubled by Nozick's observation that the Difference Principle, like all patterned conceptions of justice, can only be maintained by constant interference in people's lives? In response Rawls would argue that Nozick has painted a strange picture of how a pattern would be maintained. In the abstract it is true that to regulate society by the Difference Principle it is necessary to ban some transactions, and enforce the redistribution of property. But this could be done in a perfectly civilized, non-invasive, way, by the sort of tax and welfare system we are so familiar with. Those on large incomes will find themselves heavily taxed. Those on low incomes will receive income supplements. Tax is both a way of banning certain transactions and redistributing income—you cannot pay someone a large income without it being the case that they have to hand some of it over for the state to redistribute to others. And unpleasant though it is to pay tax, it hardly seems to amount to a grave interference in one's life.

Still, Nozick has anticipated this reply. Taxation, he says, is on a par with forced labour. And as we all object to forced labour, then we should all object to taxation. Actually not everyone does object to forced labour.

Rousseau says that he thinks forced labour is less opposed to liberty than taxation. But why should Nozick make this claim, which, on the face of it, sounds absurd? The answer is this. Suppose you work a forty-hour week, and 25 per cent of your wages is taken in taxation for redistribution to the poor. There is no way round this. If you are to do the work you do, at the wages you do, you must pay this tax. Accordingly, for ten hours of the week (25 per cent of your time), you are, in effect, forced to work for other people. For ten hours a week you are little more than a slave. Taxation, then, is slavery—a theft of your time. How can anyone who values liberty, suggests Nozick, accept such a situation?

Again, Rawls must reply that this is a massive exaggeration. There does seem to be a grain of truth in the idea that taxation forces one person to work for another, whether they wish to or not. But calling it forced labour or slavery hardly seems appropriate. And, Rawls's defenders add, we must not overlook something of perhaps even greater significance. Taxation for redistribution also increases liberty, for by increasing the income of the poor, it gives poorer people a range of choices that they would not otherwise have had. What type of system best advances liberty therefore remains a moot point. Nozick has not shown that Rawls's two principles of justice are inconsistent.

Conclusion

From all of this, what should we conclude about distributive justice? Our initial question was whether valuing liberty was enough to determine how property should be distributed. I think we can conclude that it is not. All the theories considered (with the exception of utilitarianism) have been defended on grounds of liberty, among other values, but none of the arguments is uniquely convincing.

Does this mean that the question of distributive justice cannot be settled by argument, or at least not at this level of abstraction? It would be too hasty to draw such a conclusion on the basis of what we have seen so far. Lack of success does not mean that success is impossible. If one accepts Rawls's general framework, as many philosophers are inclined to do, then we do have a way of reasoning about justice. This does not mean that Rawls's conclusions must be right, for it is possible that he has misused his own method. For example, it might be that rational people in the original position would choose utilitarian principles of distributive justice, or, more plausibly, utilitarianism subject to a 'social minimum'— a modified version of existing welfare states. But whether or not Rawls's principles of justice are correct, he has done political philosophy the great service of providing a framework in which the debate can be continued. And Rawls is now such a dominant figure in political philosophy that those who reject his methodology need to explain why.

JUSTICE FOR EVERYONE, EVERYWHERE?

'Oversights' of justice

> The entire history of social improvement has been a series of transitions, by which one custom or institution after another, from being a supposed primary necessity of social existence, has passed into the rank of a universally stigmatised injustice and tyranny. So it has been with the distinctions of slaves and freemen, nobles and serfs, patricians and plebeians; and so it will be, and in part already is, with the aristocracies of colour, race, and sex.
>
> John Stuart Mill, *'Utilitarianism'*, in *Utilitarianism and Other Writings*, ed. Mary Warnock ([1861], 2nd edn, Glasgow: Collins, 2003), 234

At various points in this book I have pointed out that some of the greatest political philosophers had suffered from we might charitably call 'oversights'. In Chapter 4, I mentioned that Karl Marx, the great revolutionary and theorist of emancipation, seems to suggest that political emancipation (i.e. the granting of civil rights and liberties) was essentially 'complete' in the United States in 1843, almost a hundred years before women were able to vote on equal terms with men, and at a time when around two-and-a-half million people of African descent, more than ten per cent of the population, were living as slaves. Now Marx did not, of course, argue in favour of slavery or against women having the vote, but at least when he was writing on the topics of liberalism and real human flourishing, as a young man in his mid-twenties, his focus on what concerned him pushed other highly significant issues into the background, even out of sight. In Chapter 3, I mentioned that Mary Wollstonecraft, champion of women's rights, seemed to assume that the women she was discussing, those of what she called 'middle rank', would have households staffed by domestic servants. And John Stuart Mill, writer of the stirring passage cited above, and author of a major book on the 'subjection of women', earned his living working for the East India Company, which was the British colonial administrator of India. This puts in context his comments about children and 'barbarians' being unsuited for liberty, although his actual views about India remain a matter of scholarly debate. I have picked out Marx, Wollstonecraft, and Mill merely as examples. Virtually all the thinkers I have discussed in this book have been criticized, fairly or unfairly, for overlooking what justice requires for women, racial or ethnic minorities, people who are LGBTQ (lesbian, gay, bisexual, transsexual, or questioning), those living in other countries, or those who will live in the future, taking too much of their own society's practices for granted.

Inequality is persistent. Nevertheless, great progress has been made, even if perhaps more recently than is sometimes assumed. Consider access to higher education. In England, until 1826, it was impossible to obtain a university education unless you were prepared to accept the articles of the Church of England, and as a result Catholics, Jews, Muslims, Atheists, and Christian non-conformists could not enter university. Women were not admitted on equal terms to men anywhere in England until 1878. Even though women had first been admitted to Cambridge University in 1869, it was, astonishingly, not until 1948 that they were able to graduate and receive a degree in the same way as men. A similar story can be told about the United States. For example, female applicants seeking entry to Harvard were admitted instead to the women-only Radcliffe College, founded in 1879, gaining full equality at Harvard only after the Second World War. The occasional male African-American did gain access to Harvard from around 1870 onwards. For example, the pioneering intellectual, academic and activist W. E. B. Du Bois (1868–1963), who will be mentioned again below, was the first African-American to gain a Ph.D. there in 1895, having also studied at the University of Berlin. Unfortunately, female African-Americans have had an even harder time. It is said that the first female African-American to graduate from Harvard Business School was Lillian Lincoln Lambert, who graduated as recently as 1969. While we still struggle to achieve full equality now, it is startling how different the world was just one or two generations ago.

In this chapter we will briefly explore some of these oversights of justice. We start by looking at issues of gender equality, then at racial justice, followed by issues of disability and sexual orientation, each from the standpoint of what has been called 'domestic justice': justice as it operates within a single state. We then broaden our perspective, first by looking at questions of global justice, including immigration, and global inequalities of wealth, and then justice to future generations, especially in relation to climate change. These discussions are necessarily brief, but they reflect areas of great contemporary concern, both in political philosophy and real life.

Justice for everyone?

... in no domain has woman ever really had her chance. That is why a great many women today demand a new status; and ... their demand is not that they be exalted in their femininity ... they wish to be accorded at last the abstract rights and concrete possibilities without the concurrence of which liberty is only a mockery. (Simone de Beauvoir, *The Second Sex* ([1949], London: Vintage Classics, 1997), 164)

Rights for women

Perhaps the most obvious feminist demand is for equal rights for women. And the demand is not surprising when we recognize how unequally women have been treated, as pointed out by the French feminist and philosopher Simone de Beauvoir (1908–86) in 1949, in the passage just quoted.

Du Beauvoir is right that even in the 1940s women were subordinated to an extraordinary degree. In an earlier chapter, we saw that British women were denied the vote until the twentieth century. And until the various Married Women's Property Acts of the late nineteenth century, a woman's property on marriage automatically became her husband's. Even in the 1960s, before the Equal Pay Act of 1970, it was standard practice in the United Kingdom to offer jobs with two rates of pay: one (higher) rate for men, and another for women. This is now illegal, but, as with equality in higher education discussed above, it is quite astonishing how recently the change was made. The political theorist Carole Pateman points out that until the 1970s, a married woman in the United Kingdom could not even obtain credit, such as make a hire purchase agreement, without her husband's signature.

Society has certainly made great strides towards equal rights for women. Open and explicit discrimination in employment is now much more rare than it was even a decade ago, and there are reasons to believe that the situation will continue to improve. A married woman's access to credit now depends on her financial circumstances, not her husband's approval. More women attend university than men in many countries. So if women have—or shortly will have—equal rights, what more could a feminist want?

It does not take much to see that a policy of equal rights, while highly desirable in itself, is not enough to satisfy demands for equality. Even if women rarely now suffer open and explicit discrimination in employment, more subtle forms of discrimination still exist. It is illegal to have different pay scales for men and women, but women still tend to cluster near the bottom of the scale. According to a recent report, in the United Kingdom in 1970, before the first Equal Pay Act, women on average earned 63 per cent of men's hourly pay. By 2005, women in full-time work still earned 18 per cent less than men, and for part-time work the difference was a remarkable 40 per cent. By 2014, the gap for full-time pay had fallen to just below 10 per cent, albeit partially because male pay fell more rapidly than female pay after the recession of 2008. Why does the gap persist? While it is illegal to discriminate in employment practices, the state simply does not have the resources to supervise every employment panel or promotion decision. In other words, as Karl Marx observed, and we noted in an earlier chapter, laws can be free of a defect without society being free of that defect. Making discrimination illegal has not made it stop.

But even if we could achieve a policy of genuinely equal rights there may still be problems. Again, as Marx argued, a right to equality in one respect can lead to inequality in another. Equal incomes will not ensure equal living standards if one person has elderly dependants and another has not, or if one is disabled and another not. Therefore if men's and women's needs differ in significant ways, then a policy of equal rights will not be a way of achieving equality. Is there, in fact, a relevant difference? Here feminists have sometimes felt themselves to be in a dilemma. Suggesting that women's needs are different to those of men, and, furthermore, arguing that such needs give rise to specific claims, has sometimes been taken as weakness or special pleading: a tacit admission of inferiority. As a result, some feminists have been tempted to deny that women need their own distinctive rights.

Yet there is no reason why an acceptance that differences exist between men and women should imply that women are weaker or inferior: this is simply how we often construe the position. Men have special needs too: for example, a man generally needs a higher daily intake of calories than a woman. But this has never been thought of as a sign of men's inferiority to women; if anything, it is a sign of strength and an entitlement to extra food. Accepting that a group has special needs is not, in itself, to say that they are weaker. And a refusal to admit that women have special needs—particularly those connected with their biological nature—may be a way of ensuring women an inferior standing. So, for example, we can hardly ignore the fact that women, not men, give birth to children. This fact gives rise to special needs, and with it the need for special rights.

However, this type of argument needs to be handled very carefully. How much of what is considered distinctive about women is really due to biology? One way to highlight this question is by drawing a distinction between 'sex' and 'gender'. Sex is identified as a purely biological category; gender a social category. Gender roles can differ quite arbitrarily from society to society. To take one apparently trivial example, in some societies only men tend goats, in others only women do so. Clearly there is no biological reason why this should be: the difference is obviously a matter of social custom that societies take for granted as 'second nature'. But there is nothing natural about it, and apparently no reason why it could not be reconfigured some other way. Gender roles seem open to evaluation and change, in principle at least.

The point is that even if there are biological differences between the sexes this does not mean that we must endorse all traditional differences in gender roles. Yet our imaginations are often very limited. In almost all societies it has been treated as a virtually inescapable fact that women are the primary carers for young children, at least in the first few months of a child's life. As a response to this difference, which generates differences in need, modern societies have in recent decades devised various systems of maternity leave as a way of trying to treat women and men as equals.

Yet maternity leave alone is not sufficient to guarantee women equality in the workplace. However generous her leave, a mother's career is almost certain to be affected by the birth of a child in a way in which a father's rarely is. Generous maternity leave may even stand in the way of a woman's career development, particularly when we remember that a woman's childbearing age coincides with the stage of her life when she is likely to be building a career, if she is to have a good chance of achieving at a high level. As the feminist political philosopher Susan Moller Okin (1946–2004) has put the point, at the root of the problem

> ... are two commonly made but inconsistent presumptions: that women are primarily responsible for the rearing of children; and that serious and committed members of the workforce ... do not have primary responsibility, or even shared responsibility, for the rearing of children. The old assumption of the workplace, still implicit, is that workers have wives at home. (*Justice, Gender, and the Family* (New York: Basic Books, 1989), 5)

Many feminists have sought to challenge the assumptions upon which the policy of maternity leave is based. Why is it assumed that a mother will be the person to look after her child in the first few months? There is no longer any biological necessity. Why should the father not take on this responsibility, if that is more appropriate in the circumstances? Here is Mary Wollstonecraft on the issue, as long ago as 1792:

> Many men attend to the breeding of horses, and ... the management of the stable, [but] would ... think themselves degraded by paying any attention to the nursery. (*Vindication of the Rights of Woman* ([1792], rev. edn Harmondsworth: Penguin, 2004), Section 13.5, 236)

Maternity leave is increasingly being replaced by 'parental leave', which can be taken by either parent (or both for a shorter time). This seems a liberating proposal. Ideally it will become a matter of choice whether the mother or father takes on the role traditionally assumed by the mother, although it may take a long time for expectations to change. Not everyone, of course, will be happy with this suggestion. Some women will feel that the apparent 'choice' offered is simply another avenue of oppression: to be forced back to work when they would rather spend time with their newborn baby. Nevertheless, the general point remains. Social policy can be used to help reconstruct gender roles when these are seen as unfair.

This example also makes connections between two domains of particular concern to feminists: the workplace and the family. For much of history, marriage, for a woman, was seen as a refuge from unsatisfying and low-grade work. Often, though, it was not much of an improvement, and, even at best, perpetuated women's subservient social role. However, the attempt—through choice or through economic necessity—to combine a career and a family has led many women into an exhausting 'double day' of work and housework, which in turn has often hampered their career prospects. Are men prepared to share domestic burdens with their working wives? In the mid-1980s it was claimed that: 'husbands of wives with full-time jobs averaged about two minutes more housework per day than did husbands in housewife-maintaining families, hardly enough additional time to prepare a soft-boiled egg' (Barbara R. Bergmann, cited in *Justice, Gender, and the Family*, 153). Have things changed? Whether in paid employment or not, a wife often lacks the power, status, and economic autonomy enjoyed by her husband, and this, in part, explains why even a working wife normally has primary responsibility for domestic chores. These inequalities need to be addressed both in themselves and as a means of allowing women equal opportunity in the workplace.

But what else is to be done? One additional suggestion is that women should be the beneficiaries of programmes of 'affirmative action'—active policies to favour the careers of a disadvantaged group. Affirmative action has been proposed for many other groups besides women, and I will discuss a variety of examples and cases.

Affirmative action

Affirmative action takes many forms. It could simply be a matter of encouraging people from particular groups to apply for jobs or for promotion through a policy of active recruitment. More significantly and controversially, affirmative action can also involve 'preferential' hiring or admissions policies. Again, there are different ways this can be done. Imagine the case of a university that wishes to have more female staff on the faculty. It might have a strict quota of places to be awarded to female candidates. Or it might have no quota, but view applications from women more favourably. Or it might simply use gender as a tiebreaker between equally able candidates. No doubt other policies are possible too. Broadly, the point of affirmative action is to advance freedom of occupational choice and equality.

However, many people, including some who call themselves 'liberals', react very strongly against affirmative action programmes. It is frequently objected that the policy is self-contradictory. After all, affirmative action programmes are supposed to be a remedy for discrimination, but all they seem to do is discriminate on different grounds. Common though it is, this is a very superficial objection as it stands. Any policy must discriminate on some grounds. The university selection committee ought to discriminate between the accomplished scholar and the beginner, for example. We cannot possibly say that all discrimination is unjust. The real question is whether the discrimination involved in affirmative action programmes is acceptable or not.

Why might it not be? Objectionable discrimination might be defined as 'choosing on non-relevant grounds'. And, it is said, gender or race (which we will look at in more detail in the next section) are never relevant grounds for choice. Perhaps it is wrong to treat people as members of groups, rather than as individuals. The fact that someone has black skin or white skin, or is male or female, should be irrelevant to the treatment they receive, particularly when the allocation of scarce resources is at issue. The argument against racial or sexual discrimination can be turned into an argument against affirmative action. Everyone should be treated on their individual merits. To do otherwise is unjust. Furthermore, it can even make things worse. What is the justice, for example, of helping middle-class women into medical school if they do not have the qualifications of some male candidates, perhaps from less fortunate backgrounds, who will lose out?

A further objection to affirmative action is that it can be counterproductive. Those who owe their place to a policy of affirmative action may be stigmatized by this fact. Even worse, those members of disadvantaged groups who would have gained a job or a place anyway will be treated as if they are beneficiaries of the programme, and so stigmatized too. They cannot win. Affirmative action, on this view, is patronizing and degrading, and, in the long term, may do more harm than good.

These are forceful criticisms. Can affirmative action be rescued? Various defences are possible, not all of equal power. One argument is that affirmative action is little more than an extension of the idea of equality of opportunity. In any meritocratic system positions should go to the most able, but relying on formal qualifications will systematically discriminate in favour of those who went to better schools, or had more affluent family backgrounds, or more support and encouragement at home. Affirmative action can be a way of compensating for the exaggerated qualifications of the advantaged.

If the advantaged simply looked better on their application forms than they were in real life, then this argument would be persuasive. But often those who have achieved high qualifications have acquired valuable skills as well as a certificate, and so are in a better position to use an opportunity offered, or to perform well in a job. Inequality of opportunity tends to be cumulative, and getting one advantage puts you in a better position to compete for the next. Even if their underlying potential is no greater, the privileged may well have acquired more highly developed skills, and so would have greater relevant merits, in competition with those from more difficult circumstances. As a response, it can be argued that justice requires equality of opportunity in the acquisition of skill; this is Rawls's view. But that would seem to demand intervention at the level of education, not affirmative action later on.

A second argument defends affirmative action on the grounds of social utility. It is claimed that people feel more comfortable dealing with professionals of their own race and sex. Female and black doctors and lawyers are needed by society, and law and medical schools have a social duty to train people from all backgrounds to fill these roles. Again, this is an argument that needs handling with great care. Apart from the fact that the argument is very limited in scope, applying only to professional roles, is it really true that people have preferences for professionals of their own race and sex? And should we simply accept these preferences without further question if people do have them? Furthermore, why should we assume that female or black doctors and lawyers will choose to work in the neighbourhoods where they are needed if they can earn more elsewhere?

A third argument is based on the idea of reparation or compensation for past injustices. This is particularly clear in the case of many African-Americans, or British Afro-Caribbeans, whose current disadvantages are, in part at least, a legacy of the slave trade. Affirmative action is one policy in a package that tries to compensate for these past injustices.

Against this, it is argued that whites living today do not have slaves, and so have not acted unjustly to blacks. But this misses the point. Whites are the beneficiaries of past injustices, even if they are not the cause of them. And men are the beneficiaries of a culture in which they have been more favourably treated than women. Hence there is reason to make reparation.

Each of these arguments has some force, but we are not finished yet. A fourth argument points to the symbolic power of a policy of affirmative action. It is a way of symbolizing the idea that black people and women are welcome in the universities and professions, and that their earlier exclusion is a matter for regret. For the time being at least, their way must be eased if they are to make a contribution and imbalances redressed. This goes hand in hand with a fifth argument: that it is essential to break the mould by which certain opportunities have seemed closed to women and minorities. Affirmative action provides role models, opening the eyes of a new generation to what is possible for them.

The great advantage of these final two arguments is that they allow us to make the concession that a world that includes affirmative action is not an ideal one. As a long-term policy, affirmative action is undesirable, and in certain respects unjust. People should be treated on their individual merits, as critics of affirmative action claim. But without a temporary policy of affirmative action it will be much harder to create a world in which affirmative action is unnecessary: in which people *are* treated on their individual merits. So we should see affirmative action as a transitional policy in a step towards a more just world.

Justice and race

The discussion of affirmative action makes clear that there are similarities between issues of gender equality and racial equality. We saw that Simone de Beauvoir, in 1949, said that women had never been given their chance. Compare her words with those of W. E. B. Du Bois in 1900, at the start of a speech called 'To The Nations of the World', at the first Pan-African Convention, held in London:

> The problem of the twentieth century is the problem of the color line, the question as to how far differences of race—which show themselves chiefly in the color of the skin and the texture of the hair—will hereafter be made the

basis of denying to over half the world the right of sharing to their utmost ability the opportunities and privileges of modern civilization. ([1900]; cited in Kwame Anthony Appiah, *Lines of Descent* (Cambridge, MA: Harvard University Press, 2014), 62)

Members of disadvantaged races, as well as women, can be victims of both direct and indirect discrimination, and policies of affirmative action have been proposed as remedies in both cases. Yet it would be wrong to think that there are no relevant differences between sexism and racism, and it is important to explore racial injustice as a topic in its own right.

We saw in the last section that one way of attempting to justify discriminatory practices against women starts from the undeniable observation that men and women play different biological roles in human reproduction. Relatively innocent claims about biology can then be extended, more worryingly, into highly contestable claims about different 'natures', different abilities, and the mutual benefit of a division of labour between men and women. Many unacceptable gender policies quite possibly had their basis in what was presumed to be well-meaning concern based on biology, different natures, and the common good.

Racial discrimination is often rooted in claims that at least look as if they are based on biology too: that races are biologically distinct; and that one race is in some relevant sense superior to another. The term 'white supremacy', for example, captures this combination of views. However, unlike the relation between men and women, there is no claim that racial difference is some sort of 'biological necessity'. It seems clear that without people occupying the biological male and female roles the human race would not, for most of human history, have been able to reproduce, although new reproductive technologies add an interesting angle. But no one can plausibly argue, surely, that racial difference is essential to human existence. It seems an artefact of human evolution that apparently different races have come into existence, and we could imagine a perfectly coherent alternative history in which human beings never left Africa (where we first evolved) and remained with no significant diversity in skin colour or other 'racialized' characteristics or bodily features.

While sexual discrimination could, in its most charitable light, be considered a highly misguided application of a biological theory, racial discrimination or prejudice is far harder to comprehend or rationalize. What is it about another person's appearance that could lead an employer or landlord to decide that a particular individual is unsuited for a particular job, or to be an appropriate tenant, for example? One possible explanation could be brute prejudice, based on fear of difference or some other aspect of individual or group pathology. Here we leave the realm of philosophy and enter some murky and controversial areas of psychology. However, insofar as an individual is likely to attempt to justify their discriminatory attitude by some form of reasoning or argument, it is likely that they will attribute a certain characteristic to members of a particular race. To justify discrimination in the job market it might be claimed, for example, that members of the race in question are intellectually inferior or have poor working habits, or, to justify discrimination in the housing market, that members of a race are unreliable tenants because they make irregular payments, or favour strong-smelling food or loud parties.

These attempts at justification can be contested on a number of levels. Is there really any evidence for the generalizations? And even if the generalizations are true, what does that tell you about the individual standing in front of you? To see the force of this question, consider the fact that the average Dutch person is taller than the average Spanish person. But that on its own does not tell you whether the particular Dutch person trying out for the basketball team is taller than the Spanish person who also hopes for a place. Of course, if all the information you had was that one is Dutch and one is Spanish, you might conclude that it is more likely that the Dutch person is taller. But that is very weak evidence, and it is much better to meet them both and see. And finally, even if the generalization in question is true, and is true of the particular individual, it could still be very unfair to discriminate on these grounds. In each case further investigation or argument is necessary to judge how relevant the characteristic is to the opportunity offered.

Yet the philosophical literature also includes a deeper response to attempts to justify discrimination on grounds of race, pointing out that the debate makes the important assumption that the notion of race has a biological basis. In response, it is increasingly now argued that the concept of race is pseudo-scientific, with no foundation in genetics. What, after all, is the biological claim about race? We are used to the concept of 'species'. The normally accepted definition is that a male and a female of the same species can mate and produce fertile offspring. Donkeys and

zebras are, by the criterion, separate species, as any offspring they produce are infertile. Races are not species in this sense, for 'inter-breeding'
creates fertile offspring at the normal rate. Investigations have not revealed significant genetic variations between different races, for there
is as much or more genetic variation within a race as between races.
Features such as skin colour, body shape and size, and facial features are,
genetically, superficial characteristics rather than markers of some deep
difference. Skin colour is genetically no more significant than hair colour,
eye colour, or the very many other ways in which humans beings vary.

Some philosophers have used these findings to deny that there is such a
thing as race. However this is, arguably, to go further than the science justifies. Although race may not be a biological category it is surely a sociological
one: most people still think in terms of race, and consciously or uncon-
sciously it influences their attitudes towards, and expectations of, different people. Historians now suggest that the concept of race as we know it
developed in the seventeenth and eighteenth centuries, around the same
time as the start of the modern slave trade in which European slavers captured West Africans and transported them to the Americas to work on
plantations. Some have argued that the concept of race, and racial superi-
ority of whites and inferiority of blacks, was developed as a rationalization
of the slave trade. Others claim that pre-existing racial classification was
what allowed the slave trade to take place. And others are sceptical of both
claims, because forms of the slave trade have existed throughout human
history. But although historically there has always been division, even
domination, between different social and religious groups there is general
agreement that the concept of race as we now have it is a relatively recent
invention. It is an unfortunate product of a type of scientific outlook on the
world that tried to look behind different appearances to posit a deeper biological explanation. But there is no deeper explanation to be found.

These arguments, then, suggest that racial concepts, like those of
gender, developed for particular purposes and then exert real and detrimental effects on very many people. Even if there are no 'races', biologically speaking, individuals are nevertheless 'racialized'. This means that
although well-meaning liberals may argue that our social policies should
be 'colour-blind', and ignore race, doing so can be highly problematic.
Trying to ignore race without a deeper investigation into our institutions and structures also ignores the fact that racialization has created

sustained privileges for some and stubborn and severe disadvantages for others. These differences are very well documented, especially in the United States. For example, it is said that in certain parts of the United States a black man is more likely to spend time in prison than go to college. Throughout the world discrimination exists, and members of disfavoured races or ethnicities, or of lower castes, are more likely to be unemployed, to experience lower pay, to live in worse housing, and to suffer greater illness and die younger. This remains the case whether the disfavoured peoples are descendants of former slaves as in the United States, whether they are indigenous people victimized by colonial powers, as in Australia, New Zealand, Canada, South Africa, and also the United States and elsewhere, whether they are the victims of long-standing caste distinctions, as in India, or they are recent immigrants, as in many countries of the world. These effects will not go away even if, from tomorrow, no discrimination of any form takes place. Members of dominant races, religions, or castes will have typically acquired the skills, social networks, and habits of life that will make it easier for them to 'fit in' and 'get on'. 'Colour-blind' policies, in the world in which we live, will not change the dominant ways of doing things, and those who are the best fit for the dominant culture will continue to do best. This is not to deny that a truly colour-blind world would be one way of achieving a form of racial justice, and is an inspiring ideal. The point, rather, is that we have not yet made the background changes to the world that would allow colour-blind policies to do the work we would hope for them.

More fundamental changes are needed, although understanding that there are several different paths by which modern societies have become multi-racial suggests that remedies for racial injustice may also need to take different forms. Those groups that have been the victim of historic injustice would seem to have a strong case for reparation. Just as descendants of Jews murdered in the holocaust have received payments in reparation from the German government, it has been argued that the descendants of those brought to the Americas as slaves are owed compensation from the countries that profited from (and still profit from the capital accumulated by) slavery. It has also been argued that indigenous peoples who were turned off the land should have the land returned to them, as has happened in Canada and New Zealand. Recent immigrants are much less likely to have claims for reparation, although it does remain possible. For example, Afro-Caribbeans in the United Kingdom are likely to be descended from slaves who were part of a slave trade from which the United Kingdom benefited.

In the modern world, many of our towns and cities contain large numbers of people with different histories, cultures, and languages. In major cities such as New York or London several hundred languages are spoken, which illustrates the further point that racial difference is not the only way in which societies divide: religion, ethnicity, and nationality, as well as social class, also generate social fault-lines. In some cities a form of semi-voluntary segregation takes place, with members of different groups living in different neighbourhoods, often at different levels of prosperity and opportunity. In other countries there is much more geographic mixing, which may or may not be accompanied by social mixing. Not all members of minority groups will face the same type of discrimination, but racial discrimination remains highly problematic virtually everywhere. Putting aside questions of compensation, a central question that faces us in the modern world now is how people regarded as members of different races, religions, or ethnicities can live together as equals.

In public discussion two main approaches to this problem are 'assimilation' and 'multi-culturalism'. The underlying idea of assimilation could be expressed as 'Everyone is welcome in this country, as long as they behave like us.' This attitude can be seen in those who believe that immigrants have a duty to learn the language of their new country, and to obey its laws, even if they clash with elements of the immigrant culture. For example, regulations for slaughtering animals according to kosher or halal practices can conflict with animal welfare laws, and some countries restrict the wearing of the Islamic face-covering burqa, arguing that religious dress has no place in the public sphere. Those who favour assimilation do not necessarily want to obliterate cultural difference, but rather regard cultural difference as a personal, private matter, rather than something to be accommodated at a political level. Such an attitude seems consistent with 'colour-blind' policies, discussed above, and to have the same flaws. If, for example, members of one religion find that their religious holy days are treated as national holidays, as in the case of Christians in Europe, then they are in a privileged position relative to those who have to lose days of work or schooling in order to celebrate their religious holy days, such as Jews and Muslims.

The policy of 'assimilation' contrasts with an alternative approach of 'multi-culturalism' which accepts that individuals have a right to live according to their cultural traditions even when those traditions conflict with majority norms. For example, some religions use drugs for religious festivals. If those drugs are illegal in the host country should there be a special dispensation for members of the particular religion? Those who believe in multi-culturalism are more likely to accept a dispensation than those who favour assimilation. Equally, in the examples discussed above, multi-culturalists will look for solutions that do not favour one group over another, even if historically one group has lived in the country for much longer. Multi-culturalists are also more likely to support the use of public money to subsidize and celebrate the art, literature, history, and culture of minority groups.

Multi-culturalists appear to be more welcoming of individual difference than assimilationists, who are happy to give people from minorities rights, but largely on the terms of the majority culture. Multi-culturalists face some tough questions, though. First, some cultures engage in practices that western liberals find barbaric or even an abuse of human rights, such as arranged child marriage or the genital cutting of young women. Should members of a religion be allowed to impose and enforce their own laws, such as the Sharia Law of Islam, which is often thought to be much more restrictive of women's rights than western liberal legal systems? What are the limits to multi-cultural toleration? Second, some cultural groups strongly reject the values of the country in which they are citizens and even plot its overthrow, as we have seen with some terrorist actions carried out in the name of religion even by citizens born into the country against which they protest. Of course, any country has the right to defend itself against terrorism, but the question is how far it can go to suppress the cultures that are thought to be conducive to terrorism. For example, should speakers who encourage terrorism be banned? Should there be limits to free speech even on a university campus?

Difficulties with assimilation and multi-culturalism lead to a third approach, known as 'integration'. It shares with assimilation the idea that there should be a single public culture that all should join. Where it differs, however, is that it acknowledges that the currently dominant culture also needs to change to accommodate a wide range of different ways of life. Elizabeth Anderson, for example, who is especially interested in racial integration in the United States, powerfully argues that when dominant norms and practices create disadvantages for subordinated groups, those norms have to change. But, according to Anderson, this is not a matter of granting 'group rights' for minorities as multi-culturalists might seek, but rather changing our practices so all can flourish. In the United States policies of racial integration have, most notably, been attempted in housing and education, and Anderson documents both successes and failures, trying to understand the conditions under which policies have positive effects. For example, she argues that there is evidence that black schoolchildren perform better in racially integrated schools, especially if they have attended an integrated elementary school. But for this to work well, the schools themselves need to accept that their pupils come from a range of backgrounds and experience, with different needs and perhaps learning styles, at least initially. Part of the lesson is that integration requires hard work and effort. If 'quick fixes' were available, it is likely that we would have found them already.

There are, in fact, parallels between policies of racial integration and policies that flow from the 'social model of disability', which we will look at in the following section. In both cases we need to start by reflecting on what the dominant group takes for granted, how standard practices damage others, and, most challengingly, how those practices could be changed. Of course, different societies find themselves in different situations with different questions to answer. A wide package of measures seems necessary if everyone of different races or ethnic origin will be able, eventually, to live together as equals. Certainly there are different cultural practices among different groups, and indeed, different races. How much is in need of changing? How much can we accept or even celebrate as rich and joyful diversity? Perhaps these questions will always be subject to disagreement. But nevertheless we can attempt to adjust patterns of education, housing, and employment so that all have fair treatment. Progress is there, but painfully slow, and what for some counts as progress is seen by others as a retrograde step.

Disability

Like gender and race, disability is a difficult social and philosophical issue. Even the language presents challenges. Not long ago it was perfectly acceptable to use the language of 'cripple' for someone with a physical impairment. Now it is considered insulting as, often, is 'handicapped'. Sometimes it is said that the term 'handicapped' has its origin in the degrading 'cap-in-hand' pose of a beggar, although this claimed origin is disputed. However, the term could still be objectionable, as it seems to be a sporting metaphor, implying that some people are fated to do less well in the 'game of life'. Today the term 'person with a disability' is often used, to emphasize the fact that the person 'comes before' the disability. Some favour the term 'differently abled', and other new terms have been introduced, such as 'neuro-diversity' for what were previously regarded as some mental disabilities. Alternatively, some activists prefer the term 'disabled person' because, they claim, it is society that disables people. This may be a surprising claim. Surely, it will be said, some people are simply born disabled, and others become disabled through tragic accidents. Why should anyone think that society disables people?

Those who argue for the idea that society disables people—often known as the 'social model of disability'—readily accept that people are born with different bodily and mental characteristics. But how well you can function given those characteristics depends to a very large extent on social facts. For example, a study was carried out exploring the lives of people with spinal cord injuries who had lost the use of their legs. The study compared living in modern urban Sydney, in Australia, with rural Cameroon, in Africa. In Australia the people studied were able to use high-quality wheelchairs, and had a normal range of employment and leisure opportunities, which took place in modern, well-designed buildings that were constructed bearing in mind the needs of people with mobility problems. However, in rural Cameroon, in the rain forest, there is a good deal of flooding for much of the year, few well-made roads or paths, and buildings lack accessibility features, or even modern sanitation. Wheelchairs, even if available, are close to useless. Medical facilities are also scarce and people with severe mobility problems typically have short life expectancies, often dying from infections that took hold in bed sores, caused by spending almost their entire life lying down in unhygienic conditions. The study showed that life for people with severe mobility problems can be a torment in some parts of the world, but very close to 'normal' experience in others. In this sense, at least, how severe a disability is depends on social and material factors outside the capacities of the individual.

Some radical defenders of the social model of disability attempt to go further and deny that there is anything to disability beyond the way in which we have constructed the world to favour some types of people over others. Here there are analogies with some discussions about race and gender. Yes, it is admitted, there are some 'natural' differences in function and body shape. But these natural differences do not on their own explain the dramatically different ways in which people are treated or that some people have lives of great richness and achievement while others struggle on the margins. In the case of disability, our building practices, the way we configure the workplace, our technologies, our attitudes to each other, and our inherited culture has made life much more difficult and challenging for some people than it is for others. Society has 'disabled' some people and rewarded others, without any justification.

The social model of disability is often contrasted with a medical model. The medical model is, perhaps, our inherited 'common sense', suggesting that disability is a medical matter, to be treated by surgery or medical intervention wherever possible. On this view, action for people with disabilities takes place in hospitals. The social model contests this by suggesting that it would be like trying to deal with racism by medically changing everyone's skin colour so that it is the same. But is this a good analogy? If someone has a mobility problem that is amenable to surgery, is that really like a skin-colour-changing procedure? Rather it seems valuable in itself. Even though there is surely something right about the social model, to deny that disability is ever a medical issue is too extreme. Neither the medical nor the social model can be accepted as the whole truth, but the social model is a powerful corrective to our medicalized assumptions.

In practice the social model encourages us to consider the ways in which the things we take for granted exclude people with disabilities. And different disabilities present different challenges. Societies are getting better at dealing with mobility issues, as the example of modern Sydney illustrates. Technology is helping us find ways for people with sensory impairments, such as problems with eyesight and hearing, to work and enjoy leisure activities. We have, unfortunately, been less successful in applying the social model to some cognitive disabilities. How would we need to change the world so that people can have equally rich and fulfilling lives whatever their levels of intellectual development? No doubt changes are possible but societies have not been very imaginative so far.

Furthermore, we should also bear in mind that not everyone regards the same things as a disability. One well-known example concerns people who are profoundly deaf. Some deaf people strongly wish to hear and would welcome any technological or medical intervention if it held out hope of better hearing. But other deaf people reject technological interventions such as cochlear implants, and prefer to remain an accomplished and secure member of a complex and vivid sign-language culture rather than haltingly enter an unfamiliar and perhaps unsympathetic 'hearing world'. Similar debates take place with respect to conditions such as autism and manic depression. Medication can make people feel that their real nature is being suppressed, and many would rather 'be themselves' rather than take medication in order to fit in with other people's expectations.

What seems clear is that even people who appear to be in similar circumstances can want and need very different things. Starting with the questions 'How can we treat everyone as an equal?' and 'In what ways does society make a bad situation worse?' at least brings out some of the problems.

Sexual orientation

Once we start looking for ways in which the world we have found ourselves in favours some people or groups over others, it is striking how many examples appear. In recent years intense scrutiny has been paid to questions of sexual orientation, and in particular to how society has treated gay, lesbian, bisexual, and transsexual people. In Chapter 4, I mentioned how recently homosexuality was decriminalized in the United Kingdom, and it remains proscribed in many countries. Yet initial legal reform was only the start of a drive towards equality. For example, in the United Kingdom initially the 'age of consent' for gay sex for men (homosexuality for women was never legally prohibited—a case, perhaps, of ignorance, neglect, or embarrassment rather than enlightenment) was 21, compared to 16 for heterosexual sex. Further equalizing policies have been introduced, with the question of gay marriage a recent issue of interest and controversy. For some people it may be surprising that the issue of marriage is treated as so important. Why should gay people want anything to do with the patriarchal, bourgeois, conservative institution of marriage? But whether or not marriage is a patriarchal, bourgeois, conservative institution, it does confer important rights on individuals (for example, the right to inherit without paying estate duty). Furthermore, marriage is a public celebration and validation of a relationship. To offer it to some types of relationship but not to others seems to send a message that we as a society prefer some ways of living to others. And what right do we have as a society to express such a preference in this way? The symbolic value and prestige of marriage should not be underestimated. As we saw with arguments about women and voting, whatever the facts about individual preferences, denying some people rights that others have is insulting and treats people as belonging to different moral categories. Each couple should decide for themselves whether to get married, rather than have the choice against made for them by the law.

There do, however, remain other questions. Society has begun to accept gay marriage, but what should be said about polygamy and polyandry? Are our restrictive practices discriminatory? If, for example, two men and one woman decide that they want to spend their lives together as a single household, do we have good reason, as a society, to refuse to give this the official public sanction and extended rights of marriage? And on what grounds? But taking the questions even further, should there even be such a thing as marriage? What message does the formal recognition of marriage convey in respect of those who, for whatever reason, never marry? Does it imply that their lives are, in some way, a failure? What entitles us to that judgement?

And marriage, of course, is only one of many issues. Those who have transitioned from one gender to another have a special concern about their legal status and personality. For someone born of one gender who has transitioned to another, what should it say on their passport or driving licence? (Why do we insist on putting someone's gender on their driving licence in any case? What possible purpose does it serve?) Which public bathrooms should someone in the process of transitioning be permitted, or required, to use? And consider someone with children who then transitions and divorces. Should their transitioning have any relevance to whether they should be granted custody? These are new questions that are only beginning to be discussed publicly and philosophically. Saying that we must overcome prejudice and recognize rights is easy. What that means in practice is always much more difficult.

Traditional values

At this point it may be understandable if someone were to object that this discussion of 'oversights' of justice has an oversight of its own. By focusing on the ways in which our institutions can be deeply unfair to individuals and groups we have concentrated solely on the assertion of individual rights and liberties. To do so is to pre-suppose a form of progressive liberalism in which it is taken for granted that our goal is to produce a fair society that is respectful to all, granting each person the right to live their life their own way on equals terms with all others. But as we discussed in Chapter 4, this is not the only way of looking at the relation between the individual and society, and liberalism can come under severe attack for ignoring other social values, especially those related to tradition and community.

Some people who oppose gay marriage, or feel that even raising the question of state approval of polygamous marriage goes beyond the bounds of decency, may well argue that the traditional value of the family provides a sound reason for refusing to extend the privilege of marriage to novel forms of relationship. It is important, those of a more conservative turn of mind will argue, that we follow the moral traditions of the past, otherwise we will lose our way. We will become rootless, lacking guidance in how to plan and live our lives, or what to expect from others. Change can be very harmful. Just as we should be very careful before we decide to bulldoze ancient buildings and construct new ones, we should be very careful before we tear up older moral traditions. Where progressive liberals see irrational prejudice to be broken down by enlightened reason, conservatives see great wisdom, painfully accumulated over the generations. Edmund Burke (1729–97), in his work *Reflections on the Revolution in France* (1790)—an attack on the French Revolution and the political ideas that led to it—argued against the domination of reason and theory in politics. Burke emphasized the importance of habits and traditions, which, although they may not be able to withstand criticism at the bar of reason, should not be expected to pass what he thought to be a quite inappropriate test. The theme was resumed in the twentieth century by Michael Oakeshott (1901–90) who, in various writings, including *Rationalism in Politics* (1962), argues that our traditions and inherited institutions contain more wisdom than we do and that it is both wrong and damaging to reform and rebuild except in the most slow and careful manner. On this view progressive liberal individualism is pernicious, with a mistaken view about what reason and argument in politics can achieve.

As is so often the case, it is possible to see merit on both sides. If everything had been left to custom and tradition we would not have made the emancipatory progress of the past fifty years. On the other hand, Burke and Oakeshott cannot be dismissed out of hand. We should have respect for the achievements of the past, and the humility to accept that we do not always know better. The analogy with architecture is a powerful warning: things are not bad just because they are old and would not be how we would choose to do them now. Getting the balance right will not be easy. Work needs to be done to decide which of the moral traditions of the past are still deserving of our respect, and which really are prejudices that we would be much better off without.

Oppression, knowledge, politics

Independently of the question of whether there has been an overly liberal emphasis to the discussion so far, it may have been thought that sometimes the discussion has taken place at a relatively superficial level. Yes, it will be agreed, women, minorities and people with disabilities face discrimination in the workplace and in some cases in the housing market. Marriage favours some types of relationship over others (or none at all). Yet these institutional forms of discrimination come nowhere near to characterizing the experience of members of marginalized groups. In its worst cases it is to be treated as a lesser person, or even an invisible non-person, as captured in the title of the absorbing and unsettling novel by the African-American writer Ralph Ellison, first published in 1952: *Invisible Man*. Experiencing one's life as a subject of discrimination and prejudice is much more than unfair. It can go to the core of your identity, undermining confidence in your abilities, or your belief in your right to participate in politics, or public discourse, or to attend 'elite' cultural events such as theatre or opera. The American feminist philosopher Iris Marion Young (1949–2006) has very helpfully set out what she calls the 'five faces of oppression'— exploitation, marginalization, powerlessness, cultural imperialism, and violence—all of which can be experienced to varying degrees by members of oppressed groups.

One way in which philosophers have been especially interested in how marginalization and powerlessness can come together is through practices of knowledge, creativity, and testimony. Women, even now, are often treated as unable or unlikely to make valuable contributions to group discussions, or even given credit when they do (as brilliantly demonstrated by a Rionna Duncan cartoon of a boardroom discussion in which the Chairman remarks 'That's an excellent suggestion Miss Triggs. Perhaps one of the men here would like to make it.'). Although no generalization in this area is likely to be universally true, there are certainly many times and many places when a middle-aged, middle-class white man is much more likely to be believed by the police or the law courts or others in authority than a young, working-class, black man, whatever the merits of what they have to say. When this becomes part of someone's regular experience, an accumulation of apparently rather minor episodes can create and reinforce marginalization and powerlessness. Oppression is not always, or even often, a deliberate conspiracy. It is in some ways like air pollution, the consequences of many individual, small actions.

If these structural factors create oppression for some, they create privilege for others. But those who benefit from privilege rarely see their success as a consequence of unfair structural features. Consider someone from a secure economic and social background who has benefited from an excellent education and has family contacts in the business world. Suppose they live in a country in the developed world, with a stable legal framework, and a growing and diverse economy. Under those conditions hard work may well bring success. Those who are successful may well put their success down entirely to their hard work, not noticing that with a different economic and social background, or living in a different type of country, their hard work may well have come to nothing. It can suit the privileged to have limited understanding about how their privileges came about. Others who struggle may have a much better perception of how things really are. The point was made, rather poetically, by W. E. D. Du Bois in *The Souls of Black Folk*, published in 1903. 'The Negro is ... born with a veil, and gifted with second-sight' (p. 8). The 'veil' refers to the ways in which African-Americans were treated as invisible in the United States, excluded from education and the professions and hence the opportunities to succeed. White Americans are then in a dilemma. Do they admit that their treatment of African-Americans is unjust? Or do they develop a set of views to 'justify' their privileged position, such as that whites are especially hard working, talented, or favoured by God? Du Bois's suggestion is that the dominant group, whichever it is, forms a set of myths to make themselves feel that their dominance is deserved. But the oppressed group can easily see through these myths. Hence oppression leads to 'second sight'. Similar arguments have been used to suggest that the proletariat (in Marxist thought) and women (in feminist thought) have greater insight into social injustice than their oppressors, and the argument can and has been generalized further. Disadvantage brings heightened perception of injustice.

This does not mean that everything that oppressed groups say about their oppression must be right and everything the privileged say to defend their privilege must be wrong. But it does give us a very interesting inversion of the debate. I began this part of the discussion by suggesting that women and minorities are very often excluded, in part at least, from the creation of knowledge or provision of testimony, being dismissed as less able to make a contribution. But we now see that in one sense at least oppressed people are privileged, for they have special insight into the false or misleading forms in which the dominant group justify their position. The political challenge is then to make that point persuasively and repeatedly, so that those in power take notice, and those who genuinely care about justification, not only power and protection of privilege, come to realize the injustice of the present situation. And this, of course, is the goal of political campaigning and activism.

Justice everywhere?

> The need of a constantly expanding market for its products chases the bourgeoisie over the entire surface of the globe. It must nestle everywhere, settle everywhere, establish connexions everywhere. (Karl Marx and Frederick Engels, *The Communist Manifesto* [1848])

Global justice

Up to this point, not just in this chapter but in the book as a whole, each issue has been discussed taking for granted that human beings live in different states, each with its own laws and social policies. We have looked at questions of how a state might justly distribute resources, powers, rights, and liberty. We have not, so far, had very much to say about relations between states or between different individuals in different states. Yet we live in an interconnected, increasingly globalized, world. Many people will live in more than one country in their lifetime. More significantly, perhaps, every day we use products that have their origin in many different countries. Even if you wear clothes produced in your country, and drive a car manufactured a hundred miles away, the chances are that the materials the clothes are made from, or many parts of that car, were made or designed by people living on the other side of the planet. When we think of the services we consume—medical care, banking, entertainment, sport—the globalization of our world is everywhere. Living purely on things that are made from items that are indigenous to your own region is barely conceivable. For example, unless you live in Peru or Bolivia you'd have to do without any product derived from the potato.

As soon as we start to think about our interconnected world several pressing questions of political philosophy also confront us. Here, though, we have space to raise and consider just two issues of serious current concern: first, the question of global justice, and, in the following section, immigration.

In Chapter 5, we looked at Jan Pen's income parade to illustrate the inequalities to be found even within one country. Imagine what it would be like if we were to run the parade on a global scale. Writers on global justice point out the extraordinary disparities of wealth in the world. The charity Oxfam claimed that in 2013 the richest eighty-five people in the world owned as much wealth as the bottom half put together. That bottom half amounts to around three-and-a-half billion people.

In current discussions about global justice there is general agreement on a number of points. The poorest people in the world, who mostly live in Africa and the poorest regions of Asia, survive on very little money. They are able to buy what a single dollar, or on some measures two dollars, would buy in the United States each day. Estimates vary about how many people live in these conditions, but on the higher poverty line of two dollars a day it may be more than two billion people, close to one-third of the world's population. Many of these people suffer from serious malnutrition. True, most, one way or another, will be able to obtain sufficient calories to live from day to day, but many will go to bed hungry and their diets will often lack the vitamins and other nutrients needed to keep healthy, or for children, to develop and thrive. No political philosopher seems to be happy with the fact that so many people live in such difficult circumstances, and it would be strange to think that anyone could be.

Philosophical disagreement, however, breaks out at two related levels. The first is how we should describe what is wrong with the global disparities between the super-rich and the extremely poor. The second is what sort of moral duty there is to do anything about it. Let us take the first question. The most obvious thing to say about the inequalities we have seen is that they are unjust. But there is more to the issue than meets the eye, and some philosophers, while being very sympathetic to the plight of the poor, have denied that global inequality and poverty are, strictly speaking, unjust. While they absolutely agree that rich people and nations should do much more to assist those in need around the world, they say that nevertheless failure to do so is not an injustice.

To understand this issue we need to explore the debate between what are called the 'cosmopolitans' and the 'nationalists'. Both terms, unfortunately, are rather misleading. In ordinary language a 'cosmopolitan' normally refers to some sort of sophisticated urbanite with a global outlook. The philosophical view also thinks of a cosmopolitan as a 'citizen of the world', but in this case it is a theory of justice rather than a lifestyle. A philosophical cosmopolitan, broadly, believes that principles of justice apply in the same way to everyone in the world. On this view national borders may be important historically and politically, for it may be impossible to organize a single world political system, but philosophically and morally they are of no fundamental significance. All human beings are equally human beings and we all owe the same moral obligations to everyone else in the world. Therefore rich people often have duties of justice to assist the very poor, wherever they live. Philosophical nationalists disagree. Philosophical nationalists are not all fiercely loyal to their own country, unlike 'nationalists' as the term is used in ordinary language. Rather they claim that there is, in fact, an important moral significance to national borders. Nationalists argue that most duties of justice apply only within a state. In any particular state the wealthy are likely to have duties of justice to help the poor, but between states, so they argue, this is not so (unless special circumstances apply—we will return to this). True, they say, the global wealthy do have moral duties to help the global poor. But generally these are duties of charity rather than justice.

Now you may think that it doesn't matter what we call our moral duties: both sides agree we are morally obliged to help the world's poorest people and so why worry whether they are duties of justice or charity? But one reason why it does matter is that typically different types of moral duty call for different types of action. Justice is often thought to give rise to duties that can be enforced against you, whereas duties of charity are generally regarded as voluntary. For example, within a state we are all subject to taxation, and a significant portion of the tax we pay goes to help support, or pay for services, used by people who are unable to support themselves. In effect, then, we accept that there are duties of justice that arise within a state and we use the institution of compulsory taxation to enforce those duties. Those who evade their taxes are fined, or even sent to prison. In many countries transfers from rich to poor are significant. Poorer people are provided with subsidized housing, free medical care, free education for their children, and money for food and clothes. But when we think about our duties to poor people who live in other countries it is, perhaps surprisingly, the nationalist position that reflects what most people think. Yes, we should help poor people wherever they live, but first, our duties to people who live outside our national borders are much less extensive than our duties to people who live in our own country, and second, it is up to each of us individually to decide whether and how much to give. It is not for the government to tax me to give to people living outside the country (apart perhaps from small amounts of foreign aid which could well be given for strategic, self-interested, reasons rather than reasons of justice).

This debate should make us feel rather uncomfortable. The nationalist position, though it is the position many adopt unthinkingly, seems rather narrow-minded, perhaps tinged with racism, or at least collective selfishness. On what basis can we justify privileging fellow citizens over other human beings who happen to live elsewhere in the world? But on the other hand, we are quite used to putting our friends and families before strangers. Perhaps national solidarity, built upon traditional values as discussed above, provides a similar justification for preferring co-citizens to those outside our borders. And furthermore, what is the cosmopolitan asking for? Should we, for example, argue that justice requires us to extend Rawls' Difference Principle (discussed in Chapter 5) to the world as a whole? That would mean we have a duty of justice to make the worst-off people in the world as well off as possible. It would seem to require a mind-boggling transfer of wealth from prosperous countries to the developing world. Even poor people in rich countries are, in terms of resources, part of the global elite, and therefore everyone in wealthy countries would be required to transfer a very significant portion of what they own and most of their income. Is that what justice requires?

Some will think that justice does indeed require huge transfers of wealth, and the fact that rich countries will not do this shows only that the world is deeply unjust. Others may take some comfort in the nationalist position, suggesting that failure to transfer resources is a defect of charity rather than justice, and we must redouble our efforts to bring people to understand our common humanity and moral duties. A third view is, however, becoming increasingly popular. It attempts to work out a compromise or middle way by which we do have duties of justice to people all over the world, but these duties are less extensive than, or at least different to, the duties of justice between citizens. For example, some may argue that globally there is a duty of justice to relieve malnutrition and to provide basic sanitation, medical care, and education for all, but it is not for the citizens of one country to provide unemployment benefit for the citizens of another. It is a subtle question to work out how and why we can have different levels and duties of justice to different groups, but it is not impossible. For example, it could be argued that the higher level of cooperation and interaction between citizens within a state creates more stringent conditions for justice than the looser relations that transcend state boundaries. If justice is relative to degrees of interaction, then there is a justification for different principles of justice to regulate different circumstances of interaction.

A supplementary approach to thinking about possible duties of justice between countries, or citizens in different countries, appeals to 'corrective' justice, or what Robert Nozick called 'justice in rectification'. After all, the difficult conditions in many poorer countries in the global South may well be a continued legacy of previous colonialism in which some countries were ruthlessly exploited by what are now much richer countries. If so, duties of justice may well fall on wealthy countries to compensate for damage done a few generations ago. Such duties of rectification might be recognized by the 'nationalist' as well as by the 'cosmopolitan'. Hence where action is a matter of recompense for past wrongs everyone can agree that the wealthy countries do have significant duties of justice. And the same argument applies if there are present wrongs too. It has been argued, for example, that rich countries have duties of justice to ensure that current terms of trade are fair to all parties, which is often not the case, as the wealthy countries can use their bargaining strength to obtain favourable trading conditions. Despite our 'nationalist' intuitions then, the cosmopolitans have a number of very strong points.

Nevertheless, it is not entirely clear what justice to the global poor requires in practice. Experience shows that transfer of resources from wealthy countries to poorer countries has not always turned out to be as effective in curing global poverty as was hoped. Enormous sums have been transferred, but in the worst cases it has led some countries to become highly dependent on foreign aid, rather than using aid as a pathway to development, which was the underlying intention. It seems that wealthy countries need to find ways to help poorer countries take control of their own fate, rather than relying on transfers. And here, it seems, the nationalist position, emphasizing the importance of national self-determination, also has something to offer too.

Immigration

Questions of global justice and redistribution are urgent and pressing. And many people's lives may well be improved as a result of wealth transfers or development programmes. Nevertheless, for a given individual the greatest transformation in life prospects will often be the result of leaving a poor country and moving to a wealthy one, whether legally or illegally. In the United States large numbers of people illegally try to cross the border from Mexico, often having travelled from further south, and in Europe and Australasia tens of thousands of people each year attempt hazardous sea journeys to move from Africa or Asia to wealthier countries, as well as crossing by land.

Current regulations around the world place tight restrictions on immigration. Most countries will accept political 'asylum seekers' if they can show that they are fleeing from danger of persecution in their home country. But in other cases immigration is much more limited, with countries offering work permits only to those who have some special skill, such as in medicine or engineering. While this is in the interests of those rich countries that do not train enough people to meet the demand for high-skilled professionals, it can be highly problematic for poorer countries, which will lose the people most desperately needed. These people will often have been trained at great public expense. Admittedly, people who move to wealthier countries often send back 'remittances' from their wages to their families, which will be of great benefit. But the point of training doctors is to have a medical workforce, not to receive a flow of income. Two pressing questions, then, are first, whether it is within the rights of wealthy countries to restrict entry in the way they do, trying to keep immigrants out of the country unless they have something special to offer; and second, whether poorer countries have the right to restrict emigration, for example, requiring that those trained at pubic expense remain to work in their country of origin at least for a certain period before they may leave.

To take first the question of immigration, the nationalist position, discussed above, has a relatively straightforward answer to the question of whom a country should allow to enter and live within its borders. A country's citizens have the right to control their particular territory and it should be a collective decision who can enter and who should not. It is part of the right to a country's self-determination for it to make up whatever rules on immigration suit it best. The cosmopolitan, though, is in a more delicate position. If national boundaries have no moral relevance, then moving from one country to another should be like moving from one town to another in the same country. This is how things are with regard to moving between states in the United States and in Australia, between provinces in Canada, or between countries in the European Union. On the cosmopolitan view it appears that this is how the world should be. On what basis can one group of people prevent another person from purchasing or renting property and coming to live in the part of the world in which that group happens to reside?

The cosmopolitan ideal, then, would seem to dismantle customs and immigration posts and to open up all borders. Yet could we really do that? Suppose, for example, the United States announced that anyone could come and live and work there without needing a permit or visa. The most immediate effect, most likely, would be a vast influx of people from poor and middle-income countries who, experience suggests, would be prepared to work for low wages and to live in very crowded conditions. This is likely to push wages down and rents up, which is good news for those who run businesses and own property but highly problematic for those already living in the United States, working for low pay and renting property, for they would be squeezed in both directions. There could also be problems about access to schools and medical care. Should the cosmopolitan simply respond that these adverse effects are the price of justice, and they fall on people who, in global terms, are relatively privileged, even if it doesn't feel like that to them? Or should the cosmopolitan make a distinction between the ideal state of affairs, and what we can achieve in the real world without causing huge disruption? The underlying problem is really the enormous disparity in life prospects in different parts of the world that makes migration so attractive to some. In other words, it is the problem of global inequality that causes the questions of immigration to be so difficult.

Global inequality also generates the separate and difficult question of whether a developing country should be permitted to impose conditions on exit. Refusing to let people leave the country has been a tactic of repressive states, such as the Soviet Union before the fall of communism. Hence in recent times there has been great support for the idea of freedom of movement, even to the point where it is regarded as a human right. But consider a low-income country with a grave shortage of doctors and nurses. In order to address that need the country trains students, at great expense, but as soon as they are trained the best may well be recruited by wealthier countries with a shortage of medical professionals. Should the newly qualified doctors and nurses be permitted to leave? On the one hand, it seems unacceptable to make individuals remain 'prisoners' in their own country, especially when their life prospects may be so much worse than they might be able to achieve elsewhere. On the other hand, if they have been trained at public expense then leaving right away, before giving something back, can surely be criticized. Perhaps anyone who receives training at public expense should sign a contract committing them to stay in the country for a certain period, or otherwise pay back the cost of the training. However, does this really solve the problem? The developing country needs professionals who will remain in the country for their working life, developing seniority and leadership positions in the community. Staying for five or even ten years will not achieve this, and receiving a refund of the cost of training, while better than nothing, is not what the country hoped to achieve by offering the training. It is very hard to devise a solution that seems fair to all.

Future generations

What do we owe to people who will come to inhabit the planet in the future but are not alive now? Interestingly, it does not seem that this has been a question much discussed in political philosophy until fairly recently. Of course, particular individuals have always been concerned about their legacy, in the sense of what property they will be able to leave to their children, or in the case of exceptional writers, artists, engineers, architects and other creative workers, what they may leave to posterity as a whole. But the question of what we as a society may leave for future generations was not widely debated by philosophers before the twentieth century. For much of human history it was probably assumed that life would simply continue much as it had. Eventually, the industrial revolution, starting in the late eighteenth century, introduced rapid economic growth and the assumption may well have changed to the belief that each generation will be richer than the previous one, and so the future will be well placed to look after itself. However, in the mid-twentieth century a new anxiety took hold. The process of industrialization, combined with the associated population explosion, uses up natural resources on an unprecedented scale, and spews out pollution that could endanger future life. The current concern, of course, is that the use of fossil fuels is leading to emissions of carbon dioxide—a 'greenhouse gas'—that is causing a general rise in global temperatures, to be experienced in different ways in different parts of the planet, but with potentially catastrophic effects on future human health and well-being. Some argue that we are already past the point of no return and climate change is certain to have very significant effects. Of course, there are some who deny that climate change is taking place, or if it is that humans are the cause, but among scientists who study the climate in detail there is very broad consensus that 'anthropocentric'—i.e. human-caused—climate change is taking place and steps need to be taken to deal with it.

This is tricky terrain for philosophers. Suppose there is scientific agreement that climate change is taking place, largely as a result of the rapid development of wealthy countries, and at the expense of poorer people living on land that, for the next generation, will not be able to sustain agriculture or even human settlement. What should be done? We can divide the difficulties into two. First, scientifically, what are our options? And second, from a moral and political point of view, which are the right options to follow?

To take the first question, there are broadly three types of scientific view. The most pessimistic scenario is that we are now stuck with irreversible climate change, in that we have passed a tipping point. In that case our only options are to prepare for, and adapt to, a difficult future. In our coming world food and water supplies across the globe will be put in jeopardy. Rising sea levels from melting polar ice will cause catastrophic flooding in vulnerable coastal areas in countries such as Bangladesh and the Philippines, and will devastate smaller island countries such as the Maldives. It may even lead to the loss of parts of major low-lying cities, including London and New York. If so, then the future will be one of attempted mass migration of people, and possibly violent conflict over the occupation of the remaining hospitable land. It is, though, very hard to predict likely future weather patterns. For example, it is thought by some experts that as global temperatures rise, the Gulf Stream in the Atlantic Ocean that warms northern Europe will be knocked off course or disappear. If so, temperatures in northern Europe will remain stable, or even fall, while the rest of the world warms, and Europe will be the target of mass immigration. But at this point such predictions are pure speculation and many different effects seem possible. It is hard, therefore, to provide a philosophical response to unknown problems.

If the first approach suggested, pessimistically, that we are past a tipping point, then the second approach, optimistically, assumes that human ingenuity will come up with some sort of 'technological fix'. On this view we can simply carry on 'business as usual' and scientists will come to our rescue. Some technologies under discussion at the moment are 'carbon capture', which takes carbon dioxide out of the atmosphere. Far-fetched as this may sound, one suggestion is to put iron filings in the sea to stimulate the growth of algae that will absorb carbon dioxide and then die and sink to the bottom of the ocean. A different type of proposal is to spray sulphur dioxide into the atmosphere to reflect back sunlight and act as a type of filter. However, these technologies are very controversial. Even if they work they may also have unwelcome side-effects which do more harm than good, as we have seen with the 'technological miracles' of asbestos, which was used to fireproof buildings but turned out to be a deadly health hazard, and chlorofluorocarbons (CFCs), which were widely used in new air conditioning and refrigeration technologies, but were then found to destroy the ozone layer in the atmosphere. Technological solutions may appeal to those who greatly admire scientific progress, but must be handled with great care.

A third view is that we can, and must, reduce carbon emissions. After all, if carbon emissions cause climate change, then doesn't it stand to reason that reducing carbon emissions will reduce, even reverse, climate change? But it is not so simple, for it might already be too late, as the first scenario assumed. To argue that reducing carbon emissions will be beneficial in addressing climate change assumes, then, we are still at a point where the effects are reversible. But perhaps we are lucky and reducing carbon emissions will still have a beneficial effect; this, anyway, is the basis of the major international discussions about how to address climate change. Currently, the primary focus is setting a target for reduction of emissions, and agreeing which countries have the greatest responsibility to bear the greatest burdens.

Morally it seems clear that the highest responsibilities for reducing emissions should fall on residents of the most developed nations. First, they are currently the highest emitters, per capita. Some developed countries emit more than a hundred times as much carbon per person than some sub-Saharan African countries, and hence these countries have by far the greatest capacity to make substantial reductions in their use. Second, residents of wealthy countries have benefited the most from the use of fossil fuels and have a moral duty to 'pay back' for the harm done as a result. Third, only the wealthy countries can afford to take the necessary cut in their standard of living, by reducing energy use in their homes, workplaces, and transport systems, to the degree necessary to make significant inroads on carbon emissions. In fact, many argue that the poorer countries should be allowed to increase their emissions, as doing so is a necessary correlate of development.

The moral arguments seem compelling. The political challenges of implementing them, though, are immense. Can we really imagine wealthy nations electing into government a political party that promises to cut their living standards, if another political party offers to keep things as they are? If climate change is the threat many scientists think it is, then we may need to go back to the themes of Chapter 3. Is democracy—at least in the forms we currently know it—the right approach to political decision making in the face of a looming crisis? Is there an acceptable alternative approach? At the very least we need to think of ways of encouraging the electorate to think in terms not just of their own interests but those of future generations.

Final word

I hope to have conveyed in this book some of the reasons why political philosophy has been an object of study and fascination for 2,500 years. But I also hope to have made clear that it is far from complete. There are unsolved problems and unexplored byways at every turn. Does this mean we can never make any progress? That, I think, is more pessimistic a view than is warranted. One type of progress, perhaps a discouraging form, is to discover new problems, such as those discussed in this chapter, that have been unseen by previous theorists. A more encouraging form of progress is to find new arguments for and against positions to help address and reflect on the problems that concern us most. That is what the best philosophers have done through the ages, as I hope to have demonstrated in this book. But it is one thing to reflect on problems, it is another to solve them. Are solutions possible? Mill claimed that for the most fundamental questions in political philosophy 'considerations may be presented capable of determining the intellect either to give or withhold its assent to the doctrine', which is surely correct. He went on to add, rather hopefully, that 'this is equivalent to proof' (*Utilitarianism*, 184). Yet it is unclear how. Mill himself, in *On*

Liberty, argued that considerations seen at one time as decisive can later be overturned by more powerful considerations in favour of an opposing view. Thus while there can be more and less plausible positions and arguments, there can be no final word in political philosophy. Still, for the time being, this is where we shall end.

GUIDE TO FURTHER READING

A list of the principal works discussed in this book appears at the end of this guide.

Preface

As indicated in the Preface, this book is not meant to be a systematic account of the present state of play in political philosophy, nor a scholarly history of the subject. But there are excellent books that do these things. Of the many introductions to contemporary political philosophy I would particularly recommend: Will Kymlicka, *Contemporary Political Philosophy: An Introduction* (2nd edn, Oxford: Oxford University Press, 2002) and Adam Swift, *Political Philosophy: A Beginners, Guide for Students and Politicians* (3rd edn, Oxford: Polity, 2013) as well as David Miller, *Political Philosophy: A Very Short Introduction* (Oxford: Oxford University Press, 2003), which, though very short, covers historical as well as contemporary issues. *A Companion to Contemporary Political Philosophy*, ed. Robert E. Goodin and Philip Pettit (2nd edn, Oxford: Blackwell, 2006), contains many useful introductory articles. An excellent introduction to the history of political theory is Iain Hampsher-Monk, *A History of Modern Political Thought* (Oxford: Blackwell, 1992), providing reliable and readable accounts of the views of many of the philosophers discussed here, including Hobbes, Locke, Rousseau, Marx, and Mill. Selections from the texts of most of the philosophers discussed in detail here are included in Michael Rosen and Jonathan Wolff (eds), *Political Thought* (Oxford: Oxford University Press, 1999).

Introduction

The citation to Thucydides' *The Peleponnesian War* is from the 1973 Penguin edition. Locke's definition of political power is from his *Second Treatise* (see full reference below). The quotation from Engels is from his *Socialism: Utopian and Scientific*, available in many editions of Marx/Engels selected works, as well as from the astonishing internet archive <http://www.marxists.org>.

Chapter 1

The citation from William Golding's *Lord of the Flies* is taken from the 1954 Penguin edition. Aristotle's views on human beings as 'political animals' are set out in his *Politics* Book 1, of which there are many editions, including that from Oxford (Oxford University Press, 2009).

Many editions of Hobbes's *Leviathan* are available. References in the text are to the edition by C. B. MacPherson ([1651], Harmondsworth: Penguin, 1968). For an introduction to Hobbes, see Richard Tuck, *Hobbes: A Very Short Introduction* (Oxford: Oxford University Press, 2002) and Glen Newey, *The Routledge Guidebook to Hobbes' Leviathan* (2nd edn, Abingdon: Routledge, 2014). More advanced, but highly recommended, is Jean Hampton, *Hobbes and the Social Contract Tradition* (Cambridge: Cambridge University Press, 1986).

References to Locke are to *Two Treatises of Government*, ed. Peter Laslett ([1689], student edn, Cambridge: Cambridge University Press, 1988). References in the present book give section as well as page numbers, for users of other editions. David Lloyd Thomas, *Locke on Government* (London: Routledge, 1995) is an excellent introduction to Locke's political thought.

The works of Rousseau used throughout this book are taken from the Cambridge University Press two-volume set, edited by Victor Gourevitch (1997). References to *The Discourse on the Arts and Sciences* and *The Discourse on Inequality* are taken from Rousseau, *The Discourse and other Early Political Writings* (Cambridge: Cambridge University Press, 1997), while references to *Discourse on Political Economy* and *The Social Contract* are taken from *The Social Contract and other Later Political Writings* (Cambridge: Cambridge University Press 1997). Page numbers given are taken from these editions (in the case of *The Social Contract*, book and chapter numbers are also provided). This edition contains all of Rousseau's major philosophical works, with the exception of *Émile*, which is available in several editions. On Rousseau, see also Christopher Bertram, *Rousseau and 'The Social Contract'* (London: Routledge, 2003) and Joshua Cohen, *Rousseau: A Free Community of Equals* (Oxford: Oxford University Press, 2010).

An account of societies without the state is contained in Harold Barclay, *People Without Government* (London: Kahn & Averill, 1990). Many discussions of the prisoner's dilemma are available. A good introduction to this and related issues is Jon Elster, *Nuts and Bolts for the Social Sciences* (Cambridge: Cambridge University Press, 1989) (the Sartre example is taken from Elster). George Woodcock (ed.), *The Anarchist Reader* (Glasgow: Fontana, 1977) contains an interesting selection of anarchist writings, including portions of William Godwin, *Enquiry Concerning Political Justice* (1793), and Peter Kropotkin, *Mutual Aid* (1902). Full-length reprints of these two works are: Godwin,

Enquiry Concerning Political Justice, ed. Isaac Kramnick (Harmondsworth: Penguin, 1976); Kropotkin, *Mutual Aid,* ed. Paul Avrich (London: Allen Lane, 1972). A useful survey of positions is contained in David Miller, *Anarchism* (London: Dent, 1984).

Chapter 2

The page references to John Stuart Mill's *On Liberty* are to the very convenient edition of *Utilitarianism and Other Writings,* ed. Mary Warnock ([1859], 2nd edn, Oxford: Blackwell, 2003). The references to Locke are again to the Laslett edition of the *Two Treatises.* Bentham's utilitarianism is set out in his *Introduction to the Principles of Morals and Legislation,* ed. J. H. Burns and H. L. A. Hart (Oxford: Oxford University Press, 1996). The first five chapters of this are printed in the Mary Warnock edition of Mill, and there are now many other editions of this text.

Max Weber's definition of the state is presented in his paper 'Politics as a Vocation', which is widely available, for example in *From Max Weber,* trans. H. Gerth and C. W. Mills ([1946], London: Routledge, 2009), 77–127.

Two excellent general treatments of the problem of political obligation are A. John Simmons, *Moral Principles and Political Obligations* (Princeton, NJ: Princeton University Press, 1979) and John Horton, *Political Obligation* (2nd edn, London: Palgrave MacMillan, 2010). Simmons defends 'philosophical anarchism', as does R. P. Wolff in *In Defense of Anarchism* (New York: Harper, 1973). A defence of consent theory is Harry Beran, *The Consent Theory of Political Obligation* (London: Croom Helm, 1987).

The theory of participatory democracy is defended by Carole Pateman in two works: *Participation and Democratic Theory* (Cambridge: Cambridge University Press, 1970) and *The Problem of Political Obligation* (Oxford: Polity Press, 1985).

The quotation concerning tacit consent from Hume is from 'Of the Original Contract', in his *Essays Moral Political and Literary,* ed. E. F. Miller ([1748], Indianapolis: Liberty Press, 1985), 465–87, and the citation from Rousseau is from *The Social Contract,* in the Cambridge edition of *The Social Contract and Later Political Writings,* ed. Gourevitch ([1762], Cambridge: Cambridge University Press, 1997).

H. L. A. Hart presented the theory of fairness in his paper 'Are There Any Natural Rights?', reprinted in J. Waldron (ed.), *Theories of Rights* ([1955], Oxford: Oxford University Press, 1984). It has received book-length defence in George Klosko, *The Principle of Fairness and Political Obligation* (Lanham, MD: Rowman and Littlefield, 1992). Nozick's objections are set out in his *Anarchy,*

State, and Utopia (Oxford: Blackwell, 1974), and are discussed by Simmons and Horton in their books mentioned above.

Bentham's theory appears in *A Fragment on Government*, ed. Ross Harrison ([1776], Cambridge: Cambridge University Press, 1988). A good discussion of utilitarianism is J. J. C. Smart and Bernard Williams, *Utilitarianism, For and Against* (Cambridge: Cambridge University Press, 1973). The case of the Birmingham six is discussed in detail in Chris Mullin, *Error of Judgement* (rev. edn, Dublin: Poolbeg Press, 1990). For excellent discussion of Mill's *Utilitarianism*, see Roger Crisp, *Mill on Utilitarianism* (London: Routledge, 1997). Richard Layard's *Happiness* (2nd edn, London: Penguin, 2011), is a modern attempt to revive utilitarianism, drawing on contemporary methods for measuring happiness.

In addition to the essay 'Of the Original Contract', referred to above, Hume discusses justice and political obligation in Book III of his *A Treatise of Human Nature*, ed. L. A. Selby-Bigge ([1739–40], 2nd edn, Oxford: Oxford University Press, 1978). See also his *An Enquiry Concerning the Principle of Morals* in his *Enquiries*, ed. L. A. Selby-Bigge (3rd edn, Oxford: Oxford University Press, 1975).

Chapter 3

Philosophical treatments of democracy include Ross Harrison, *Democracy* (London: Routledge, 1993), Thomas Christiano, *The Rule of the Many* (Boulder, CO: Westview Press, 1996) and David Estlund, *Democratic Authority* (Princeton, NJ: Princeton University Press, 2007). Also useful is David Held, *Models of Democracy* (Cambridge: Polity, 1987) and Keith Graham, *The Battle of Democracy* (Brighton: Wheatsheaf, 1986). A more detailed development of some of the themes of this chapter is contained in Jeremy Waldron, 'Rights and Majorities: Rousseau Revisited', in his *Liberal Rights* (Cambridge: Cambridge University Press, 1993), 392–421.

Many editions of Plato's *Republic* are available. The citations here are from H. P. D. Lee's edition ([380–360 BCE], Harmondsworth: Penguin, 1955). However, a standard numbering system is used when referring to Plato's works and I have given the reference so that the passages can be identified in other editions. A famous extended attack on Plato's view is Karl Popper, *The Open Society and Its Enemies*, I (London: Routledge, 1945). An excellent introduction to *The Republic* as a whole is Nickolas Pappas, *Plato: The Republic* (2nd edn, London: Routledge, 2003). Condorcet's argument is summarized in Brian Barry, 'The Public Interest', in A. Quinton (ed.), *Political Philosophy* (Oxford: Oxford University Press, 1967), 112–26, and set out in detail in Duncan Black, *The Theory of Committees and Elections* (Cambridge: Cambridge University Press,

1958). It is also discussed in the books by Christiano, Estlund, and Harrison mentioned above. The 'trade union' examples, illustrating the idea of the 'General Will', are adapted from Barry's paper.

References to Rousseau's *Social Contract* and *A Discourse on Political Economy* are once more to the Cambridge 1997 edition by Gourevitch. Mary Wollstonecraft's *Vindication of the Rights of Women* is available edited by Miriam Brody (rev. edn, Harmondsworth: Penguin, 2004). The distinction between positive and negative freedom is famously discussed by Isaiah Berlin in 'Two Concepts of Liberty', in his *Liberty* ([1958], 2nd edn, Oxford: Clarendon Press, 2002), 166–217. It is reprinted, with other relevant papers, including Gerald MacCallum's paper 'Negative and Positive Liberty', which proposed the 'three-place' analysis of freedom, in *Liberty* (ed.) David Miller (Oxford: Oxford University Press, 1991). Berlin's essay makes several of the criticisms of Rousseau pointed out here. MacCallum's paper was first published in *The Philosophical Review* 76 (1967): 312–34. The works of Carole Pateman on participatory democracy (cited above) are also particularly relevant, and deliberative democracy is discussed in the general texts on democracy listed above. Mill's position is set out in *Considerations on Representative Government* (1861). It is very widely available. Page numbers are given to the edition published in *Utilitarianism, On Liberty and Considerations on Representative Government*, ed. H. B. Acton (London: Dent, 1972).

Chapter 4

References to Mill's *On Liberty* and *Utilitarianism* are again to the Mary Warnock edition of *Utilitarianism*. An excellent discussion of Mill's position is contained in the essays in *J. S. Mill On Liberty In Focus*, ed. John Gray and G. W. Smith (London: Routledge, 1991). For a treatment of Mill's political ideas in the broader context of his thought, see John Skorupski, *John Stuart Mill* (London: Routledge, 1989) and, for a briefer presentation, John Skorupski, *Why Read Mill Today?* (London: Routledge, 2006). The reference to Rousseau is again to the Cambridge edition by Gourevitch of *The Social Contract and Later Political Writings*. Mill's defence of freedom of thought is critically discussed in detail by R. P. Wolff, *The Poverty of Liberalism* (Boston, MA: Beacon Press, 1968). The 'rich aunt' example is taken from David Lloyd Thomas, 'Rights, Consequences, and Mill on Liberty', in *Of Liberty*, ed. A. Phillips Griffiths (Cambridge: Cambridge University Press, 1983), 167–80. Bentham's attack on natural rights is set out in his 'Anarchical Fallacies', reprinted in *Nonsense on Stilts*, ed. Jeremy Waldron (London: Methuen, 1987), which also contains the cited text 'Supply without Burthen'. As well as a good general discussion of the concept of a right, this volume also contains a version of Marx's 'On the Jewish Question', which is also widely available in anthologies of Marx's writings. Particularly recommended is *Karl Marx: Selected Writings*, ed. D. McLellan (2nd edn, Oxford: Oxford University Press, 2000), from which citations of 'On the Jewish Question' in the present book are taken. For an introduction to Karl Marx, see my *Why Read Marx Today?* (Oxford: Oxford University Press, 2002).

Henry Sidgwick's position is set out in his *The Methods of Ethics* (London: Macmillan, 1907), of which many reprints are available. The term 'government-house utilitarianism' comes from the introduction to Amartya Sen and Bernard Williams (eds), *Utilitarianism and Beyond* (Cambridge: Cambridge University Press, 1982). James Fitzjames Stephen, *Liberty, Equality, Fraternity* is available in a reprint ([1873], Chicago: Chicago University Press, 1991), as well as several other editions. Patrick Devlin's 'Morals and the Criminal Law', first published in 1958, is reprinted in his *The Enforcement of Morals* (Oxford: Oxford University Press, 1965) and has been critically discussed by H. L. A. Hart in *Law, Liberty, and Morality* (London: Oxford University Press, 1963). For the communitarian critiques of liberalism, see the essays in *Communitarianism and Individualism*, ed. Shlomo Avineri and Avner de-Shalit (Oxford: Oxford University Press, 1992), especially those of Michael Sandel, Charles Taylor, Alisdair MacIntyre, and Michael Walzer, the philosophical founders of modern communitarianism. Michael Sandel, *Liberalism and Limits of Justice* (2nd edn, Cambridge: Cambridge University Press, 1998) is an influential full-length presentation of a communitarian position, concentrating on criticism of John Rawls, *A Theory of Justice* ([1971], rev. edn, Oxford: Oxford University Press, 1999). See also Stephen Mulhall and Adam Swift, *Liberals and Communitarians: An Introduction* (2nd edn, Oxford: Blackwell Publishers, 1996).

Chapter 5

The quotation from Hume's *Second Enquiry* is from the Selby-Bigge edition. Mill's *Chapters on Socialism* is available in *On Liberty and Other Writings*, ed. Stefan Collini (Cambridge: Cambridge University Press, 1989). Nozick's *Anarchy, State, and Utopia* is discussed at length in my own *Robert Nozick: Property, Justice and the Minimal State* (Cambridge: Polity, 1991). See also G. A. Cohen, *Self-Ownership, Freedom, and Equality* (Cambridge: Cambridge University Press, 1995), and the essays in Jeffrey Paul (ed.), *Reading Nozick* (Oxford: Blackwell, 1982). References in the present volume to Rawls, *A Theory of Justice* give page numbers for both the original 1971 edition and the revised 1999 edition, with the latter in square brackets. An excellent collection of essays on Rawls, *A Theory of Justice* is Norman Daniels (ed.), *Reading Rawls* (Oxford: Blackwell, 1975; reissued

Stanford, CA.: Stanford University Press, 1989). Rawls went on to publish other important works, including *Political Liberalism* (New York: Columbia University Press, 1993; expanded edn, 2005), and *Justice as Fairness: A Restatement* (Cambridge, MA: Harvard University Press, 2001). An excellent guide to Rawls is Samuel Freeman, *Rawls* (London: Routledge, 2007).

Jan Pen's *Income Distribution* is published by Penguin (1971). Much more up-to- date income distribution figures are presented by Thomas Piketty, *Capital in the Twenty-First Century* (Cambridge, MA: Harvard University Press, 2014). The quotation from Rousseau is again taken from the Cambridge edition of *The Discourses and other Earlier Political Writings*. Locke's discussion of property is contained in Chapter 5 of his *Second Treatise* (citations from the Laslett edition). Useful treatments of the topic of property rights are Lawrence C. Becker, *Property Rights* (Boston, MA: Routledge & Kegan Paul, 1977) and Jeremy Waldron, *The Right to Private Property* (Oxford: Oxford University Press, 1990).

A good general philosophical discussion of the market is Allen Buchanan, *Ethics, Efficiency and the Market* (Totowa, NJ: Rowman & Allanheld, 1985). It contains a useful brief summary of F. A. von Hayek's position, which is set out by Hayek at great length in various writings, but especially in *The Constitution of Liberty* ([1960], rev. edn, London: Routledge, 2006). The writings of Milton Friedman are more accessible: see particularly his *Capitalism and Freedom* (rev. edn, Chicago: Chicago University Press, 2002), and (jointly written with Rose Friedman), *Free to Choose* (Harmondsworth: Penguin, 1980). John Kay's *The Truth About Markets* (London: Allen Lane, 2003) is a very interesting and accessible account of the strengths and weaknesses of markets. A discussion of Marx's reasons for advocating the planned economy is contained in my book *Why Read Marx Today?* (Oxford: Oxford University Press, 2002). Engels's *Speeches in Elberfeld* are reprinted in K. Marx, F. Engels, and V. I. Lenin, *On Communist Society* ([1845], Moscow: Progress Press, 1974). The edition of Marx cited is *Early Writings*, ed. Lucio Colletti (Harmondsworth: Penguin, 1975).

The quotation from Adam Smith is from *The Wealth of Nations*, first published in 1776 (Harmondsworth: Penguin, 1970), although many other versions are available. The quotation from Alec Nove's *The Economics of Feasible Socialism* is from the first edition (London: George Allen & Unwin, 1983). A second edition is entitled *The Economics of Feasible Socialism Revisited* (London: HarperCollins, 1991).

The main source for Marx's writings on alienation is his 1844 *Economic and Philosophical Manuscripts*, especially the 'Alienated Labour' manuscript. This is available in many editions: for example, in the two collections already mentioned above, *Karl Marx: Selected Writings*, ed. D. McLellan (2000) and *Early Writings*, ed. Lucio Colletti (1985). On the phenomenon of 'de-skilling' under capitalism, see Henry Braverman, *Labor and Monopoly Capitalism* (New York: Monthly Review Press, 1974). The reference to Engels's work *The Condition of the Working Class in England*, first published in 1845, is taken from *Marx and Engels on Britain* (Moscow: Marx-Engels-Lenin-Stalin Institute, 1953). Other editions are also available, including electronically from <http://www.marxists.org>.

Many of the objections to Rawls are raised in the collection edited by Norman Daniels, referred to above. See in particular the papers by Ronald Dworkin (cited in the text), Thomas Nagel, and Thomas Scanlon. The idea of the 'social minimum' is usefully discussed in Jeremy Waldron's 'John Rawls and the Social Minimum' in his collection *Liberal Rights*, 250–70. For versions of 'left-wing libertarianism' see Hillel Steiner, *An Essay on Rights* (Oxford: Blackwell, 1994) and Michael Otsuka, *Libertarianism Without Inequality* (Oxford: Oxford University Press, 2003).

Chapter 6

A good introduction to the diversity of feminist political thought is contained in Jane J. Mansbridge and Susan Moller Okin, 'Feminism', in *A Companion to Contemporary Political Philosophy*, eds Robert E. Goodin and Philip Pettit (Oxford: Blackwell, 1993). This also contains a substantial bibliography. Will Kymlicka's *Introduction to Contemporary Political Philosophy* includes a (partly) sympathetic response to feminist thought from a liberal perspective. Simone De Beauvoir's quotation is from *The Second Sex* (London: Vintage Classics, 1997). Carole Pateman's observation about credit is made in her excellent exchange with Charles Mills: C. Pateman and C. Mills, *Contract and Domination* (Cambridge: Polity, 2007). Pateman and Mills both examine the theory of the social contract, as discussed here in Chapter 2, from the point of view of feminist and critical race theory, making many important arguments about how the contract tradition has typically ignored women and people of minority races. They also provide very interesting historical and sociological background information on questions of gender and race. The pay gap figures come from the Office of National Statistics, *Annual Survey of Hours and Earnings* (<http://www.ons.gov.uk>) and are regularly updated. Susan Moller Okin, *Justice, Gender and the Family* (New York: Basic Books, 1989) is a much-discussed liberal feminist position.

Useful anthologies of feminist writings include Janet A. Kourany, James P. Sterba, and Rosemarie Tong (eds), *Feminist Philosophies* (Hemel Hempstead: Harvester Wheatsheaf, 1993), Nancy Tuana and Rosemarie Tong (eds), *Feminism and Philosophy* (Boulder, CO: Westview Press, 1995), and Ann Cudd and Robin Andreasen (eds), *Feminist Theory: A Philosophical Anthology* (Oxford:

Wiley-Blackwell, 2004). Susan Moller Okin, *Women in Western Political Thought* (Princeton, NJ: Princeton University Press, 1979) is a very interesting account of the place of women in the thought of Plato, Aristotle, Rousseau, and Mill. See also Okin's *Justice, Gender and the Family*. Martha Nussbaum's *Women and Human Development* (Cambridge: Cambridge University Press, 2001) looks at issues of gender equality in the context of the developing world.

One of the best discussions of affirmative action is Thomas E. Hill Jr, 'The Message of Affirmative Action', in his *Autonomy and Self-Respect* (Cambridge: Cambridge University Press, 1991). Elizabeth Anderson's *The Imperative of Integration* (Princeton, NJ: Princeton University Press, 2010), which is the source for her defence of the policy of integration discussed in the text, also has a sophisticated discussion of affirmative action.

Kwame Anthony Appiah's *Lines of Descent: W. E. B. Du Bois and the Emergence of Identity*, from which the first Du Bois quotation is taken, is published by Harvard University Press (2014). It is a highly readable, brief account of Du Bois's remarkable life, set in the context of his intellectual formation in Germany and the United States, and also contains a useful summary of biological work on race. Bernard Boxill (ed.), *Race and Racism* (Oxford: Oxford University Press 2001) is a very good philosophical anthology of writings on race. Boxill's introduction also examines the debates about the concept of race and its history.

A very good introduction to the academic study of disability is Tom Shakespeare, *Disability Rights and Wrongs Revisited* (2nd edn, London: Routledge, 2013). I also recommend Anita Silvers, David Wasserman, and Mary Mahowald, *Disability, Difference, Discrimination* (Lanham, MD: Rowman & Littlefield, 1998). My *Ethics and Public Policy* (London: Routledge, 2011) has a chapter on disability. The study comparing the experience of disability in Australia and Cameroon is P. Allotey, P. D. Reidpath, A. Kouamé, & R. Cummins, 'The DALY, Context and the Determinants of the Severity of Disease: An Exploratory Comparison of Paraplegia in Australia and Cameroon', *Social Science and Medicine* 57(2003): 949–58.

Stephen Macedo's *Just Married: Same-Sex Couples, Monogamy, and the Future of Marriage* (Princeton, NJ: Princeton University Press, 2015) covers in much greater detail the issues concerning gay marriage touched on here. Burke's *Reflections on the Revolution in France* is available in a 1968 Penguin edition, among others. Michael Oakeshott's *Rationalism in Politics* is published by Methuen (1962). Also see Roger Scruton, *The Meaning of Conservatism* (3rd edn, London: Macmillan, 2001).

Many editions of Ralph Ellison's *Invisible Man* are available, including Penguin (2014). Iris Marion Young's 'five faces of oppression' are set out in her *Justice and the Politics of Difference* (Princeton, NJ: Princeton University Press,

1990). On the relationships between power, knowledge, and justice see Miranda Fricker, *Epistemic Injustice* (Oxford: Oxford University Press, 2007). W. E. B. Du Bois, *The Souls of Black Folk*, is available in an edition published in the Oxford World Classics series (Oxford: Oxford University Press, 2007).

Marx and Engels' *Communist Manifesto* is available in dozens of different editions, including freely from the website <http://www.marxists.org>. The Oxfam report is called *Wealth: Having it All and Wanting More*, and is downloadable from the Oxfam website: <http://policy-practice.oxfam.org.uk/publications/wealth-having-it-all-and-wanting-more-338125/>. A classic text on global justice is Thomas Pogge, *World Poverty and Human Rights* (Oxford: Polity, 2007). For an excellent guide to the debates, see Gillian Brock, *Global Justice: A Cosmopolitan Account* (Oxford: Oxford University Press, 2009). Versions of 'nationalist' positions are defended by John Rawls, *The Law of Peoples* (Cambridge, MA: Harvard University Press, 2001), David Miller, *National Responsibility and Global Justice* (Oxford: Oxford University Press, 2007), and Yael Tamir, *Liberal Nationalism* (Princeton, NJ: Princeton University Press, 1995). The reference to Robert Nozick is again to *Anarchy, State, and Utopia*. Paul Collier, *The Bottom Billion* (Oxford: Oxford University Press, 2008), discusses the effectiveness of different forms of aid, and Dambisa Moya's *Dead Aid* (London: Penguin, 2010) is a controversial book by a Zambian-born economist arguing for the end of aid in some of its current forms.

On immigration, see Joseph Carens, *The Ethics of Immigration* (Oxford: Oxford University Press, 2013). On duties to future generations, see Avner de-Shalit, *Why Posterity Matters* (London: Routledge, 1993). John Broome, *Climate Matters* (New York: W. W. Norton, 2014) is an up-to-date account of the ethics of climate change. See also Anthony Costello, Mustafa Abbas, Adriana Allen et al 'Managing The Health Effect of Climate Change', *The Lancet* 373 (2009): 1693–733.

Principal works discussed in the text

BENTHAM, JEREMY, *Anarchical Fallacies, and Supply Without Burthen* in *Nonsense on Stilts*, ed. Jeremy Waldron ([1795], London: Methuen, 1987).

——, *An Introduction to the Principles of Morals and Legislation*, ed. J. H. Burns and H. L. A. Hart ([1781], London: Methuen, 1982).

——, *A Fragment on Government*, ed. Ross Harrison ([1776], Cambridge: Cambridge University Press, 1988).

BERLIN, ISAIAH, 'Two Concepts of Liberty', in his *Liberty* ([1958], 2nd edn, Oxford: Clarendon Press, 2002), 116–217.

HART, H. L. A., 'Are There Any Natural Rights?', repr. in J. Waldron (ed.), *Theories of Rights* ([1955], Oxford: Oxford University Press, 1984), 77–90.

HOBBES, THOMAS, *Leviathan*, ed. C. B. MacPherson ([1651], Harmondsworth: Penguin, 1968).

HUME, DAVID, *An Enquiry Concerning the Principles of Morals*, in *Enquiries*, ed. L. A. Selby-Bigge ([1751], Oxford: Oxford University Press, 3rd edn., 1975), 169-313.

——, *A Treatise of Human Nature*, ed. L. A. Selby-Bigge ([1739–40], 2nd edn, Oxford: Oxford University Press, 1978).

——, 'Of the Original Contract', in *Essays Moral, Political and Literary*, ed. E. F. Miller ([1748], Indianapolis, IN: Liberty Press, 1985), 465–487.

KROPOTKIN, PETER, *Mutual Aid*, ed. Paul Avrich ([1902], London: Allen Lane, 1972).

LOCKE, JOHN, *Two Treatises of Government*, ed. Peter Laslett ([1689], student edn, Cambridge: Cambridge University Press, 1988).

MARX, KARL, *Early Writings*, ed. Lucio Colletti ([1843], Harmondsworth: Penguin, 1975).

——, 'On the Jewish Question', in *Karl Marx: Selected Writings*, ed. D. McLellan (2nd edn, Oxford: Oxford University Press, 2000).

MILL, JOHN STUART, 'Considerations on Representative Government', in *Utilitarianism*, ed. H. B. Acton ([1861], London: Dent, 1972).

——, *Chapters on Socialism*, in *On Liberty and Other Writings*, ed. Stefan Collini ([1879], Cambridge: Cambridge University Press, 1989).

——, '*On Liberty*', in *Utilitarianism and Other Writings*, ed. Mary Warnock ([1859], 2nd edn, Glasgow: Collins, 2003).

——, '*Utilitarianism*', in *Utilitarianism and Other Writings*, ed. Mary Warnock ([1861], 2nd edn, Glasgow: Collins, 2003).

NOZICK, ROBERT, *Anarchy, State, and Utopia* (Oxford: Blackwell, 1974).

PLATO, *The Republic*, ed. H. P. D. Lee ([380–360BCE], Harmondsworth: Penguin, 1955).

RAWLS, JOHN, *Political Liberalism* (New York: Columbia University Press, 1993).

——, *A Theory of Justice* ([1971], rev. edn. Oxford: Oxford University Press, 1999).

ROUSSEAU, JEAN-JACQUES, *Émile* ([1762], London: Everyman, 1974).

——, *The Discourse and other Early Political Writings*, ed. S. Gourevitch (Cambridge: Cambridge University Press, 1997).

——, *The Social Contract and other Later Political Writings*, ed. S. Gourevitch (Cambridge: Cambridge University Press, 1997).

STEPHEN, JAMES FITZJAMES, *Liberty, Equality, Fraternity* ([1873], Chicago: Chicago University Press, 1991).

VON HAYEK, F. A., *The Constitution of Liberty* ([1960], rev. edn, London: Routledge, 2006).

WOLLSTONECRAFT, MARY, *Vindication of the Rights of Women*, ed. Miriam Brody ([1792], rev. edn, Harmondsworth: Penguin, 2004).

INDEX